A History of Christian–Muslim Relations

Hugh Goddard

NEW AMSTERDAM BOOKS
Ivan R. Dee, Publisher
Chicago

To Jane

 For information, address: New Amsterdam Books, c/o Ivan R. Dee, Publisher, 1332 North Halsted Street, Chicago 60622.

ISBN paper: 1-56663-340-0
ISBN cloth: 1-56663-341-9

First published in Great Britain by Edinburgh University Press Ltd.

Library of Congress Cataloging-in-Publication Data:
Goddard, Hugh.
A history of Christian-Muslim relations / Hugh Goddard.
p. cm.
Includes bibliographical references and index.
ISBN: 978-1-56663-340-6
ISBN: 1-56663-340-0
1. Islam--Relations--Christianity--History. 2. Christianity and other religions--Islam--History. I. Title.

BP172 .G6 2001
261.2'7'09--dc21

00-042371

A History of Christian–Muslim Relations

Contents

Preface vii
Note on Transliteration and Dates viii
Chronology ix

Map 1: The Christian and Muslim Worlds c. 830/215 51
Map 2: The Christian and Muslim Worlds Today 178–9

Introduction 1

1 The Christian Background to the Coming of Islam 5
Early Christian Thinking about Other Religions 5
The History of the Christian Church in the Middle East 11

2 The Islamic Impact 19
Muḥammad's Contacts with Christians 19
The Qur'ān's View of Christians 24
Precedents for Muslim Treatment of Christians 29

3 The First Age of Christian–Muslim Interaction (–c. 830/215) 34
Christian Responses to the Coming of Islam 34
Muslim Treatment of Christians I 41

4 The Medieval Period I: Confrontation or Interaction in the East? 50
Contacts and Exchanges 50
Developing Mutual Perceptions 56
Muslim Treatment of Christians II 66
Conversion to Islam 68

5 The Medieval Period II: Confrontation or Interaction in the West? 79
Western Christian Reactions to the Coming of Islam 79
The Crusades 84
Alternative Perceptions of Islam 92
The Transmission of Knowledge from the Islamic World to the West 96

6 The Changing Balance of Power: Mission and Imperialism? 109
The Growth of European Power 109
The Establishment of Christian Missions 113
The Heyday of European Influence 123
Muslim Responses 127

7 New Thinking in the 19th/13th and 20th/14th Centuries 142
The Growth of Western Academic Study of Islam 142
Changing Christian Thinking about Islam 149
Changing Muslim Thinking about Christianity 158

8 Dialogue or Confrontation? 177
The Dialogue Movement 177
The Political Context 186
Fellow-Pilgrims? 188

Bibliography 199
Index 201

Preface

Publishing projects often take a little longer than expected, but some take quite a lot longer than originally planned, so I am very grateful to my editors at Edinburgh University Press, Jane Feore and Nicola Carr, for their patience when a family crisis caused a delay in the submission of my typescript.

I am also grateful to Carole Hillenbrand, the Editor of the Islamic Surveys Series, and to David Kerr, my PhD supervisor many years ago and my on-going mentor. David is Director of Edinburgh's Centre for the Study of Christianity in the non-Western world, and it was he who originally suggested the composition of this book. He also organised two very stimulating conferences in Edinburgh, which re-enthused me for the completion of the book when energy levels were flagging.

Note on Transliteration and Dates

I have transliterated Arabic names and terms in accordance with the system of the *Encyclopaedia of Islam*, with the exception of the Arabic letter *jīm*, for which I have used 'j' rather than 'dj', and the Arabic letter *qāf*, for which I have used 'q' rather than 'k' with a dot underneath it. I have not used the full transliteration system for names and terms from other Islamic languages such as Persian, Turkish, or Urdu.

In order to provide a sense of where the individuals and movements discussed in this book fit into the historical development of the Christian and Muslim traditions, I have usually provided dates according to both the Christian (i.e. Common Era) and Islamic calendars. (In the early chapters, where only one date is given, it refers to the Christian Common Era calendar, since the Islamic calendar had not yet commenced.) This may appear somewhat complicated since the former is a solar calendar and the latter a lunar calendar, with the result that an Islamic year is ten or eleven days shorter than a Christian/Common Era one, and an Islamic century is thus some three years shorter than a Christian/Common Era one. However, full conversion tables can be found in G. S. P. Freeman-Granville, *The Muslim and Christian Calendars*, 2nd edn., London: Collings, 1977 (which only goes up to 2000 CE), and a convenient summary is as follows:

The start of the Islamic calendar [AH1] = 622 CE.
AH 700 began on 20 September 1300 CE.
2000 CE began in 1420 AH.

Chronology

Christian history	*Interaction*	*Muslim history*
313 Conversion of Roman Emperor Constantine to Christianity		
451 Council of Chalcedon		
		c.570–632/11 Muḥammad
		622/1 Hijra from Mecca to Yathrib/Medina
	634/13 Fall of Jerusalem to Muslims	
	711/92 Muslim invasion of Spain	
	732/114 Battle of Tours	
John of Damascus (c. 652/32–750/132)		
		al-Ma'mūn caliph (813/198–833/218)
	850/235 Edict of al-Mutawakkil	
c. 850/235 Nicetas of Byzantium		
850/235–860/246 Spanish Martyrs' Movement		
	Ḥunayn ibn Isḥāq (809/193–873/260) (translator)	
		Abū'l-Ḥasan al-Ash'arī (874/260–936/324)
		Abū Manṣūr al-Māturīdī (?873/261–944/333)
		al-Fārābī (c. 870/256–950/339)
Yaḥyā ibn 'Adī (893/280–974/363)		
	1099/492 First Crusade captures Jerusalem	

Christian history	*Interaction*	*Muslim history*
		al-Ghazālī (1058/450–1111/505)
Peter the Venerable (c. 1092/485–1156/541)		
c. 1150/545 Paul of Antioch		
	Gerard of Cremona (1114/508–1187/583) (translator)	
	1187/583 Salāḥ al-Dīn recaptures Jerusalem	
	1189/585 Richard I leaves England for the Crusades	
		Ibn Rushd (1126/520–1198/595)
	1204/600 Fourth Crusade sacks Constantinople	
Francis of Assisi (1182/578–1226/623)		
Thomas Aquinas (c. 1225/622–1274/672)		
Ramon Lull (c. 1235/632–1316/716)		
	1291/690 Fall of Acre – end of crusading kingdoms	
		Ibn Taimiyya (1263/661–1328/728)
	1389/791 Battle of Kosovo	
	1453/857 Ottoman conquest of Constantinople	
	1492/897 Fall of Granada – completion of Reconquista	
	1497/903 Vasco da Gama sails around Cape of Good Hope	
	1579/987–1583/991 and 1593/1001–1613/1022 Jesuits at Moghul court	

Christian history	*Interaction*	*Muslim history*
	1604/1013 and 1621/1030 Carmelites at court of Shah 'Abbās I	
	1614/1023 Sir Thomas Roe at the Court of Ajmir	
Henry Martyn (1781/1195–1812/1227)		
Karl Pfander (1803/1218–1865/1282)		Raḥmat Allāh al-Kairanāwī (1834/1250–1891/1308)
	1854/1271 Agra debate between Pfander and al-Hindi	
William Muir (1819/1234–1905/1323)		Sayyid Ahmad Khan (1817/1232–1898/1316)
Temple Gairdner (1873/1290–1928/1346)		Jamāl al-dīn al-Afghānī (1838/1254–1897/1314)
Samuel Zwemer (1867/1283–1952/1371)		Muḥammad 'Abduh (1849/1265–1905/1323)
Hendrik Kraemer (1888/1305–1965/1385)		Ismā'īl al-Farūqī (1921/1339–1986/1406)
Louis Massignon (1883/1300–1962/1382)		Muḥammad al-Ṭālbī (b. 1921/1339)
Wilfred Cantwell Smith (1916/1334–2000/1420)		
1965/1385 Second Vatican Council statement on Islam		1985/1405 King Hassan II invites Pope John Paul II to Morocco

Introduction

On 22 October 1997, in the House of Commons in London, a report by a Commission of the Runnymede Trust, an independent London-based trust which sponsors research in the field of social policy, was launched. The title of the report was *Islamophobia: a challenge for us all*, and in the report the members of the Commission, who included eight Muslims and two Jews, investigated the nature of anti-Muslim prejudice (Islamophobia), the situation of Muslim communities in Britain, media coverage of issues involving Muslims, and how areas such as the law, education and community projects might address some of the difficulties which Muslims encounter in the United Kingdom, not least violent attacks on their persons.[1]

Some of the comments which were made at the launch, and some of the media comment about the report, suggested that concern with Islam in Britain was a relatively new phenomenon, arising from the growth of a significant Muslim community in the country since 1945/1364. There was a certain irony, therefore, in the fact that those who attended the launch, in the Members' Dining Room of the House of Commons, had, on their way in, passed two pictures which, had they noticed them, would have made it very clear that this is not the case. Involvement with Islam, in different ways, goes back a considerable way in British history.

The two pictures hang in St Stephen's Hall, the main access route for the public to the Central Lobby, which links the House of Commons and the House of Lords, and they are part of a series of eight paintings which together depict 'The Building of Britain'.[2] The subjects of the paintings are as follows: King Alfred's longships defeat the Danes (877/263); King John assents to Magna Carta (1215/612); The English people reading Wycliffe's Bible (fourteenth/eighth century); Sir Thomas More refusing to grant Wolsey a subsidy (1523/929); Queen Elizabeth commissions Raleigh to sail for America (1584/992); the Parliamentary Union of England and Scotland (1707/1119); and then the two paintings which involve Islam in different ways, namely Richard I leaving England for the Crusades (1189/585), and Sir Thomas Roe at the Court of Ajmir (1614/1023).[3]

Taken together these two paintings, which are reproduced in miniature on the cover of this book, point firstly to the length of time during which one small part of the Christian world, England, has had some contact with the world of Islam, and secondly to the different forms which that relationship has taken over the course of the centuries. Richard I's departure for the Third Crusade is an instance of Christians taking up the sword for the purpose of recovering the city of Jerusalem from its Muslim rulers – of Christians as aggressors against Muslims, in other words – whereas Sir Thomas Roe's visit to the Moghul Emperor Jahangir is an example of Christians as supplicants to Muslims, seeking in this case trading privileges on behalf of King James I. The two pictures therefore portray Christian–Muslim relationships of a very different kind.

In the context of the history of the world as a whole, the relationship between the Christian and Muslim worlds is thus a long and tortuous one. Both communities have their geographical and historical origins in the Middle East, but during the course of their subsequent histories they have expanded in different directions and become influential in different regions of the world – Christianity in Europe and the Americas, Islam in Africa and Asia. During the past two centuries, however, as a result of trade, the growth of empires, and migration, both communities have become truly universal; there are now very few regions of the world in which Christians and Muslims are not found, even if in hugely different proportions.

In addition, over the course of the centuries, what might be called the balance of power between the two communities has swung backwards and forwards. Sometimes the initiative seems to have lain with the Muslim community, with the Christian world simply being compelled to react to developments outside itself, and sometimes the situation seems to have been reversed, with the initiative lying with the Christian world and the Muslim world finding itself in the position of responding. Broadly speaking these descriptions could be seen as fitting the medieval era and the modern era respectively, but today in some respects the situation may be seen as demonstrating a greater degree of balance between Christians and Muslims. Military and technological power may thus be seen as residing more in the Christian world, but religious conviction and motivation may be discerned as being more powerful in Islamic societies. Increasing globalisation in the fields of commerce and information also does much to facilitate interchange and encounter between Christians and Muslims.

In many situations, however, encounter and interchange lead not to the growth of mutual understanding and sympathy but to conflict. The 1990s/1410s have witnessed this most dramatically in Europe, in different regions of the former Federal Republic of Yugoslavia, particularly Bosnia and Kosovo. But in other continents too, from the

Philippines to the Sudan to Nigeria, conflicts have also arisen and continue to cause suspicion and mistrust. The legacy of past conflicts, from the Muslim Age of Expansion in the early centuries to the Crusades and European imperialism, thus continues to wield a powerful influence, and some of the mutual misunderstandings which have arisen in the past seem to persist with great vigour despite the efforts of some in both communities to foster a more accurate understanding of the other and a more positive attitude towards members of the other community.

In this situation, then, it is important for material to be available which may help both Christians and Muslims to understand how the two communities have reached the situation in which they find themselves today. A book which attempts to survey the relationship between Christians and Muslims over the centuries and across the whole geographical range of their encounter may therefore be timely.

The main structure of the book will be historical, surveying the development of the relationship between Christians and Muslims as it has unfolded across the centuries. Given the thesis outlined above, namely that at certain stages one community has been compelled to react to developments in the other while at other stages that situation has been reversed, it is important to make clear that Christian–Muslim relations over the centuries have developed on a kind of layer by layer basis: what happened in one community in one generation produced a reaction in the other community which in turn contributed to the development of formulations and attitudes in the first community in later generations. In Christian–Muslim relations, memories are long and thus the Crusades, for example, still exercise a powerful influence, many centuries later, in some parts of both the Christian and Muslim worlds.

Attention will also be given to the diversity of opinion which has usually existed in each community at any one time. For all their insistence on unity and unanimity neither Christians nor Muslims have managed to achieve these things for very long except with respect to a very few essential or core teachings and practices. There has thus usually been a spectrum of opinion in each community with reference to the other too. This is as true in the medieval Islamic world, with the divergent opinions of, for example, the ninth/third-century thinker al-Jāḥiẓ and the tenth/fourth-century group of philosophers known as the Ikhwān al-Ṣafā (Brethren of Purity) concerning Christianity, as it is in the modern Christian world with the contrasting views of two Christian thinkers from the Reformed tradition, the Dutchman Hendrik Kraemer and the Canadian Wilfred Cantwell Smith, concerning Islam. The book will thus attempt to make clear the diversity which has existed and still exists within each community on the subject of the relationship with the other.

My hope is that a better understanding of the past, of the history of the relationship between Christians and Muslims, may help to promote deeper mutual comprehension in the present and a greater measure of collaboration rather than conflict in the future. There should be no illusions, however, about the extent of the obstacles which militate against the realisation of these hopes. Some Christians and some Muslims, perhaps even an increasing proportion of the membership of both communities, see the relationship as being intrinsically and essentially an adversarial one, but history itself points to the existence of a more positive irenical way of thinking among both Muslims and Christians at certain stages of their history. My hope is that this book may be a small contribution towards the promotion and expansion in influence of this latter perspective.[4]

NOTES

1. The full report was published by the Runnymede Trust in October 1997.
2. A brief description of all of the paintings may be found in Hay, M., and Riding, J. (eds.), *Art in Parliament: a descriptive catalogue*, Norwich: Jarrold, 1996, pp. 98–101.
3. A certain amount of political and constitutional sensitivity is, of course, necessary at this point, since although the series as a whole is entitled 'The Building of Britain', with only two exceptions all of the events portrayed are actually significant moments in the building of England. (The two exceptions are the Parliamentary Union of England and Scotland, and Sir Thomas Roe's trip to Ajmir, since it was undertaken at the instigation of the first king to unite the crowns of England and Scotland, James I, who had previously been James VI of Scotland.)
4. One example of a book which seems to posit an essentially adversarial relationship between the West and the world of Islam (which is not quite the same as the relationship between Christians and Muslims), is S. P. Huntington's *The Clash of Civilizations and the Remaking of World Order*, New York: Simon and Schuster, 1996. The author suggests that of the nine major civilizations in the world today, the Western, the Confucian/Sinic, the Japanese, the Islamic, the Hindu, the Orthodox, the Latin American, the African, and the Buddhist, it is the relationship between the Western and the Islamic which poses the main threat to future world peace. See especially pp. 109–20, 174–9, 209–18, and 246–98.

I

The Christian Background to the Coming of Islam

EARLY CHRISTIAN THINKING ABOUT OTHER RELIGIONS

When the Islamic community was established in the seventh/first century and the Christian community found itself having to respond to this new phenomenon, it did so on the basis of an already well-established tradition of thought about other religions. This was based partly on the scriptures which it had inherited from the Jewish community, the Old Testament/Hebrew Bible, partly on developments found within its own distinctive scriptures, the New Testament, and partly on the tradition of Christian thought and practice as it developed in the Patristic period, the period of the Fathers (*patres*) of the Christian church.

Thus in the Old Testament/Hebrew Bible there was a well-established tension between what might be called exclusivism or antagonism on the one hand, and inclusivism or universalism on the other. In some places the dominant theme is the chosen-ness of the Children of Israel, with the emphasis on their being set apart and enjoying a special relationship with God, expressed in the concept of covenant. This sometimes resulted in confrontation between them and the surrounding nations and religions, as expressed most memorably in 1 Kings 18, the challenge of the prophet Elijah to the prophets of Baal and Asherah, but in many of these confrontations the extent to which the main cause of conflict was religious and the extent to which it was political or territorial is not always clear. On the other hand the Hebrew scriptures often point to individuals outside the community of the Children of Israel who are recognised as knowing something of God and who may either be accepted into the community, as was the case with Ruth the Moabitess, or be explicitly recognised as being agents of God, as was the case with Cyrus the King of Persia, who in Isaiah 45: 1 was described as having been anointed by God.

The long series of battles between Israelites and Amalekites, Canaanites, Philistines, Syrians and others, and between their gods, suggest that the dominant motif in the relationship between the communities was that of confrontation, even enmity. But the more inclusive tradition was always there, and the universalist dimension is perhaps most clearly expressed at the start of what in the Christian arrangement of the Hebrew scriptures is the last book, Malachi, of the Old Testament:

> For from the rising of the sun to its setting my name is great among the nations, and in every place incense is offered to my name, and a pure offering; for my name is great among the nations, says the Lord of hosts. (Malachi 1: 11)

The two contrasting attitudes are also well illustrated in the messages of two short prophetic books from the latter part of the Old Testament, both of which focus on the city of Nineveh, the capital city of the Assyrian Empire. The book of Nahum celebrates the fall of the city, and glories in it, celebrating and indeed exulting in its destruction. The book of Jonah, by contrast, tells a story of the population of the city responding positively to the call to repentance which is proclaimed by the prophet, thereby escaping divine judgement and leading to Jonah's recognition of an important truth about God. This seems in a way to foreshadow certain parts of the teaching of the Qur'ān, namely that God is gracious and merciful (Jonah 4:2).

The Inter-testamental period too, roughly the four centuries before the time of Jesus, saw a similar spectrum of attitude developing among the Jewish people. On the one hand was an attitude of militant separatism and exclusivism, as represented by the Maccabees who revolted against Greek rule over Palestine in the second century BCE. They displayed an attitude of hostility both to foreign rule and to foreign religion and culture, an attitude which was continued in the time of Jesus by the Zealots, who were quite prepared to use violence in pursuit of their religious and political ambitions. In contrast to this, particularly among the Jews of the Diaspora, those living outside Palestine, an attitude of much greater openness was evident. This is best seen in the first-century CE figure of Philo, a Jew from Alexandria, who sought to expound Judaism in terms of Hellenistic philosophy and who was willing to draw on philosophical language and terminology in order to do so. The translation of the Hebrew scriptures into Greek, which was undertaken in the same city in the second or third century BCE, and which came to be known as the Septuagint because of the seventy scholars who were thought to have done the translation, is also evidence of a greater openness towards religious ideas emanating from outside the Jewish community.

For the early Christian community there were two main aspects to its thinking about other religious traditions. Firstly its relationship to the Jewish community from which it had grown, and secondly its attitude towards the prevailing patterns of Graeco-Roman religion and philosophy by which it was surrounded.

Over the course of the past fifty years much research and reflection has been undertaken about what is commonly called 'The Parting of the Ways', the process by which the Christian church became established as a community separate and distinct from the Judaism within which it had its roots.[1] One important theme which has been pushed into renewed prominence, thanks to the work of Geza Vermes in particular, is the Jewishness of Jesus: contrary to much later Christian thinking which developed after the separation of the Christian church from Judaism, Jesus in much of his teaching and practice was a very Jewish figure, in the prophetic tradition of Jewish religion.[2] All of his most intimate disciples were Jewish, he prayed and worshipped in synagogue and temple, and the earliest records of his teaching seem to make it clear that he regarded his message as being targeted primarily at his own Jewish community. Some aspects of his teaching, however, caused considerable resentment and controversy within the Jewish community, and it was these which led to Jesus's crucifixion at the hands of the Romans.

Even after this, Jesus's early disciples continued at first to regard themselves as Jews and to pray in the Temple and the synagogue. They were not always welcomed, however, and efforts on the part of some Jewish leaders to purge the followers of Jesus from Jewish congregations led to the beginnings of a separate Christian community. This was accelerated by the conversion of Saul, according to the Book of Acts a leader in the campaign against the followers of Jesus. After Saul's change of heart he began to argue for the abandonment of some Jewish practices by Christians and thus contributed towards the establishment of separate Christian congregations. The Council of Jerusalem, referred to in Acts 15, discussed the question of whether or not non-Jewish converts should be required to undergo circumcision, and by seeming to suggest that they need not it accelerated the process.

What began as a parting, or separation, gradually became a focus of more antagonism and even vitriol. After the destruction of the Jewish Temple in Jerusalem by the Romans in 70 CE, following a Jewish revolt against Roman authority, the two communities began to define themselves more explicitly as separate and distinct from each other. At first both communities were suspect in the eyes of the Roman authorities, and both on occasion suffered persecution, but the level of polemic between the two began to increase. Even within the New Testament some of the animus which some Christians evidently felt towards Judaism is clear, especially in the writings of John.

In the early Christian centuries New Testament texts such as Matthew 27: 25 (in which in his account of the trial of Jesus before Pontius Pilate Matthew writes that, in response to the Roman governor's protest that he could find no evil in Jesus, the crowd, most of whose members were Jews, shouted 'His blood be on us and on our children!') and Acts 2: 23 (where in his first major public sermon after the death of Jesus his disciple Peter says to his mainly Jewish audience 'This Jesus whom you crucified') began to be used to justify violence and persecution of members of the Jewish community. Later, when at the start of the fourth century Christianity became the official religion of the Roman Empire, the power of the state also began to be used against Jews, so that the burning of synagogues was sanctioned and the forced conversion of Jews to Christianity was legitimised. Christian-Jewish relations therefore deteriorated dramatically, and despite their common ancestry the two traditions increasingly adopted mutually hostile attitudes.[3]

A particularly graphic example of this comes in a series of eight sermons delivered by John Chrysostom (literally 'the golden-tongued') in the Syrian city of Antioch in 387 CE, where he describes the Jews as dogs who have descended to gluttony, drunkenness and sensuality, whose synagogues are no better than theatres, brothels or dens of thieves, whose souls have become the seats of demons and places of idolatry, and who are to be shunned as a filthy plague threatening the whole world. There is even a suggestion that they are no longer fit for anything but slaughter.[4] Recent research has suggested that these remarks need to be located in the context of a Christian community in Antioch which still found aspects of Judaism attractive, and that their vitriolic tone should be seen as rhetoric intended to remind Christians of their separate and distinct identity. But it must be acknowledged that their negative tone was a major contributory factor to the emergence of the ghetto in medieval and modern Christian societies.[5]

On the other hand, alongside the diatribes of Chrysostom and others, more positive attitudes towards the Jews were sometimes evident, with individual friendships between Christians and Jews not unheard of, and the overall picture of Christian–Jewish relationships after the conversion of Constantine is not one of unremitting darkness.

Christian attitudes towards Hellenism and Graeco-Roman philosophy were more varied. Within the New Testament itself, even if Jesus's message seems to have been directed primarily at the Jews, there are nevertheless, as in the Old Testament/Hebrew scriptures, a number of encounters and stories which present individuals outside the Jewish community in a favourable light: there are positive encounters with a Roman centurion and a Samaritan woman, and one of Jesus's most famous parables has at its heart a Samaritan as the model who is commended for his compassion and charity.

Partly as a result of the deterioration in the relationship between many Jews and the followers of Jesus, the early Christians began to demonstrate their conviction that the message of Jesus was not only for Jews but also for non-Jews. This is reflected in the New Testament by the story of the Three Wise Men (Matthew 2: 1–12), who came from the East in order to give gifts to Jesus, and in the Book of Acts in the vision of Peter concerning the Roman centurion Cornelius (Acts 10). It is once again Paul, though, who drives the process forward, and the Book of Acts, as it tells of his travels around the Mediterranean seeking to make Jesus more widely known, provides several accounts of his attitude towards the Greek religion of his day. Firstly, in Athens, as recorded in Acts 17, Paul seems to adopt a remarkably positive and open attitude towards Greek philosophy, suggesting that what the Athenians worship as the 'unknown god' is the God whom he proclaims; his message, he suggests, is perhaps therefore the fulfilment rather than the antithesis of what they believe. But later, in Ephesus, as recorded in Acts 19 and 20, there seems to have been a greater element of confrontation and rejection in his message, with the suggestion that the worship of Diana/Artemis of the Ephesians was of no value.

In the Patristic period too, different attitudes towards Greek philosophy grew up in different parts of the Christian church. One stream of Christian thought, more influential in the Western, Latin-speaking half of the Roman Empire, emphasised the distinctiveness of the Christian message and the need for the Christian community to separate itself from surrounding intellectual influences. This view is most succinctly represented in the famous statement of the North African Christian Tertullian (c. 170–220 CE): 'What has Athens [the home of philosophy] to do with Jerusalem [the home of revelation]?' In the Eastern part of the Empire, however, where most Christians were Greek-speaking, a more inclusive/universalist tradition grew up, as represented by such figures as Justin Martyr (c. 100–65 CE), who proclaimed Christianity as the true philosophy, and Clement of Alexandria (c. 155–c. 220 CE), who suggested that the salvation brought by Jesus would be universal in scope. Thus Justin wrote:

> It is our belief that those . . . who strive to do the good which is enjoined on us have a share in God, . . . [and] will by God's grace share his dwelling . . . in principle this holds good for all . . .

and Clement argued that:

> By reflection and direct vision those among the Greeks who have philosophized accurately see God.[6]

In this tradition the giants of the Greek philosophical tradition such as Plato and Aristotle were in a sense baptised as honorary Christians. Passages such as the one in Plato's *Republic,* which refers to the Just Man being crucified, were seen as in some way prophetic, and the emphasis seems to have lain much more on synthesis and compatibility than on antagonism or separation.[7]

Some parts of the New Testament and the writings of some of the Church Fathers do on some occasions, however, use extremely strong language concerning those with whom their authors disagree. The first letter of John speaks of the Antichrist:

> Who is the liar but he who denies that Jesus is the Christ?[8] This is the antichrist . . . (1 John 2: 22)

and

> Every spirit which confesses that Jesus Christ has come in the flesh is of God, and every spirit which does not confess Jesus is not of God. This is the spirit of antichrist . . . (1 John 4: 2–3)

This is strong language indeed, but it is very important to note that its original target was those within the Christian community who seemed to the writer to be developing opinions about Jesus which were extremely suspect. The most plausible suggestions concerning the nature of these threatening beliefs is that they involved some kind of combination of Ebionism and Gnosticism, as represented by the opinions of a figure such as Cerinthus around the end of the first century CE. He argued that Jesus was an ordinary man who was chosen by God at his baptism for a special ministry; he received special wisdom for this at his baptism, which disappeared before his crucifixion. This strongly negative judgement, in other words, was not made upon people outside the community altogether, but rather on those inside who were perceived to be threatening its identity in some way. In the same way many of the most polemical statements from the mouth of Jesus in the New Testament were originally directed towards members of his own (Jewish) community with whom he disagreed (e.g. Matthew 3: 7).

Context also needs to be kept in mind when considering some of the statements in the New Testament which have often been interpreted exclusively by Christians, in other words as meaning that only Christians will be saved. The two verses most commonly referred to in this context are John 14: 6 (Jesus said: 'I am the way, the truth and the life; no one comes to the father, but by me.'), and Acts 4: 12 (Peter said:

'There is salvation in no one else, for there is no other name under heaven . . . by which we must be saved'). It has been suggested by modern scholars that the Johannine saying in particular must be understood in the context of a vigorously sectarian Johannine community, whose exclusive social identity was therefore reinforced by such exclusive statements. Peter's saying in Acts needs to be seen against its immediate background, which is that of a spirited defence by Peter of the healing of a lame man in the Temple.[9]

Other parts of the New Testament also use extremely strong language concerning the Roman state, which as it began to persecute Christians from the time of Nero (54–68 CE) came to be referred to in apocalyptic terms as 'the beast', especially in the Book of Revelation. Earlier attitudes, whereby Christians attempted to establish their position as loyal citizens of the Empire, therefore came to be substantially revised by changing circumstances, and not surprisingly a far greater measure of antagonism becomes evident and persists through the early centuries.

When the Islamic community came onto the scene, therefore, in the seventh/first century, these were some of the traditions which the Christian community was able to draw on and develop in seeking to formulate its response to and interpretation of Islam. We shall see later that a considerable variety of Christian response emerged at that time, with no single universally accepted Christian view ever gaining complete acceptance. Given the spectrum of opinion which we have seen existing within both the Christian scriptures and early Christian thought, this is not really surprising.

THE HISTORY OF THE CHRISTIAN CHURCH IN THE MIDDLE EAST

One of the aspects of its history which the Christian church shares with the Islamic community is that it has its historical origins in the Middle East. It is therefore important that some account is given of the history and development of the Christian church after its origins as described in the New Testament, with which most modern Christians are broadly familiar; the 600 or so years of further development are less familiar, at least to many modern Western Christians, and it is important to outline the main features of evolution in the centuries prior to the establishment of the Islamic *umma* (community).

Probably the most important change in this period was a result of the conversion to Christianity of the Roman Emperor Constantine in the second decade of the fourth century. From being a minority community with little or no political influence and power, the Christian church suddenly became the established religion of the most powerful state of the Mediterranean world. Close links were thus established between church and state, with Christian bishops sometimes becoming powerful players in the political arena, and with the power of the state sometimes being used to further the influence of particular groups within the Christian community.[10]

Part of the reason for Constantine's decision to accept Christianity himself was his hope that the Christian religion might serve as a focus for unity and thus bring about renewed strength within the Empire. Developments in the next few centuries, however, quickly made it clear that this was to be a vain hope, as more and more division took place within the Christian church, leading to the emergence and establishment of a number of different Christian communities. Argument and division were not new, of course, with many fierce debates being waged in the first three centuries, but somehow the minority status of the Christians, together with the persecution which they had intermittently suffered, meant that these early divisions did not become institutionalised in the way that was the case with those which came after the time of Constantine.

By the seventh/first century, therefore, the Christian church was deeply divided, and this was one of the charges which the Qur'ān quite explicitly made against Christians as it sought to challenge their claim to possess the truth:

> And with those who say: 'Lo! We are Christians,' We made a covenant, but they forgot a part of that whereof they were admonished. Therefore We have stirred up enmity and hatred among them till the Day of Resurrection, when Allah will inform them of their handiwork. (5: 14)

In part these divisions simply bore some correspondence to the split which the Roman Empire itself underwent in the fourth century when it was divided into an Eastern and a Western half. The Christian church in the Western, Latin-speaking, half of the Empire, began to develop its own understanding of the Christian faith, with an emphasis on law, which gave rise to redemption becoming the central focus of Western theology, expressed in worship through sacrifice being at the heart of the Mass. The church in the Eastern half of the Empire, by contrast, mainly Greek-speaking, was more at home with the language of philosophy, and thus Eastern Christian theology came to focus more on the idea of deification, with the emphasis in worship lying much more on Eucharist (Thanksgiving). To some extent East and West therefore quite simply drifted apart, a process which accelerated when the Western half of the Empire collapsed in 476, while the Eastern half lived on for almost another millennium, and although a split between the Eastern and Western churches was not formalised until 1054/446, the year of the so-called Great Schism, the real separation had taken place centuries earlier, even before the establishment of the Islamic community.[11]

One difference, which was not an original cause of the division between East and West but which grew up somewhat later, concerned what was known as the *filioque* clause, that part of the Christian creed as it evolved in the early centuries which elaborated on what Christians were to believe about the Holy Spirit. In the East it was affirmed that the Spirit 'proceeded from the Father', but in the West, beginning probably in Spain towards the end of the eighth/second century, it began to be affirmed that the Spirit 'proceeded from the Father and the Son' (*filioque* being simply the Latin for 'and the Son'). As well as being one of the most serious and bitterly contested differences between the Eastern and Western churches until today, this difference also, as we shall see, gave rise to some significant differences between the Eastern and the Western churches in their reactions and attitudes towards Islam.

A further difference between East and West in the early centuries centred on differing concepts of leadership and authority. Of the leading centres of the early Christian community only one, Rome, lay in the West, while Jerusalem, Antioch and Alexandria lay in the East. When the new city of Constantinople (today's Istanbul), founded by Constantine in 324, was also recognised as a patriarchate, this meant that four important ecclesiastical centres lay in the East. One consequence of this was that it was harder for any one centre in the East to claim pre-eminence, so Eastern views of authority tended to be more conciliar, whereas the existence of only one centre in the West resulted in a greater degree of concentration of power, with the papacy sometimes claiming supreme authority for itself.

If the division between West and East was the most serious division in the Christian church before the coming of the Islamic community, other differences soon followed, especially within the Eastern church. In the West it was perhaps Donatism in north Africa, beginning in the fourth century, which created the deepest split, even, on some accounts, providing part of the explanation for the virtually complete disappearance of the Christian church from north Africa under Islamic rule. But it was in the East that the deepest splits occurred, with their focus on Christology, the Christian teaching concerning the nature of the Person of Christ.

These splits have their roots in the emergence of schools of thought within the church in the early centuries which had different emphases concerning Christology. On the one hand the Antiochene school, based on Antioch in Syria, the place at which the term 'Christian' had first been used for the followers of Jesus (Acts 11: 26), tended to emphasise the full humanity of Jesus, as well as displaying some admiration for Aristotelian empiricism in its philosophical inclination; the Alexandrian school, by contrast, leaned more in the direction of a Logos Christology, emphasising Jesus's role as Word of God, a concept developed by the Jewish Alexandrian thinker Philo, as we have seen above. It also displayed a preference for Platonic mysticism in its drawing upon the Greek philosophical tradition.

For several centuries these schools remained trends or emphases, often interacting fruitfully with each other even when they differed, but in the fifth century extra animus became apparent in their disagreements, and as a result separate communities and hierarchies were established. This happened first in the fifth century when Nestorius, the Patriarch of Constantinople, was accused of drawing too rigid a separation between the human and the divine natures of Christ, which led to his being declared a heretic at the Council of Ephesus in 431. He was deposed and exiled, but his views were sufficiently attractive to a significant number of Christians, particularly in Syria and further to the east, in Iraq and Iran, for a separate Nestorian church to be established. In the next few years, partly as a reaction to the views of Nestorius, a view emerged which laid particular stress on the divine nature of Christ, at the expense of his humanity, and twenty years after the Council of Ephesus a further Council, this time held at Chalcedon, not far from Constantinople, rejected this view, as put forward by Eutyches, a monk in Constantinople. The opinions of Eutyches, which came to be widely known as Monophysitism (*mono*/one *physis*/nature), were declared heretical, but again they proved popular in some provinces of the Byzantine Empire, particularly in Syria and Egypt, and the result was the establishment of distinct Monophysite churches in these regions.

By the end of the fifth century, therefore, the Eastern church was no longer united, and even if all of these churches continue to be described as 'Orthodox' churches, meaning that they are all Eastern churches and they all share a common philosophy and style of worship, bitter opposition grew up between the Greek church, based in Constantinople, which accepted the decisions of the Councils of Ephesus and Chalcedon, and the Nestorian and Monophysite churches, which did not. It is important to note, too, that it was not only theology which was at issue here since political factors also played a part. On the one hand, the spread of the Christian church outside the frontiers of the Roman Empire was significant here, since the views of Nestorius were popular among the Christian subjects of the Persian Empire, and this made the loyalty of Nestorians inside the Roman Empire somewhat suspect. On the other hand, resentment against the central powers of the Byzantine Empire in its more distant provinces such as Egypt and Syria was also a factor behind theological separatism. The result, whatever the causes, was further deep division within the Christian church, along both theological and geographical lines, and the significance of this as part of the background to the coming of the Islamic community cannot be emphasised enough.[12]

This is most obvious if we turn now to investigate the position of the Christian church in Arabia, the historical and geographical heartland of the Islamic community. In the sixth century Arabia was in a sense a world of its own, independent and not a part of either of the major states of the day, the Byzantine Empire and the Sassanian Persian Empire. Its landward boundaries, however, were surrounded by those two empires, and, indeed, in one sense it straddled the frontier between them. One consequence of this is that it was not immune from their influence, and prior to the time of the prophet Muḥammad both of these states were endeavouring to expand their control over certain regions of Arabia.

If we look, therefore, at Arabia around the year 600, just before Muḥammad's call to prophethood, we find that different elements of the Christian church were well-established on the frontiers of Arabia. To the north-west, in the direction of Jerusalem and the Mediterranean, some Arab tribes on the Byzantine frontier had accepted Christianity, beginning in the fourth century; one Roman Emperor, Marcus Julius Philippus, indeed, commonly known as Philip the Arab, who ruled between 244 and 249, was a Christian, though in his official role as emperor he did not seem to make this explicit, restricting his Christian faith to his private capacity.[13] Later, an important Arab tribe, the Banū Ghassān, was among several tribes which possibly accepted Christianity in the fourth century, and in the sixth century the Ghassānids acquired a position of political dominance in the region as a result of the designation of their leader Ḥārith ibn Jabala by the Byzantines as 'phylarch' or tribal leader.

It should be made clear at this point that the acceptance of Christianity by several Arab tribes in this period was not simply a matter of religious or theological conviction. It was also a statement of cultural affinity and a marker of political allegiance, so that in a sense the spread of Christianity sometimes served as an extension of Byzantine foreign policy. But this did not mean that it was Orthodox (in the sense of accepting the decrees of the Council of Chalcedon) Christianity which spread on the frontier; rather it was Monophysite Christianity which became dominant, including the Ghassānids among its adherents, and this was to be significant for the future. The whole character of the Christian church in the region, indeed, was somewhat removed from the main stream of Christian thought and practice, not least because of the emergence of monasticism in the Syrian desert in the fourth century as a kind of protest against developments within the church at large.

On the north-eastern frontier of Arabia, the area bordering on Iraq, which was then a province of the Sassanian Empire, a similar process of the diffusion of the Christian message among some of the Arab tribes took place, but it was a different branch of the church which took root here. Politically an important tribe in this region was the tribe of Lakhm, which was the main rival of the Ghassānids during the sixth century, and enjoyed a similar kind of relationship of patronage to the Sassanian Empire as the Ghassānids did to Byzantium. Its ruler between 583 and 602, Nu'mān ibn Mundhir, was a convert to Christianity, but it was the Nestorian church to which he became affiliated, and this reflected the influence of Nestorianism within the Persian empire: the Lakhmid capital, al-Ḥīra, had been a centre of Nestorianism since the fourth century, and further south, on the eastern shores of the Gulf, Nestorianism had also taken root, again partly in connection with the diffusion of Persian cultural and political influence, so that Baḥrain (a term then used to describe the eastern shores of Arabia rather than the island off them as it is today) had Nestorian bishops.[14]

The third area on the fringes of Arabia which is important for our examination is the south-western corner of the Arabian peninsula, the area today known as Yemen. Here too Christianity had become established in the centuries prior to the establishment of the Islamic community, and the agent of its diffusion here was the Christian kingdom of Axum on the opposite shore of the Red Sea, in present-day Ethiopia and Eritrea. Once again it was Monophysite Christianity which was involved here, and although the Christian church does not seem to have had a great impact on South Arabia it did enjoy considerable influence at least in one place, the town of Najrān.

All of the instances of some kind of Christian influence in Arabia which we have looked at so far have involved the fringes of the region. Evidence for the spread of Christianity is therefore relatively easy to obtain, given the references to the process in the records of the states surrounding Arabia, which as we have seen were often intimately involved in the process anyway. What is much more difficult to chronicle and to assess is the influence of the Christian church in the more central regions of Arabia, including those where the Islamic community first became established. With respect to Najd, the central area of the peninsula, there is evidence of the tribe of Taghlib accepting

Christianity, of the Monophysite variety, towards the end of the sixth century, and of the ruling clan of the more important tribe of Kinda also adopting Christianity at roughly the same time. In the latter case it is not clear either which form of Christianity was involved or the extent to which the tribe as a whole was affected. The evidence is then even less clear with reference to the Hijaz, on the western side of the peninsula, where Muḥammad was born. It seems that there was some Christian presence, but not necessarily an indigenous one and not one which enjoyed very much influence among the ruling elements of the region.[15]

In summary, then, it is fair to suggest that the Christian church was present in and enjoyed considerable influence on the areas on the borders of Arabia, especially in the north-west and the north-east. It was also established on the east coast and in South Arabia, especially at Najrān, but even taking all this together, for all its influence on the frontiers of Arabia, Christianity had not become a major player in developments in the heartlands of Arabia. There it was to be another religious force which was to become pre-eminent.

NOTES

1. See, for example, J. D. G. Dunn, *The Partings of the Ways: between Christianity and Judaism and their significance for the character of Christianity*, London: SCM, 1991, and the earlier work of E. P. Sanders et al. (eds), *Jewish and Christian Self-Definition*, London: SCM, 3 Vols, 1980–2.
2. See G. Vermes, *Jesus the Jew*, London: Collins, 1973.
3. A classic study of this process is J. Parkes, *The Conflict of the Church and the Synagogue: a Study in the Origins of Antisemitism*, London: Socino Press, 1934.
4. See U. Simon, *Verus Israel: a Study of the Relations between Christians and Jews in the Roman Empire (135–425)*, (ET by H. McKeating), Oxford University Press, 1986, pp. 217–23, and J. N. D. Kelly, *Golden Mouth: the Story of John Chrysostom: Ascetic, Preacher, Bishop*, London: Duckworth, 1995, pp. 63–6.
5. See R. L. Wilken, *Chrysostom and the Jews: Rhetoric and Reality in the Late Fourth Century*, University of California Press, 1983.
6. Justin, *First Apology*: 10, and Clement, *Miscellanies*: 6: 5, quoted by K. Cracknell, *Considering Dialogue*, London: British Council of Churches, 1981, p. 30. For a fuller discussion of Justin and Clement, together with Origen (c. 185–c. 254) see H. Chadwick, *Early Christian Thought and the Classical Tradition*, Oxford University Press, 1966; and for a survey of relevant Biblical and patristic material (including Justin), see R. Plantinga (ed.), *Christianity and Plurality*, Oxford: Blackwell, 1999, pp. 9–89.
7. The relevant passage in *The Republic* can be found on pp. 107–8 of the 1974 Penguin Classics edition of the work.
8. 'Christ' is the Greek word meaning 'the one anointed by God'.
9. On the Johannine sayings see W. Meeks, 'The man from heaven in Johannine Sectarianism' in *Journal of Biblical Literature*, 91 (1972), pp.

44–72, and for discussion of both sayings see K. Cracknell 'A Christology for Religious Pluralism' in his *Towards a New Relationship*, London: Epworth, 1986, pp. 69–109.

10. An accessible account of Constantine's period is A. H. M. Jones, *Constantine and the Conversion of Europe*, Harmondsworth: Penguin, 1972.
11. See Chapter 1 of S. Runciman, *The Eastern Schism*, Oxford University Press, 1955.
12. On the Monophysite churches see W. H. C. Frend, *The Rise of the Monophysites*, Cambridge University Press, 1972; and on the Nestorian church, sometimes referred to as 'The Church of the East', see *Bulletin of the John Rylands Library*, 78:3 (1996), which contains a dozen or so papers on the life and thought of that church. On the history of all the non-Chalcedonian Orthodox churches, see A. S. Atiya, *A History of Eastern Christianity*, London: Methuen, 1968.
13. J. S. Trimingham, *Christianity Among the Arabs in Pre-Islamic Times*, London: Longman, 1979, pp. 58–9.
14. Ibid., p. 280.
15. Ibid., p. 260.

2

The Islamic Impact

MUḤAMMAD'S CONTACTS WITH CHRISTIANS

Muḥammad received his call to prophethood in the year 610, and during the course of the next twenty-two years, until his death in 632/11, he proclaimed his message of monotheism and its ethical consequences firstly in Mecca, until his Hijra (migration) in 622/1, and then in the neighbouring town of Yathrib (which later became known as Medina).

The extent of his contact with Christians, and also with Jews, both before and during the period of his public ministry is a subject of considerable controversy, both among and between Muslim and non-Muslim scholars. Some of the former, in order to maximise claims concerning the originality of the message and provide support for the traditional argument that the source of Muḥammad's message was God/Allāh rather than Muḥammad himself, downplay contact with Christians and tend to conclude that there was no influence from any source, Christian or Jewish or other, on his message. Some of the latter, by contrast, portray the message as having no originality at all, but simply being derivative from either Judaism, or Christianity, or pre-Islamic Arabian religion, or possibly from some kind of synthesis of one or more of those elements.[1]

Both of these views are almost certainly overstatements or oversimplifications.[2] Traditional Muslim biographies of Muḥammad contain accounts of a number of incidents when he encountered Christians, and even if the status and reliability of these biographies is also, as is the case with the New Testament, a focus of scholarly dispute, there seems to be no good reason to discount the accounts completely, even if the question of the extent to which these encounters might have shaped or contributed to the development of Muḥammad's message is a more difficult and controversial one.[3]

If we look at the main traditional biographical source for the life of Muḥammad, the *Sīrat Rasūl Allāh* (The Life of the Prophet of God) by Ibn Isḥāq (d. 767/150), we find that there are five main instances in which it is recorded that Muḥammad and the early Muslim community had some kind of direct encounter with Christians.[4]

The first comes from the period even before Muḥammad's call to prophethood. According to Ibn Isḥāq, while travelling in a merchant caravan with his uncle Abū Ṭālib to Syria, aged around 12, Muḥammad met a monk in the desert who was called Baḥīrā. As the caravan was passing by Baḥīrā's cell, the monk noticed a cloud overshadowing Muḥammad, and when the caravan stopped, the branches of a tree bent and drooped so that he was in the shade. Intrigued, the monk invited the members of the caravan to eat with him, looked carefully at Muḥammad, and saw 'the seal of prophethood', understood as being some kind of physical mark, between his shoulders. He therefore told the other members of the caravan to guard Muḥammad carefully in order to ensure that he came to no harm.[5]

The second instance then comes at a moment not long after Muḥammad's call to prophethood. In the wake of that traumatic experience, which involved some kind of vision of the angel Gabriel and a commissioning to recite a message which later became the first five verses of chapter 96 of the Qur'ān, Muḥammad is struggling to make sense of the experience, even possibly thinking that he is mad. Reassurance is provided to him by a cousin of his wife Khadīja, Waraqa ibn Nawfal, who is described by Ibn Isḥāq as 'a Christian who had studied the scriptures and was a scholar', and someone 'who had become a Christian and read the scriptures and learned from those that follow the Torah and the Gospel'; when he heard about Muḥammad's experience, Waraqa's response was that it showed that Muḥammad was to be the prophet of the Arabs, and that he should therefore be of good heart.[6]

The next encounter involves not the prophet himself but the group of Muslims who, at his command, around the year 615 performed their own hijra (migration) away from Mecca to the kingdom of Axum (Abyssinia).[7] Axum, as we have already seen, was a Christian kingdom, adhering to the Monophysite understanding of Christianity, and the choice of Axum as the first place of refuge for the early Muslims when circumstances in Mecca became difficult is surely significant. The title of the ruler of Axum at this time was the Negus. When the rulers of Mecca, the Quraish tribe, sent an embassy to Axum in order to seek the return of the Muslims to Mecca, Ibn Isḥāq records a very interesting conversation between the Negus, accompanied by his bishops with their sacred books, and the leaders of the refugee Muslims. When the Negus asked the Muslims about their religion, their leader, Ja'far ibn Abū Ṭālib replied:

> O King, we were an uncivilized people, worshipping idols, eating corpses, committing abominations, breaking natural ties, treating guests badly, and our strong devoured our weak. Thus we were until God sent us an apostle whose lineage, truth, trust-

> worthiness, and clemency we know. He summoned us to acknowledge God's unity and to worship him and to renounce the stones and images which we and our fathers formerly worshipped. He commanded us to speak the truth, be faithful to our engagements, mindful of the ties of kinship and kindly hospitality, and to refrain from crimes and bloodshed. He forbade us to commit abominations and to speak lies, and to devour the property of orphans, to vilify chaste women. He commanded us to worship God alone and not to associate anything with Him, and he gave us orders about prayer, almsgiving, and fasting (enumerating the commands of Islam). We confessed the truth and believed in him, and we followed him in what he had brought from God, and we worshipped God alone without associating aught with Him. We treated as forbidden what he forbade, and as lawful what he declared lawful. Thereupon our people attacked us, treated us harshly and seduced us from our faith to try to make us go back to the worship of idols instead of the worship of God, and to regard as lawful the evil deeds we once committed. So when they got the better of us, treated us unjustly and circumscribed our lives, and came between us and our religion, we came to your country, having chosen you above all others. Here we have been happy in your protection, and we hope that we shall not be treated unjustly while we are with you, O King.

The Negus then asked whether the Muslims had with them anything which came from God – in other words, any of their revelation – so Ja'far read a passage from chapter 19 of the Qur'ān, which describes the miraculous conception and birth of Jesus. When the Negus heard it, Ibn Isḥāq records that '[t]he Negus wept until his beard was wet and the bishops wept until their scrolls were wet', and the Negus said: 'Of a truth, this and what Jesus brought have come from the same niche', so he promises not to give the Muslims up to the Meccans. The Meccans have one more attempt at persuading the Negus to withdraw his protection, by telling him that the Muslims believe that Jesus is a creature (rather than in any sense God), but Ja'far replies once again by quoting the Qur'ān to the effect that Jesus is the slave of God, and his apostle, and his spirit, and his word, which he cast into Mary the blessed virgin (4: 171). The Negus replies by picking up a stick and affirming that the difference between what he believes about Jesus and what the Muslims believe is no greater than the length of the stick.[8]

The fourth incident recounted by Ibn Isḥāq is then a kind of mirror image of the third, in that the power relationship is reversed. This incident comes from the years after the Hijra in 622/1, so that Muḥammad is now securely established as a figure of some power and influence in Yathrib/Medina. There, probably somewhere around the year 628/7, he receives a delegation of Christians from the town of Najrān, the town which as we have seen already was an important centre of (Monophysite) Christian influence in South Arabia. The delegation, according to Ibn Isḥāq, was led by three people, the *'Āqib* or leader of the people, their *Sayyid* or administrator, and their Bishop. The name of the leader, significantly, was 'Abd al-Masīḥ (Servant of Christ), and the Bishop was described as a great student, with excellent knowledge of the Christian religion, to the extent that he had been honoured by the emperors of Byzantium because of his knowledge and zeal for their religion.

The purpose of the visit was essentially political, namely to negotiate a kind of treaty with Muḥammad. When the Christians arrived, Muḥammad was praying the afternoon prayer, and when the time came for their prayers they too were permitted to pray in the mosque. Later, when discussions began, the Christians were invited to submit, which they claimed they had already done, the language of submission being somewhat ambiguous since it was not clear whether submission to God/Allāh or to Muḥammad was being called for. The Christians claimed that they had submitted before Muḥammad, at least, but Ibn Isḥāq records that Muḥammad's response was that their belief that God had a son, their worship of the cross, and their eating pork held them back from submission. A lengthy Christological discussion follows, centring around many of the Qur'ānic verses about Jesus, and at the end of this a challenge was issued, namely that the issue should be decided by the mutual invocation of a curse. After some deliberation, the Christians declined and returned home, preferring to agree to differ peacefully and to be permitted to continue to practise their faith.[9]

The last major incident involving some kind of encounter between Muḥammad and Christians comes towards the end of his life, when Ibn Isḥāq tells of his sending letters to the rulers of the states which neighboured Arabia, calling on them to accept the faith of Islam. These letters were not only sent to Christian rulers such as the Byzantine emperor Heraclius and the Negus of Axum; the account tells of a messenger also being sent to the Sassanian emperor Chosroes/Khusro.[10]

What are we to make of these accounts? In some cases a greater measure of historical scepticism may be appropriate than in others, for particularly with respect to the first and the last incidents it is easier to discern what might be called a theological motivation for the stories. The Baḥīrā incident, for example, may be seen as validating the claim that even before his call, here was a Christian accepting, indeed predicting, that Muḥammad was to be a prophet. It is important to note here that there are also Christian accounts of this encounter, from Syrian Orthodox sources, which may seem to offer external and independent corroboration of the encounter, but that they too may be explained to some extent by the wish of later generations of Syrian Orthodox Christians to claim some kind of special position under Islamic rule on the basis of their having been the first Christians to recognise Muḥammad's claim to prophethood.[11]

To some extent this may also be true of the second incident, involving Waraqa, since he too affirms Muḥammad's prophethood, but two factors combine to give it a greater degree of credibility overall: firstly the fact that it takes place after Muḥammad's call, so that it is a reaction to an event of whose happening we can be fairly certain; and secondly the fact that it takes place in Mecca, where it seems to be compatible with the admittedly little we know for sure of the extent of the Christian presence in that town.

What casts some doubt on the letters to Heraclius and the other rulers is again the suspicion that the account of their being sent may serve as a legitimation for a development which took place at a rather later stage of Islamic history, namely the claim that the message of the prophet was not simply directed at the people of Arabia but was rather a universal one. The call to foreign rulers to accept it even in the lifetime of Muḥammad may thus serve to root this claim in the experience of the prophet himself.

A possible Christian parallel may be helpful here, namely the New Testament story of the Three Wise Men who came from the East in order to acknowledge and worship Jesus (Matthew 2: 1–12). Does this refer to a historical event? We cannot be absolutely sure, but it is at least not implausible that it represents a story which was told later in order to justify the suggestion that Jesus's message was a universal one. The fact that the story also involves the recognition of Jesus's significance even before his baptism and call is highly suggestive too when put alongside the Baḥīrā story.

It is the two encounters in Axum and in Medina, however, which probably have the greatest historical foundation, and the contrast between them in terms of the relative power and influence of the two communities is instructive too, with the Muslims being the supplicants in Axum and the Christians occupying that position in Yathrib/Medina.

These are not the only accounts of contacts of one kind or another between Muḥammad and Christians. Just to take two further examples, in Mecca, in addition to the person of Waraqa ibn Nawfal who was discussed above, there seems to have been a small community of Christians which consisted of foreigners and slaves as well as local converts;[12] and in Yathrib/Medina, towards the end of his life Muḥammad had as a concubine a Coptic Christian girl called Māriya, who played a significant role in his last years in that she gave birth to his only son, who was given the name Ibrāhīm (Abraham). However, the boy died before Muḥammad, probably before his second birthday.[13]

As we turn now to investigate the statements in the Qur'ān about Christians, we will see that they manifest a considerable degree of development and evolution, in common with the Qur'ānic message as a whole, and it is very important, therefore, to look at the different statements in their contexts. If, in other words, it is possible to discern different periods in the Qur'ānic message, these may correspond to the successive periods of Muḥammad's career. One of the factors which distinguishes one period from another may be the different relationships which were enjoyed between the Muslim community and the already existing communities of Jews and Christians.

THE QUR'ĀN'S VIEW OF CHRISTIANS

An article written by Professor Jacques Waardenburg, of the Universities of Utrecht and Lausanne, will be helpful in elaborating on this thesis.[14] Building on the earlier researches of scholars such as Hurgronje, Andrae and others, Waardenburg suggests that the development of Muḥammad's message may be partly explained by his encounter with the three main systems of religious belief and practice which were present in the Arabia of his day, namely the Meccan polytheists, the Jews of Yathrib/Medina, and the Christians of Arabia. There is clearly a process of both chronological and geographical development here as the prophet's horizons were expanded.

Put another way it should not be surprising if the Qur'ānic message seems to reflect a tension between Muḥammad's conviction and consciousness of his being a prophet of God, with a message to bear to his contemporaries, and the different groups who either accepted or refused to accept the message and his claims. Part of his conviction was evidently that his was not an isolated prophetic calling but rather the latest in a line of such callings, going back firstly to figures in the Arabian religious memory such as Hūd, Ṣāliḥ and Shu'ayb, who were regarded as having proclaimed the message of monotheism in earlier times in Arabia, and secondly to figures who were of deep religious significance to earlier monotheists in the wider world, especially the Jews and the Christians, such as Ibrāhīm/Abraham, Mūsā/Moses and 'Īsā/Jesus. Muḥammad's expectation seems to have been that on this basis his claims would be accepted by the Jews and Christians of Arabia. Experience, however, fairly quickly made clear that this was not generally going to be the case, and an extremely important element in the development of the Qur'ānic message is that the prophet encountered Jews before he encountered Christians in any depth.

The Christian presence in Arabia, as we have already seen, was most significant on the fringes of the region, on its frontiers with the neighbouring states. The Jewish presence, by contrast, was significant to a much greater extent in the heartlands of Arabia, not least in one of the two towns which was of vital significance for Muḥammad's message and ministry, namely Yathrib/Medina.[15] Mecca, the focus of the first half of the prophet's career, does not seem to have had a significant Jewish presence among its population, just as Christians were few and far between; something would probably have been known about both traditions, as a result both of Jews and Christians visiting the city and of Meccans travelling outside it, but neither community had a substantial number of adherents resident in the city. In Yathrib/Medina, by contrast, there was a well-attested and considerable Jewish presence, made up of not less than three Jewish tribes, the treatment of whom by the prophet has been the focus of a considerable amount of both scholarly and apologetic discussion in recent years.[16]

Muḥammad therefore encountered Jews in significant number before he encountered Christians to the same extent. In Yathrib/Medina, however, it fairly quickly became clear that Muḥammad's claims to prophethood were not going to be accepted by the majority of the Jews of the city, and it should not be surprising if a certain animus begins to appear in some of the Qur'ānic statements about the Medina Jews. One of the strongest of these statements comes in the first half of 5: 82: 'You will find the most vehement . . . in hostility to those who believe [i.e. the Muslims] to be the Jews and the idolaters.' Hopes may have continued to be maintained, however, about the willingness of Christians to accept Muḥammad, and the same Qur'ānic verse continues 'and you will find the nearest in affection to those who believe to be those who say "We are Christians".' The rest of the verse and the following verse elaborate on the reasons for this positive judgement on the Christians:

> This is because there are priests and monks among them, and because they are not proud; when they hear what has been sent down to the Prophet, you see their eyes overflowing with tears as they recognize the truth, and they say: 'Lord, we believe; count us with those who witness.'

Others among the Qur'ān's more positive statements about Jesus and about Christians probably also come from this period.

Later, however, as the tensions and conflicts with the Jewish tribes of Medina are resolved, either by force or by conversion, and as the range and extent of Muḥammad's vision expand to include a larger part of Arabia, more first-hand encounters with Christians begin to take place, as exemplified by the visit of the delegation of Christians from Najrān which we have already discussed. These encounters had a political dimension, in that one question at issue was the submission of the Christians to the rule of the Muslim community, but there was also a theological dimension in that Muḥammad's claims and Christian convictions were also discussed. In the course of these encounters it becomes clear that, generally speaking, Muḥammad's claims concerning his prophetic vocation were not necessarily going to be accepted by Arabian Christians either, and in response to this the tone of Qur'ānic pronouncements concerning Christians too begins to become more negative and antagonistic. Context is thus extremely important in assessing all that the Qur'ān says about Christians.

A Qur'ānic verse such as 9: 29, which commands Muslims to 'Fight against such of those who have been given the Scripture as believe not in Allah nor the Last Day, and forbid not that which God has forbidden by His Messenger, and follow not the religion of truth, until they pay the tribute readily, being brought low' is thus probably later in date than 5: 82–3, and reflects a situation in which there is some tension between Muḥammad and both Jews and Christians (those who have been given the Scripture).

In her very detailed study of how Muslim commentaries on the Qur'ān understand the Qur'ānic references to Christians, Jane McAuliffe suggests that there are seven Qur'ānic texts which are generally recognised as referring positively towards at least some Christians: in addition to 5:82–3, which has been discussed above, they are

> 2: 62 Those who believe, and those who are Jews, Christians, and Sabaeans, whoever believes in God and the Last Day and does right, their reward is with their Lord; no fear will come upon them, neither will they grieve.

> 3: 55 When God said: 'O Jesus, I will take you and raise you to Me and cleanse you from those who disbelieve, and I will place those who follow you above those who disbelieve until the Day of Resurrection; then you [plural] will return to me and I will judge between you in what you differ over.'

> 3: 199 Among the People of the Book there are some who believe in God and what was sent down to you and what was sent down to them, humbling themselves before God, and not selling the verses [*ayāt*] of God cheaply; their reward is with their Lord, who is swift to reckon.

> 5: 66 If they [the People of the Book] had observed the Torah and the Gospel and what was sent down to them from their Lord, they would have eaten from above them and from below their feet; among them are those who keep to the right path, but many of them do evil.

> 28: 52–5 [There are] those to whom We gave the Scripture beforehand who believe in it, and when it is recited to them they say: 'We believe in it; it is the truth from our Lord, and we have already submitted to it.' They will be given their reward twice, because they have been steadfast, they have repaid evil with good, and they have been generous with what we have provided them with; when they hear idle chatter they turn away from it and say: 'We have our works, and you have yours; peace be upon you; we do not seek ignorant people.'

> 57: 27 Then we caused Our messengers to follow in their [Noah and Abraham's] footsteps; We sent Jesus, the son of Mary, and gave him the Gospel, and We placed compassion and mercy in the hearts of those who followed him, but they invented monasticism; We did not prescribe it for them, seeking only God's pleasure, and they did not practise it properly, so We gave those of them who believed their reward, but many of them are evildoers.

Her conclusion, however, makes clear that in the eyes of later interpreters of the Qur'ān, the acceptance of Christians which is envisaged here is at best conditional, so that what she calls 'Qur'ānic Christians' are those 'who either accepted the prophethood of Muḥammad and the revelation entrusted to him or would have done had their historical circumstances permitted.'[17]

Alongside these broadly, if conditionally positive statements about Christians, however, there are others which seem much more negative, and many of these occur in the context of discussion of *shirk* (polytheism/idolatry), and *kufr* (unbelief). Nowhere in the Qur'ān are Christians specifically described as either *mushrikūn* (those guilty of *shirk*) or *kāfirūn* (unbelievers), terms usually referring respectively to

Meccan and Arabian polytheists and to those who reject Muḥammad's message, but in some verses it does appear to be suggested that Christians are guilty of both *kufr* and *shirk*. This is particularly the case in 5: 72: 'They disbelieve [*kafara*] who say "God is the Messiah, son of Mary" . . . God prohibits paradise to anyone who ascribes partners [*yushrik*] to God'; and 5:73: 'They disbelieve [*kafara*] who say "God is the third of three" . . . If they do not desist from what they say, a painful punishment will befall those who disbelieve [*kafarū*]'.

These verses are difficult to interpret, not least because the accusations which are made, saying that God is Jesus or that God is the third of three, are not statements which would usually be made by most Christians. However, it seems clear that it is probably Christians who were the original target of the accusations, and that is certainly the way in which the verses have been understood by most later Muslim commentators. In addition to 9: 29, therefore, which has been discussed above and which refers to both Jews and Christians, other verses are extremely hostile to Christians in particular, suggesting that they both 'disbelieve' (*kafara*) and are guilty of *shirk*.

As such, Christians are seen as coming in some sense under judgement. As a recent study of the Qur'ān, which investigates the Qur'ānic verses about 'unbelievers' in considerable detail, makes clear, although it does not address itself primarily to the question of their identity, the development of Qur'ānic attitudes towards 'unbelievers' is clear enough, from the Meccan period, with its assertion that judgement will befall them through direct intervention by God, to the Medina period with its increasing conviction that the divine judgement will be mediated through the community of believers.[18]

With respect to the Qur'ān's statements about Christians, therefore, some are more positive, suggesting that they, with the Jews, should be seen primarily as *ahl al-kitāb* (people of the book). However, some are much more negative, implying that Christians, sometimes linked with the Jews but sometimes being seen independently, should be seen as being guilty of *shirk* or *kufr*. This conclusion, then, suggests that today it is important to remember that the Qur'ānic references to Jews and Christians should be seen as having as their primary point of reference the members of those communities resident in Arabia, rather than the worldwide community of Jews and Christians of the day. It is this which explains apparently puzzling references to Jews saying that Ezra is the son of God (9: 30), and Christians taking Jesus and his mother as gods (5: 116), neither of which is a statement which would be made by most Jews or Christians.[19]

The Qur'ān's statements about Christians must therefore be seen as part of a three-cornered discussion, so that its pronouncements about

Christians are also part of a discussion with Jews. It is in that context, therefore, that the Qur'ān affirms Jesus's prophethood despite the rejection of that claim by Jews, yet also rejects aspects of the traditional Christian claims about Jesus, particularly any idea that he may be described as being in any sense 'son of God'.[20]

In exactly the same way that early Christian views of Judaism and the Jews were substantially affected by the nature of the relationship between the followers of Jesus and the Jewish communities at different stages, so the Qur'ān's views reflect the state of the relations between the different communities in Arabia, and the way in which they warmed and cooled at different stages of Muḥammad's career. We have seen something very similar already too with reference to the attitude of the early Christians towards the Roman state: in periods of tolerance and relatively benign rule, Christians were happy to proclaim their loyalty to the state and to regard it positively, but if the state began to persecute Christians then their view of it not surprisingly changed, so that in some cases it becomes described as 'The Beast', as in the book of Revelation. Here too context had a considerable effect on text.

PRECEDENTS FOR MUSLIM TREATMENT OF CHRISTIANS

So far, we have looked firstly at the extent of Muḥammad's contacts with Christians during his lifetime, and secondly at the various statements about Christians which can be found in the Qur'ān and how they need to be located in the context of Muḥammad's developing discussions with Jews as well as Christians. We now need to look at how the practical relationships between the Muslim community and the Christians of Arabia were worked out, and in this area too we shall see that relationships with Jews were again hugely important.

Upon Muḥammad's arrival in Yathrib/Medina, an extremely important document of early Islamic history, the so-called Constitution of Medina, served to regulate the relationships between the community of the newly arrived Muslims and the different tribal communities which were already present in the city, some Jewish and some Arab. Consisting of some fifty clauses, the document as it exists today has been dated by Watt as probably coming from the period after 627/6, but reflecting the circumstances which existed either as far back as 622/1 or in around 624/3. On the one hand this document describes the Muslims and those who are attached to them and fight with them as 'one community' (Clause 1), and it is affirmed that a Jew who follows the Muslims has the same right as them to help and support (Clause 16). On the other hand, religious diversity is recognised and tolerated: '. . . To the Jews their religion and to the Muslims their religion . . .'

(Clause 25); and 'It is for the Jews to bear their expenses and for the Muslims to bear their expenses. There is to be [mutual] "help" between them against whoever wars against the people of this document. Between them there is to be [mutual] giving of advice, consultation, and honourable dealing, not treachery . . .' (Clause 37).[21]

Here, then, we have what might even in modern terms be described as quite a 'liberal' document, in the sense that it seems broadly tolerant of diversity even in matters of religion, and is happy to affirm that each religious community present in Yathrib/Medina has both rights and responsibilities in the relationship between the two groups.

Some years later in Muḥammad's career, however, we find a rather different model or precedent for the relationship between the Muslim and the Jewish communities, involving the oasis of Khaybar. Situated some ninety miles south of Yathrib/Medina, Khaybar was a rich agricultural settlement, whose population was overwhelmingly Jewish. One of the Jewish tribes of Medina, the Banū Naḍīr, who had been expelled from the city by Muḥammad in 625/4, had taken refuge in Khaybar, and the population of that city had entered into an alliance with Mecca and some local Bedouin tribes to frustrate Muḥammad's ambitions. In 628/7, therefore, Muḥammad launched a military attack on Khaybar and besieged its population, which resisted. After a six-week siege, the population surrendered, the terms agreed being that the land would be handed over to Muḥammad, but the Jews would be allowed to continue to cultivate it, with half of the produce being handed over to the Muslims. The Muslims reserved the right to break the agreement at any time, however, and to expel the Jews if they wished to do so.[22]

This model of the relationship between Muḥammad and a Jewish community therefore seems rather less positive than the one we have seen testified to in the Constitution of Medina. The context, of course, is one of a military confrontation, and although there is no threat to the lives of the Jews, nor to their continuing to practise their faith, the tone of the agreement is rather harsher, and the position of the Jews after the making of the agreement is somewhat more vulnerable.

A third and final instance of an agreement between Muḥammad and other religious communities comes from around the year 630/9, when deputations came from different parts of Arabia to Muḥammad in order to negotiate concerning their relationship with the Muslim community. According to Ibn Isḥāq, the deputation from the kings of Ḥimyar declared their submission to Islam and their abandonment of polytheism, and in return they were instructed to obey God and Muḥammad, and to practise Islam properly with respect to such things as prayer and almsgiving. An interesting statement then follows concerning Jews and Christians: 'If a Jew or a Christian becomes a Muslim he is a believer with his rights and obligations. He who holds fast to his religion, Jew or Christian, is not to be turned from it. He must pay the poll-tax . . .'[23]

A few months later, according to Ibn Isḥāq, a delegation was then sent, under the leadership of Khālid ibn al-Walīd, to Najrān, probably in 631/10. This delegation was instructed to give a rather peremptory summons to the population, of whom some were Christian but not all, to accept Islam within three days or to be attacked. Most accepted, but once again it was stated that 'A Jew or a Christian who becomes a sincere Muslim of his own accord and obeys the religion of Islam is a believer with the same rights and obligations. If one of them holds fast to his religion he is not to be turned from it.'[24]

Other early Islamic historians record slightly different versions of this agreement. Ibn Sa'd, for example, provided far more detail about the nature and extent of the tribute which the people of Najrān were required to pay, and adds that they were to refrain from the practice of usury, but in return they were assured that their lives and property were safe, and that their churches and religious leaders would also be protected.[25]

A variety of models for the relationship between Muslims and non-Muslims can therefore be found in Muḥammad's career between 622/1 and 632/11 in Yathrib/Medina, and this is a natural enough outworking of the diversity in the scriptural statements concerning Jews and Christians which we have looked at in the preceding section. The Qur'ān contains some positive statements about Jesus and Christians, probably from the middle part of Muḥammad's career when relations with the Arabian Jews were tense; it also contains some more critical statements, probably from the latter end of Muḥammad's ministry. Reflecting this, in his attitude towards Jewish communities, Muḥammad's actions sometimes manifest a broadly tolerant attitude, as seen in the Constitution of Medina, and sometimes a more antagonistic one, as seen at Khaybar. Towards the end of his life, however, as seen in the negotiations with Ḥimyar and Najrān, a kind of mediating position emerges, where both Jews and Christians are given a kind of conditional acceptance, whereby they may retain their faith on condition that they submit peacefully to Islamic rule and pay some kind of tribute to the Muslim community.

Given the natural tendency for the more recent to supersede the older, it might be expected that after the prophet's death the earlier more positive Qur'ānic statements about Christians would simply have been forgotten, and passed over in favour of the later more negative ones. But one of the interesting things about the next phase of Christian–Muslim interaction is the extent to which this was not always the case, so that we see a whole range of Muslim attitudes towards Christians emerging.

NOTES

1. See the widely differing theses of C. C. Torrey, *The Jewish Foundation of Islam*, 2nd edn, New York: Ktav, 1967; R. Bell, *The Origin of Islam in its Christian environment*, London: Cass, 1968; and P. Crone and M. Cook, *Hagarism: the Making of the Islamic World*, Cambridge University Press, 1977, which suggests some Samaritan influence. An older article considers all three traditions: see J. Finkel, 'Jewish, Christian, and Samaritan Influences on Arabia' in W. G. Shellabear, E. E. Calverley, et al. (eds), *MacDonald Presentation Volume*, Princeton University Press, 1933, pp. 147–66.
2. An invaluable discussion of the whole question of origins may be found in D. Waines, *An Introduction to Islam*, Cambridge University Press, 1995, pp. 265–79.
3. Two articles which stress the originality of Muḥammad's ideas are J. Fueck, 'The Originality of the Arabian Prophet', English translation in M. Swartz (ed.), *Studies on Islam*, Oxford University Press, 1991, pp. 86–98, and T. Kronholm, 'Dependence and Prophetic Originality in the Koran' in *Orientalia Suecana*, 31–2 (1982–3), pp. 47–70.
4. See A. von Denffer, *Christians in the Qur'ān and the Sunna*, Leicester: The Islamic Foundation, 1979, pp. 10–29. Von Denffer also refers to two other brief references to Christians in the *Sīra*.
5. See A. Guillaume, *The Life of Muḥammad*, Oxford University Press, 1955, pp. 79–81.
6. Ibid., pp. 83 and 107.
7. Ibid., pp. 146–50.
8. Ibid., pp. 150–3.
9. Ibid., pp. 270–7.
10. Ibid., pp. 652–9.
11. See the unpublished MA thesis of M. A. Shabot, *An Evaluative Study of the Bahira Story in the Muslim and Christian Traditions*, University of Birmingham, 1983.
12. A paper was presented on this topic to the 1996 conference of the Middle East Studies Association in Providence, Rhode Island, by Ghada Osman of Harvard University.
13. See W. M. Watt, *Muḥammad Prophet and Statesman*, Oxford University Press, 1961, pp. 195 and 226.
14. J. Waardenburg, 'Towards a periodization of earliest Islam according to its relations with other religions' in R. Peters (ed.), *Proceedings of the Ninth Congress of the Union Européenne des Arabisants et Islamisants*, Leiden: Brill, 1981, pp. 304–26.
15. For the whole history of the Jewish communities in Arabia, see G. D. Newby, *A History of the Jews of Arabia*, Columbia, South Carolina: University of South Carolina Press, 1988.
16. See W. N. Arafat, 'New Light on the Story of Banū Qurayẓa and the Jews of Medina' in *Journal of the Royal Asiatic Society*, 1976, pp. 100–7; B. Ahmad, *Muḥammad and the Jews: a Re-examination*, Delhi: Vikas, 1979; M. J. Kister, 'The Massacre of the Banū Qurayẓa: a re-examination

of a tradition' in *Jerusalem Studies in Arabic and Islam*, 8 (1986), pp. 61–96; and R.S. Faizer, 'Muḥammad and the Medinan Jews: a Comparison of the Texts of Ibn Ishaq's *Kitāb sīrat rasūl Allāh* with al-Waqidi's *Kitāb al-maghāzī*, in *International Journal of Middle East Studies*, 28: 4 (1996), pp. 463–89.

17. J. D. McAuliffe, *Qur'ānic Christians: an Analysis of Classical and Modern Exegesis*, Cambridge University Press, 1991, p. 287.
18. D. Marshall, *God, Muḥammad and the Unbelievers*, London: Curzon, 1999.
19. On Ezra see M. Ayoub, ''Uzayr in the Qur'ān and Muslim Tradition' in W. M Brinner and S. D. Ricks (eds), *Studies in Islamic and Judaic Traditions*, vol. I, Atlanta: Scholars' Press, 1986, pp. 3–18; on Mary see G. Parrinder, *Jesus in the Qur'ān*, London: Faber, 1965, pp. 133–41.
20. For more detail on this see my *Muslim Perceptions of Christianity*, London: Grey Seal, 1996, Chapter 1.
21. See Guillaume, *The Life of Muḥammad*, pp. 231–3. A full English translation of the document can also be found in W. M. Watt, *Islamic Political Thought*, Edinburgh University Press, 1968, pp. 130–4; see also the discussion of the document in Watt, pp. 4–6; R. B. Serjeant, 'The "Constitution of Medina"' in *Islamic Quarterly*, 8 (1964), pp. 1–16; and F. M. Denny '*Ummah* in the Constitution of Medina' in *Journal of Near Eastern Studies*, 36 (1977), pp. 39–47.
22. Guillaume, pp. 510–18.
23. Ibid., p. 643.
24. Ibid., pp. 647–8.
25. See W. M. Watt, *Muḥammad at Medina*, Oxford University Press, 1981, pp. 359–60, for a translation of Ibn Sa'd's text.

3

The First Age of Christian–Muslim Interaction (–c. 830/215)

CHRISTIAN RESPONSES TO THE COMING OF ISLAM

There is no denying the impact made by the Islamic community on world history in the few decades after the death of Muḥammad in 632/11. A community which, in the course of the ten years since the Hijra in 622, had made its mark by becoming the dominant force in Arabia, very quickly also made its mark on the wider world in pretty much the same length of time. By 642/21 the Muslim state had conquered and established its control over the majority of the Sassanian Persian Empire, following the battles of Qadisiyya [637/16] in Iraq and Nihawand [642/21] in Iran, and a large part of the Byzantine Empire, following the battle of the River Yarmuk [636/15] in Syria and a campaign in Egypt in 640/19. The Sassanian Empire was destroyed, its emperor Yazdagird III finally meeting an ignominious end in central Asia in 651/30, and the Byzantine Empire lost roughly one half of its territory: according to Arab tradition, following the battle of the Yarmuk, the emperor Heraclius was driven to say 'Farewell Syria. What a good country for the enemy.'[1]

Within the next century, the Islamic state continued its expansion, so that by 750/133 it had become the largest state seen up until that point in human history, having incorporated north Africa, Spain, the most fertile parts of central Asia, and much of what is now Afghanistan and Pakistan.[2] After 750/133 the process of expansion, it is true, came to a halt for several centuries, and a process of, on the one hand, consolidation, and, on the other, fragmentation began, but there is no denying the initial impression made by the Islamic community.

One obvious difference between the situation confronting Muslims during the lifetime of Muḥammad and the new situation after 632/11 is that, as we have seen, the prophet himself did not have very much first-hand encounters with Christians, whereas his followers, as a result of their success, suddenly had a great deal of contact with Christians, as well as other religious groups: the vast majority of the population of the conquered Byzantine provinces was Christian, belonging to one church or another, and in the Sassanian Empire too there was a significant Christian minority presence, consisting mostly of Nestorian Christians. The interaction between the Christian and Muslim communities in this first period of their mutual encounter is therefore extremely significant and interesting, and my suggestion is that the initial phase of this encounter should be seen as lasting for roughly 200 years, that is until the first half of the ninth/third century.

In the wake of the initial impact of the Muslim community upon the Middle East, the first Christian reaction to this new phenomenon was to interpret it in terms of certain statements of the Old Testament/Hebrew Bible which seemed highly pertinent to some of the development of the 630s/10s and 640s/20s. In particular, some of the statements of the Book of Genesis at the start of the Old Testament seemed to offer some kind of key to explain what was happening, as it was there that an attempt was made to allocate significance to the two sons of Abraham – Ishmael, chronologically the first-born, but born to Abraham's concubine Hagar, and Isaac, born second in time but eventually declared Abraham's heir since he was born to Sarah, Abraham's wife. In the course of the narrative, it is stated that certain promises were made by God to Ishmael:

> But God said to Abraham: ' . . . I will make a nation of the son of the slave woman [Hagar] also, because he is your offspring' (Genesis 21: 12–13)

and this is elaborated later in the same chapter (Genesis 21: 18), where a further promise is made by God:

> 'I will make him a great nation.'

Later in the book of Genesis, in Chapter 25, when the descendants of Abraham are being listed, Ishmael's sons are listed before Isaac's, and the fact that there are twelve of them has traditionally been interpreted as signifying that like the twelve tribes of Israel, they made up some kind of sacred unit.[3]

When, therefore, the Islamic community burst onto the scene, one interpretation which was put onto its appearance was that it was the fulfilment of these scriptural promises. The Armenian bishop Sebeos, writing before 661/41, for example, explains Muḥammad's career as follows: 'Being very learned and well-versed in the Law of Moses, he taught them [the Arabs] to know the God of Abraham.' He also, according to Sebeos, told his hearers that God was going to realise in them the promise made to Abraham and his successors, and it was for this reason that the Ishmaelites set out from the desert towards the land around Jerusalem.[4]

John Moorhead comments: 'Sebeos reports that both Jews and Arabs accepted that the Arabs were descended from the patriarch

Abraham . . . [and] . . . seems to have accepted this connection between God's Old Dispensation and the Arabs of his time.'[5] Equally, the chronicle of an anonymous Nestorian monk, written in Iraq during the 670s/50s, testifies that the Ishmaelites have been making conquests, and that this is in part a result of their following in the footsteps of Abraham who, when he went to live in the desert, built a place for the worship of God and the offering of sacrifices; in worshipping God, therefore, the Arabs are doing nothing new, but simply following an old custom. He also suggests an interesting etymological connection, whereby Yathrib's new name, Medina, is derived from the name of Midian, the fourth son Abraham had by Keturah (cf. Genesis 25: 1).[6]

In recent years an entire thesis concerning the origins and early development of Islam has been elaborated on this basis by the Western scholars Michael Cook and Patricia Crone in their book *Hagarism*, which suggests that Islam should be interpreted as being self-consciously a movement involving the descendants of Hagar.[7] The early pages of the book refer to both of the texts which have just been discussed, but rather than taking them as what they actually are, namely Christian interpretations of the coming of Islam, the authors seem to suggest that they should be taken as more valuable descriptions of early Islamic history than the traditional Muslim accounts. This seems to be going too far.[8]

This first level of interpretation of Islam, however, was fairly quickly subjected to a number of challenges, as it began to become clear that the Islamic community was not only convinced that its coming was part of God's will, but also saw itself as having a mission to be a kind of corrective to, or even fulfilment of, the message of the Christian community. Rather than its coming simply being the fulfilment of an ancient promise, therefore, it began to appear to the Christian community as rather more of a challenge; in other words, the Christian community, which had hitherto seen itself as the bearer of God's final revelation to humankind, began to become aware that this was not an idea which was acceptable to the Ishmaelites.

As a result of this, it is not long before we see a shift to a second layer of interpretation of the coming of Islam, and in this second period the divisions of the Christian world at the time begin to become evident and to make their presence felt. Clearly in the initial encounter of Christians and Muslims after the time of Muḥammad, the Christians involved were all Eastern Christians. It was only later, after the expansion of the Muslim community into North Africa and Spain, that Western Christians began to formulate their rather different interpretations of Islam, which we will look at below. But, as we have seen, the Eastern Christian world of the day was itself also divided, with the main difference being between those who accepted the definitions of the Council of Chalcedon and those who did not, and, with respect to Islam, the different judgements which began to emerge at this time reflect that split fairly clearly.

Among the non-Chalcedonian Christians, first, the way in which Islam came to be understood after the initial Abrahamic interpretation was that its coming was in some way a judgement of God, a movement whose purpose was to bring judgement on people who had erred. This view is one which can be found in the writings of both Monophysite and Nestorian Christians, as illustrated by the Coptic editor of the Egyptian *History of the Patriarchs*, Severus of Asmounein, who wrote: 'The Lord abandoned the army of the Romans as a punishment for their corrupt faith, and because of the anathemas uttered against them by the ancient fathers, on account of the Council of Chalcedon.'[9] And the twelfth/fifth century Monophysite writer Michael the Syrian commented:

> The God of vengeance . . . raised up from the south the children of Ishmael to deliver us from the hands of the Romans . . . It was no light benefit for us to be freed from the cruelty of the Romans, their wickedness, anger and ardent cruelty towards us, and to find ourselves in peace.[10]

For all their differences these two groups are thus united in their view that Islam is God's judgement, not on themselves (of course!), but rather on their theological and ecclesiastical foes, the Christians who accepted the Christological definitions of the Council of Chalcedon. Again a Biblical analogy is called into play at this point, the analogy of the Babylonian ruler Nebuchadnezzar, who destroyed Jerusalem in 587 or 586 BCE, and whose action was interpreted by some of the Old Testament prophets, such as Jeremiah, as bringing God's judgement on a decadent Israelite community.

It was not only theological factors which were involved here. Not only had Nestorians and Monophysites each differed theologically with the church authorities in the Byzantine capital Constantinople, they had also each been on the receiving end of some fairly harsh treatment from the Byzantine authorities in Egypt and Syria, encouraged by those bishops who accepted Chalcedon. So, for example, the Copts in Egypt had been fairly harshly persecuted by Cyrus, who had been appointed by the Byzantine emperor Heraclius to be both governor of Egypt and patriarch of the church in Egypt in 631/10. Between his appointment and the Arab conquest of Egypt Cyrus succeeded in alienating the vast majority of Egyptian Christians from both the definitions of the Council of Chalcedon and allegiance to the Byzantine Empire; '"The Caucasian", as he was called, opened a reign of terror the like of which the Egyptians had not experienced since the Great Persecution. In the six years 635/14–641/20 whatever loyalty had been felt towards Heraclius and the Roman Empire ebbed away.'[11] Not only that, between 608 and 629/7 the eastern provinces of the Byzantine Empire had been occupied by the Persians. During that interlude the non-Chalcedonian Christians had found themselves treated with a greater degree of tolerance and respect than had been the case under the Byzantines, so that when the representatives of Islam first appeared, many of the non-Chalcedonian Christians welcomed them, seeing them, like the Persians, as liberators from the cruelty of the rule of Byzantine emperors and ecclesiastical authorities. 'What the Persian era showed was that a foreign overlord was not necessarily a persecutor, but a Chalcedonian nearly always was.'[12]

Among those Christians who, even under the rule of Islam, retained their loyalty to the Council of Chalcedon, later coming to be known as Melkites because of their adherence to the Byzantine liturgy and the suspicion that their political loyalty was to the Byzantine Emperor, a rather different interpretation of the coming of Islam emerged during the first century or so of Islamic rule.[13] As a figure representative of this point of view we may take John of Damascus.

As his name indicates, John's family came from Damascus, where they had had considerable influence for some time, as seen in the fact that it was his grandfather, Manṣūr ibn Sargūn, who surrendered the city to the Arab invaders in 635/14.[14] Sahas observes that this name is not Greek in form, being closer to the name patterns of Syrian Christians of Arab descent, which is evidence of the diffusion of population from Arabia into Syria and the wider world. John was probably educated with Muslims until the age of twelve, so that he knew Arabic as well as Greek, and like his father and grandfather before him he went on to achieve a high position in the administration of the city in which they lived. Some sources speak of John himself as being secretary to the prince of the city, and others speak of him having some special financial responsibility. The last twenty-five years or so of his life, however, he spent in the monastery of Saint Sabas in Palestine, having retired from his work for the Muslim rulers of the city. He is commonly regarded as the last of the Fathers of the Eastern Church.[15]

On the basis of his experience and his theological reflection, John was able to articulate a novel interpretation of Islam, and the kernel of this interpretation was that Islam should be understood as a Christian heresy. As a result of his encounters with Muslims, at different levels and in different contexts, John had been able to acquire at least a reasonable first-hand knowledge of Muslim beliefs and religious practices, including some acquaintance with the Qur'ān, and it was on this basis that he concluded that Muslims had at least some convictions in common with those of Christians, even if on other points the two communities differed. The simplest way to account for this combination of commonality and distinctiveness was, in John's view, to describe Islam as a Christian heresy.

This view is outlined in two of his works. The first is an Appendix to his *De Haeresibus* (On Heresies), which was itself a supplement to his *De Fide Orthodoxa* (On the Orthodox Faith). The work on heresies lists 100 established Christian heresies, in the discussion of which John is heavily reliant on the work of earlier Christian heresiographers, and then Islam is referred to as the one hundred and first heresy. In his description John manifests both a theoretical and a practical knowledge of Islam, so that he knows, for example, about the following things: the idolatrous character of pre-Islamic religion in Arabia; Muḥammad's preaching of the message of monotheism in that context (and here John gives a fairly accurate summary of Sura 112 of the Qur'ān to the effect that there is one God, creator of all, who is neither begotten nor has begotten); some of the contents of the Qur'ān, since he quotes the titles of four Suras from it – Sura 2 (the Heifer), Sura 4 (Women), Sura 5 (The Table), and also a title which is not generally recognised, 'the she-camel of God', which Sahas thinks may refer to Sura 7 or Sura 26; and Muslim practices such as the kissing of the Black Stone in the corner of the Ka'ba in Mecca, which John describes as being extremely passionate, circumcision, not keeping the Sabbath, and abstention from some foods and wine.[16]

John also knows what the Qur'ān says about Jesus – that he is a word of (from) God, His spirit, and a servant, miraculously conceived, but not crucified – and it is perhaps on the basis of this point that he constructs his main interpretation of Islam as a Christian heresy: Muḥammad, John alleges, came across the Old and New Testaments by chance, and with the help of an Arian monk, constructed a heresy of his own. John himself makes no mention of Baḥīrā at this point, but Sahas, following Tor Andrae, suggests that this is an allusion, at least, to Baḥīrā as an agent of transmission to Muḥammad, and if Arianism was a Christian heresy it is easy enough to see how Islam might be interpreted in a similar way. Muḥammad thus claimed, according to John, that a book was sent down to him from heaven, but the resulting claim to prophethood is rejected by John, who describes Islam as 'a deceptive superstition of the Ishmaelites' and 'the fore-runner of the Antichrist'. The latter of these phrases, particularly, seems to demonstrate a particularly negative evaluation of Islam, but as Sahas makes clear, it is not a manifestation of any special animus against Islam but rather the phrase which is used as a matter of course to refer to anyone whom John considers to be a heretic; it is thus used earlier in the work with respect to Nestorius, and its usage can, indeed, be traced back to the New Testament itself:

> By this you know the Spirit of God: every spirit which confesses that Jesus Christ has come in the flesh is of God, and every spirit which does not confess Jesus is not of God. This is the spirit of antichrist, of which you heard that it was coming, and now it is in the world already. (1 John 4: 2–3)

The original target of these verses was probably Gnosticism, which leaned in the direction of denying Jesus's humanity rather than his divinity, but in later Christian thought, as exemplified by John of Damascus, the term 'antichrist' came to be used of anyone who 'does not confess that the Son of God came in flesh, is perfect God and He became perfect man while at the same time He was God.'[17]

Very importantly, John does not use the term 'forerunner of the Antichrist' to refer to Muḥammad personally, but to Islam in general. In this he differs from some later Christian writers who do personalise the epithet. Sahas therefore concludes:

> The author . . . presents the facts about Islam in an orderly and systematic way, although not at all complimentary; he demonstrates an accurate knowledge of the religion . . . he is aware of the cardinal doctrines and concepts in Islam . . . he knows well his sources and he is at home with the Muslim mentality. Chapter . . . 101 is not inflammatory of hatred, neither grandiloquent and full of self-triumph; it is an essay on Islam, in a book of Christian heresies. In this simple fact lies its significance and its weakness![18]

This assessment of Islam as a Christian heresy is also demonstrated in another work commonly attributed to John of Damascus, the *Disputatio Saraceni et Christiani* (The Disputation of a Muslim and a Christian). There is some uncertainty concerning the authorship of this document, with some suggestions being made that it comes from the pen of John's disciple Theodore Abū Qurra rather than from John himself, but Sahas is content to treat it as a product of his thought if not of his own pen.[19]

The form and format of this work is quite different from Chapter 101 of the *De Haeresibus*, in that this work is intended not so much as a theological evaluation of Islam but rather as a kind of manual of guidance for Christians who find themselves entering into theological discussion with Muslims. Two main themes are discussed; firstly the question of the relationship between divine omnipotence and human free will, and secondly the question of the identity of the 'word of God'. As has been suggested by a number of Western scholars, notably M. S. Seale in his *Muslim Theology*, these questions were among the most important in the development of the tradition of *Kalām* (Islamic Theology), and John's opinions may therefore have had some influence on the form which that tradition took. But whatever the extent or otherwise of direct influence, the *Disputatio* 'is a valuable source of information about the earliest stage of Muslim–Christian dialogue', and 'allows one to assume that John of Damascus . . . had participated in formal or informal debates [with Muslim theologians]'.[20]

These were the three main strains of Christian interpretation of Islam before the ninth/third century – fulfilment of God's promises to Abraham and his son Ishmael, judgement from God on those Christians who accepted the Christological definitions of the Council of Chalcedon, and Christian heresy. During that century, however, new, more negative interpretations of Islam begin to emerge, and they take us into the next phase of Christian–Muslim encounter which will be looked at in more detail in the next chapter. Briefly, however, what changes is that a considerably more negative view of Islam begins to emerge, firstly among Christians outside the world of Islam, in the Byzantine Empire, but shortly afterwards among Christians, both Nestorian and Monophysite, too, within the world of Islam. The ninth/third century therefore does seem to mark a transition to another stage in Christian–Muslim relations.

MUSLIM TREATMENT OF CHRISTIANS I

As has been hinted above, the way in which Christians responded to and interpreted the coming of Islam was, naturally enough, considerably influenced by the way in which they were treated by the Muslim conquerors. Here too, as in most other aspects of Christian–Muslim relations, there was no single Muslim attitude, but rather a range of attitudes which shifted over the course of time and displayed a considerable amount of diversity.

During the course of his lifetime, Muḥammad, as we have seen, had some contact with Christians and rather more contact with Jews. Out of these contacts came a number of precedents for inter-communal relations, varying with respect to the Jews from the relatively liberal model of the Constitution of Medina to the rather harsher model of the treatment of the Jews of Khaybar. An intermediate position was seen in the negotiations which took place with some of the people of South Arabia, including Jews and Christians, who were allowed to retain their faith provided that they submitted peacefully to Islamic rule.

After the death of the prophet in 632/11, therefore, when the Muslim community began to encounter Christians and, to a lesser extent, Jews in much greater numbers, as it expanded into the wider Middle East, it was these different incidents from the career of Muḥammad which provided guidance for the Muslim community as to how to treat Christians and Jews. In the two centuries or so after Muḥammad's death, these various precedents seemed to result in two main attitudes being taken: the first was seen in a fairly short phase, which involved raids outside Arabia and the expulsion of Jews and Christians from Arabia itself, and was thus rather antagonistic and confrontational; the second, which was much longer-lasting, devolped once the raids had evolved into more permanent conquests, and demonstrated more settled and conciliatory attitudes.

Towards the end of his career, as we have seen, Muḥammad's message seems to have developed a more critical approach towards both Jews and Christians, as seen in a Qur'ānic verse such as 9: 29. After his death, therefore, it was this approach, with its reference to fighting the People of the Book, which predominated. Military raids were launched into the areas bordering on Arabia, and Crone and Cook draw attention to the fact that the earliest raids seem to have displayed a particular hostility towards Christianity. This can be seen in such things as the choice given to the Byzantine garrison in Gaza, whose members were invited to abandon their faith, deny Christ and participate in Muslim worship: when they refused they were all martyred.[21] Crone and Cook point to a number of other examples of particular antipathy towards Christians in this period, such as the burning of churches, the destruction of monasteries, the profanation of crosses (as seen when the Arab raiders reached Mt Sinai), and other blasphemies against Christ and the church.

In Arabia itself, too, in the decade after Muḥammad's death, some revision of the prophet's own attitude towards Jews and Christians took place, in that the Jewish and Christian communities of Arabia were expelled from Arabia. The Muslim sources differ on the exact detail of how and when this was done, but al-Wāqidī tells of the second caliph, 'Umar ibn al-Khaṭṭāb, expelling the Jews of the Hijaz, and al-Ṭabarī refers to 'Umar expelling the Jews from Khaybar and dividing the land there between the Muslims.[22] Al-Ṭabarī does not indicate that all the Jews were expelled from Arabia, and later sources point to the continuing existence of Jewish communities in both the Hijaz and the area around Khaybar, so the commands of the caliph were not necessarily executed thoroughly, but clearly these measures resulted in the marginalisation of the Jews who remained in Arabia.

As regards the Christians of Arabia, Muslim sources speak of an order of 'Umar ibn al-Khaṭṭāb to the effect that they too must leave Arabia, and there are accounts of the Christians of Najrān migrating to Iraq, but the historicity of these events is not absolutely reliably established, and there is some evidence of a continuing Christian presence in Najrān for at least 200 years.[23] Again, therefore, we see a trend towards the establishment of religious uniformity in Arabia, which parallels the emergence of the tradition that Muḥammad, as he was dying, said that two religions could not exist together in Arabia.[24] But measures to implement that advice were clearly not put into place immediately.[25]

During the same period in the wider Middle East, as the Muslim community moved from undertaking raids to a situation where longer-term conquests and settlement were envisaged, the model for the relationship between the Muslims and the conquered population, which was largely Christian, began to change again, and it did so in the direction of the precedent provided by the behaviour of the delegation sent to Najrān under the leadership of Khālid ibn al-Walīd in 631/10. The fact that Khālid was one of the leaders of the main Muslim army in Syria during the time of the conquests is not irrelevant here. There was some evolution from that precedent, however, in that in Najrān the population had been summoned to accept Islam or be attacked, though the Jewish and Christian elements of the town had been assured that they would not be turned from their faith. In Syria and many other conquered areas, by contrast, Christians were not a minority but a majority of the population, and the terms of the discussion were somewhat different.

There are variations between the different Muslim historical sources concerning the exact pattern of events around the conquests, and particularly as regards the agreements which were made between the Muslim leaders and the cities of the conquered territories.[26] In general terms, what seems usually to have occurred is that the population of cities such as Damascus was given a choice: the people could either surrender, in which case they would be given an assurance that their lives, their property and their places of worship would be secure, or they could resist. If the cities were then forced to surrender, the terms would be much less generous, so that their places of worship would be liable to be taken over and converted into mosques, and they would not be permitted to construct new places of worship. Not surprisingly, many cities such as Damascus chose to submit peacefully, and we have seen already that it was the grandfather of the theologian John of Damascus who negotiated the surrender of the city in 635/14.

Other cities, however, resisted, including Jerusalem and Caesarea, but Jerusalem sued for peace in 640/19, and Caesarea fell in the same year. The events surrounding the surrender of Jerusalem are particularly interesting, in that it was the Greek Orthodox Archbishop Sophronius who negotiated the surrender and the second caliph, 'Umar ibn al-Khaṭṭāb, who personally visited the city in order to consolidate its conquest. While there he visited the site of the ancient Jewish Temple, which was then desolate, commanded that it be cleaned, and established it as a place of Muslim prayer. Crone and Cook use these actions as evidence for their thesis that Islam, or Hagarism, was in some sense a messianic movement, with 'Umar here behaving like a messiah, but what is certain is that the result of his actions is a major shift in the sacred geography of the city whereby the religious focus moves back from the city's western ridge, where the Church of the Holy Sepulchre and many other Christian churches and monasteries are situated, to its eastern ridge, where the Jewish Temple had been situated and where the Muslims built their main places of worship in the city.[27]

Once the situation had settled down, therefore, in the sense that the Byzantines had more or less resigned themselves to the loss of Syria and the civil administration had been set up under the leadership of Abū 'Ubaida ibn al-Jarrāḥ, some kind of stability emerged in the relationships between the Muslim conquerors and the mainly Christian population of the province. The main essentials of this relationship were that political and military power were to be firmly in the hands of the Arab rulers, but the non-Muslim population, provided it had submitted peacefully to Muslim rule, was to be given freedom of religion, in the sense of being able to worship freely in its own places of worship, in return for the payment of a special tax called the *jizya*. This was the term used in the Qur'ān in 9: 29, where the Muslims were instructed to fight against those among the People of the Book who did not believe in God and the Last Day, did not forbid what God had forbidden through Muḥammad, and did not follow the religion of truth, until they paid the tribute (*jizya*), being brought low. It was also the term used by Ibn Isḥāq as part of the negotiations between Muḥammad and the people of Ḥimyar and Najrān.[28]

The detail of these arrangements came to be enshrined in the Covenant of 'Umar, which was named after the second caliph, 'Umar, because it was claimed to be a record of the agreements made between 'Umar and the conquered population, but in fact almost certainly comes from a much later period. It can be found in different forms in some of the early Islamic historians, and Tritton gives two main versions, both found in the *History* of Ibn 'Asākir. The first takes the form of an extract from a letter from 'Umar in which he quotes from a letter from some Christians, as follows:

> When you came to us we asked of you safety for our lives, our families and property, and the people of our religion on these conditions: to pay tribute out of hand and be humiliated; not to hinder any Muslim from stopping in our churches by night or day, to entertain him there three days and give him food there and open to him their doors; to beat the gong [used in eastern churches in lieu of a bell] only gently in them and not to raise our voices in chanting; not to shelter there, nor in any of our houses, a spy of your enemies; not to build a church, convent, hermitage, or cell, nor repair those that are dilapidated, nor assemble in any that is in a Muslim quarter, nor in their presence; not to display idolatry nor invite to it, nor show a cross on our churches, nor in any of the roads or markets of the Muslims; not to learn the Qur'ān nor teach it to our children; not to prevent any of our relatives from turning Muslim if he wish it; to cut our hair in front; to tie the *zunnār* [a special belt] round our waists; to keep to our religion; not to resemble the Muslims in dress, appearance, saddles, the engraving on our seals [i.e. not to engrave them in Arabic]; not to use their *kunyas* [titles]; to honour and respect them, to stand up for them when we meet together; to guide them in their ways and goings; not to make our houses higher than theirs; not to keep weapons or swords, nor wear them in a town or on a journey in Muslim lands; not to sell wine or display it; not to light fires with our dead at a road where Muslims dwell, nor to raise our voices at their [?our] funerals, nor bring them near Muslims; not to strike a Muslim; not to keep slaves who have been the property of Muslims. We impose these terms on ourselves and our co-religionists; he who rejects them has no protection.[29]

The form of words used here in the first sentence clearly repeats the language of the Qur'ān (9: 29) in its references to paying the tribute/*jizya* and being humiliated, but there is considerably more detail given as to what this means in practice. It is clear that political loyalty is expected, as seen in the promise not to entertain anyone spying for an enemy; military involvement is rejected, as seen in the declaration that swords will not be kept; Christian worship is permitted, but it is clear that it is only to happen surreptitiously, with no public display of crosses and only quiet musical accompaniment; the building of new churches is prohibited, and those which are dilapidated are not to be repaired; Christians undertake to retain their religion, yet paradoxically also undertake not to prevent any of their relatives who wish to convert to Islam from doing so; and they are to distinguish themselves from Muslims in what they wear.

The second version quoted by Tritton again consists of a quotation from a letter, this time from the Christians of Damascus to Abū 'Ubaida. It adds a little more detail concerning some things which Christians promise not to do, such as carry a cross or the Bible in a procession, especially at Easter or on Palm Sunday, or seek to entice a Muslim to Christianity or invite him to it, or use Muslims' language, or ride on saddles or make Christian houses higher than Muslim ones.[30]

Some of these measures seem intended to demonstrate Christians' second-class status as compared to Muslims; neither they nor their houses, for example, may look down on those of Muslims. But Tritton concludes that although the documents are attributed to 'Umar, in all probability they actually come from the second Islamic century, and although they may reflect some of the policies and attitudes towards the conquered population which began to become evident in the period of the Umayyad caliph 'Umar ibn 'Abd al-'Azīz (717/99–720/101), the texts were only collected together in the form in which they exist today some time after that. 'The covenant was drawn up in the schools of law, and came to be ascribed, like so much else, to 'Umar I.'[31]

Whatever the history of this text and whatever the precise date when its measures were first introduced, it clearly reflects a much more generous attitude towards the conquered population than the rather aggressive one which we have seen in the first decade or so after the death of Muḥammad. It therefore reflects a change in the situation from one where the Muslims were raiding the areas bordering Arabia and displaying a considerable animus towards Christians and their religious symbols, to a situation where efforts are being made to establish Muslim rule and there is therefore a need to adopt a more conciliatory approach to the existing population. It is in this context, therefore, that the *ahl al-kitāb*, the People of the Book referred to in the Qur'ān as having in the past received scriptures from God, in other words Jews and Christians, also become known as the *ahl al-dhimma*, the People of the Covenant, or simply *dhimmīs*.

Dhimma is a word which is used twice in the Qur'ān (9: 8 and 10), in the context of Muḥammad's dealings with idolaters (*mushrikūn*), who are accused of not honouring their covenants or agreements with the prophet; as a result the prophet is also released from his commitments, and their position becomes rather more vulnerable. But in the period of the conquests the term comes to be used more with reference to the agreements made between the conquered population and their Muslim rulers, and therefore becomes more specific.

It has recently been suggested that many of the detailed regulations concerning what the *ahl al-dhimma* were and were not permitted to do come from an earlier historical precedent, namely the regulations which existed in the Sassanian Persian Empire with reference to its religious minorities in Iraq. Here there was a highly developed Jewish community, and separate Monophysite and Nestorian Christian communities, and during the late Sassanian period the rulers experimented with arrangements by which efforts were made to ensure the loyalty of the population by granting military protection and some degree of religious toleration in return for the payment of taxes. This tribute was even applied as a kind of poll-tax, for the collection of which the leaders of the different communities were held responsible.[32] So the detail of the agreements between the Muslims and the conquered Christian population was therefore not completely novel and original.

Having looked in some detail at the Muslim treatment of the Christians who found themselves under Muslim rule in the first period of Christian–Muslim interaction, we need to remember that not all the Christians of the day, of course, were in this situation. Most particularly, the Byzantine Empire, even if it lost roughly half of its territory, that is Egypt and Syria, to the new Muslim state, remained a powerful force, and the frontier between the caliphate and the Byzantines stabilised around the Taurus Mountains fairly quickly. Political and military rivalry continued, however, both on the land frontier and in the form of naval engagements at sea, but contemporary with some of the military confrontations it is also important to remember that more positive cultural and intellectual exchanges also took place.[33]

Thus on the one hand, naval raids were organised by the Arabs against Constantinople itself in 669/49 and 717/98, the Arab fleet on the latter occasion being rowed to the city by Coptic Christians. Yet on the other, the first mosque in Constantinople was established during the reign of Leo III (717/98–741/123), and the Byzantine emperor Justinian II, during the second period of his rule (705/86–711/92), sent craftsmen to help the caliph al-Walīd (705/86–715/96) with the decoration of not only the Great Mosque in Damascus but also the Mosque of the Prophet in Medina. There is also an account in Byzantine, though not in known Arabic sources, of the caliph ʿAbd al-Malik (685/65–705/86) being provided with columns for the mosque in Mecca by Justinian II, at the instigation of some of the Christians of

Jerusalem who wanted to prevent 'Abd al-Malik removing some columns from one of the churches in Jerusalem.[34]

During the first period of Christian–Muslim interaction, therefore, there was a considerable range of opinion and attitude in both communities. Christian interpretations of Islam varied from seeing it as: a fulfilment of God's promises to Abraham and Ishmael; a judgement of God on Christians who had erred in their Christological formulations; or quite simply as a Christian heresy. Muslim attitudes towards Christians also varied, from a fairly militant antagonism, for a relatively short period, to a much more tolerant and conciliatory attitude which still imposed certain restrictions on Christians, along with other non-Muslims, but gave them security of life and property and permitted them freedom of worship, though not freedom of religion in the modern sense.

NOTES

1. See F. Gabrieli, *Muḥammad and the Conquests of Islam*, London: Weidenfeld and Nicolson, 1968, p. 150.
2. Ibid., pp. 180–223.
3. G. Von Rad, *Genesis: a Commentary*, London: SCM, 1961, p. 258.
4. J. Moorhead, 'The Earliest Christian Theological Response to Islam' in *Religion*, 11 (1981), pp. 265–6.
5. Ibid., p. 266.
6. Ibid., pp. 266–7.
7. P. Crone and M. Cook, *Hagarism: the Making of the Islamic World*, Cambridge University Press, 1977, esp. pp. 3–15.
8. See the discussion in N. Robinson, *Discovering the Qur'ān*, London: SCM, 1996, pp. 47–59.
9. Quoted in W. H. C. Frend, *The Rise of the Monophysites*, Cambridge University Press, 1972, p. 353.
10. Quoted by J. Moorhead in 'The Monophysite Response to the Arab Invasions' in *Byzantion*, 51 (1981), p. 585.
11. Frend, *The Rise of the Monophysites*, p. 351. The Great Persecution was the programme of repression which was inaugurated by Roman Emperor Diocletian in 303 and which lasted until 312.
12. Ibid., p. 337.
13. The title originally derived from the Syriac word *malka*, meaning 'king'. In modern times 'Melkite' has commonly become used to refer to the Roman Catholic Christians of the Middle East who use the Byzantine rite rather than the Latin rite, and who are sometimes referred to as Greek Catholics.
14. D. J. Sahas, *John of Damascus on Islam*, Leiden: Brill, 1972, p. 7.
15. Ibid., pp. 38–48.
16. The full Greek text of Chapter 101, with English translation, may be found in Sahas, *John of Damascus*, pp. 132–41, and there is commentary and discussion in ibid., pp. 67–95.
17. Ibid., p. 69, quoting John of Damascus's *De Fide Orthodoxa*.
18. Ibid., p. 95.
19. The full Greek text, with English translation, may be found in Sahas,

John of Damascus, pp. 142–55, with commentary and discussion in ibid., pp. 99–122.

20. Ibid., pp. 121 and 122. See also Seale's *Muslim Theology*, London: Luzac, 1964, and 'John of Damascus: a Dialogue between a Saracen and a Christian' in Seale's *Qur'ān and Bible*, London: Croom Helm, 1978, pp. 63–70.
21. Crone and Cook, *Hagarism*, pp. 6 and 120.
22. G. Newby, *A History of the Jews of Arabia*, Columbia: University of South Carolina Press, 1988, p. 99.
23. J. S. Trimingham, *Christianity among the Arabs in pre-Islamic Times*, London: Longman, 1979, p. 307.
24. Newby, *Jews of Arabia*, p. 99.
25. For fuller discussion of the historicity of the tradition, as well as of the course of events, see S. Ward, 'A Fragment from an Unknown Work by al-Ṭabarī on the Tradition "Expel the Jews and Christians from the Arabian Peninsula [and the Lands of Islam]"' in *Bulletin of the School of Oriental and African Studies*, 53 (1990), pp. 407–20.
26. The texts have been collected and discussed by D. R. Hill in his *The Termination of Hostilities in the Early Arab Conquests A.D. 634–656*, London: Luzac, 1971. See also F. M. Donner, *The Early Islamic Conquests*, Princeton University Press, 1981, and W. Kaegi, *Byzantium and the Early Islamic Conquests*, Cambridge University Press, 1992.
27. See Crone and Cook, *Hagarism*, p. 5 and pp. 154–5. On Jerusalem, see L. I. Levine (ed.), *Jerusalem: its Sanctity and Centrality to Judaism, Christianity, and Islam*, New York: Continuum, 1999, p. xxiii.
28. See Chapter 2 above.
29. A. S. Tritton, *The Caliphs and their non-Muslim Subjects: a Critical Study of the Covenant of 'Umar*, London: Cass, 1930, pp. 5–6.
30. Ibid., pp. 6–8.
31. Ibid., p. 233.
32. See M. G. Morony, 'Religious Communities in Late Sassanian and Early Muslim Iraq' in *Journal of the Economic and Social History of the Orient*, 17 (1974), pp. 113–35. See also the same author's 'The Effects of the Muslim Conquest on the Persian Population of Iraq' in *Iran*, 14 (1976), pp. 41–59, and 'Conquerors and Conquered: Iran' in G. H. A. Juynboll (ed.), *Studies on the First Century of Islamic Society*, South Illinois University Press, 1982, pp. 73–87.
33. See C. E. Bosworth, 'Byzantium and the Arabs: War and Peace between Two World Civilizations' in his *The Arabs, Byzantium and Iran*, London: Variorum, 1996, Article XIII.
34. See H. A. R. Gibb, 'Arab-Byzantine Relations under the Umayyad caliphate' in his *Studies on the Civilization of Islam*, (ed. S. J. Shaw and W. R. Polk), Boston: Beacon Press, 1982, pp. 47–61, esp. pp. 51–8 and 61.

4

The Medieval Period I: Confrontation or Interaction in the East?

CONTACTS AND EXCHANGES

The ninth/third century was an extremely significant one for what has been called 'the elaboration of Islam'. To take but two disciplines of study within an Islamic context, the achievements of al-Shāfiʿī (d. 820/205) in the field of *sharīʿa* (Islamic Law) and of al-Kindī (d. c. 870/256) in the field of *falsafa* (Islamic Philosophy) were both crucial for the later development of Islamic thought and practice as a whole. One important factor in some aspects of this process of elaboration was a network of contacts between the Christian and Muslim communities which grew up during that century in what is today called the Middle East.

We have seen already that, on the one hand, even in the previous century cultural and religious contacts between Byzantium and the Islamic world had developed across the military frontier, so that the relationship was not simply one of confrontation between Byzantine Christians and the Muslims. Far more important, on the other hand, were the contacts between Christians and Muslims which developed within the Muslim world during the ninth/third century. Even these had their precursors, going back to the era before the establishment of the Islamic community, as a key factor in their development was the decision by the Byzantine emperor Justinian (527–65) in 529 to close the philosophy school in Athens. As a result of this some members of the school migrated to Gundeshapur in Iraq, in the territory of the Sassanian Persian Empire, and there it remained until the Islamic conquest of the region in 637/16. The only other major school of philosophy of the sixth century, that of Alexandria, also came within the ambit of the Islamic community in the same decade, and the result of this was that while Byzantium entered a period of intellectual stagnation, with the dominance of the church more or less unchallenged, the Islamic community in due course found itself in a position to interact with and draw upon the legacy of Hellenism.[1]

This did not happen immediately. The Islamic community had a great many other issues, of a military, political and economic nature as well those centred on religious concerns, to deal with, but especially after the ʿAbbasid Revolution of 750/132 issues connected with the intellectual elaboration of Islam began to become increasingly promi-

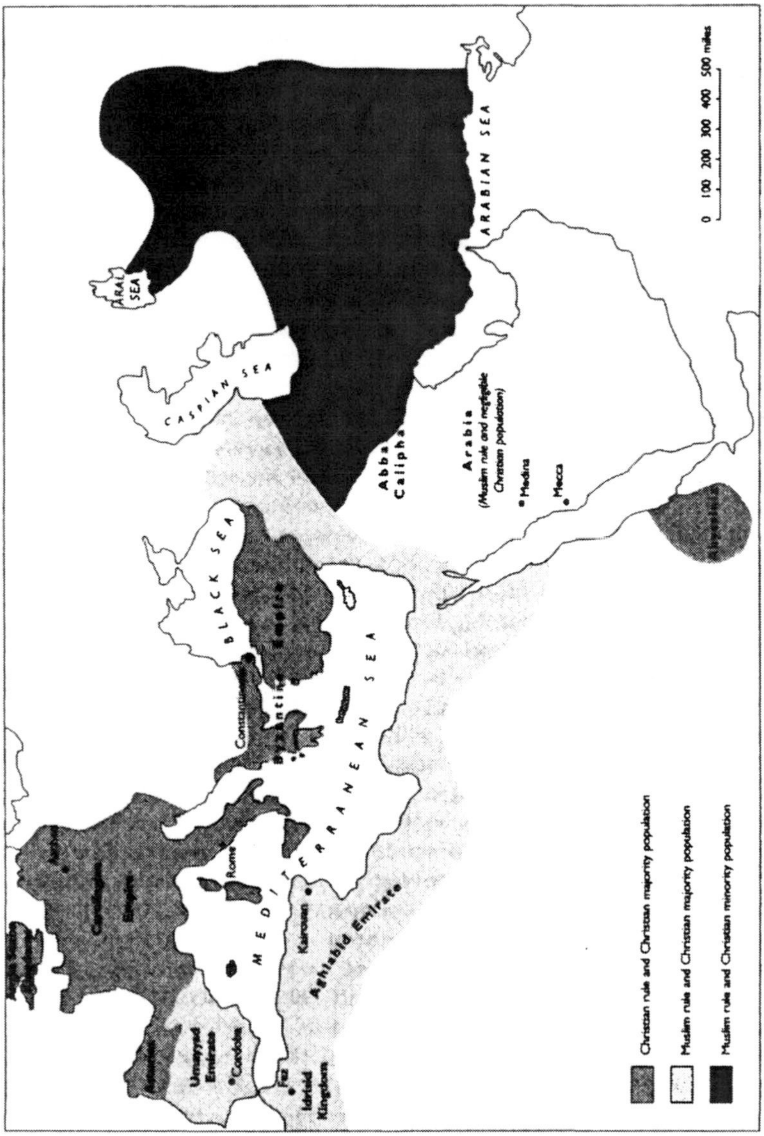

Map 1 *The Christian and Muslim Worlds c. 830/215*

nent. A particular role in this process is commonly attributed to the caliph al-Ma'mūn, who ruled from 813/198 to 833/218. It was he who in 832/217 founded, in Baghdad, the institution known as the *bayt al-ḥikma* (literally 'House of Wisdom'), whose purpose was to arrange for the translation of Greek and other works into Arabic and to encourage their dissemination within the Islamic world. Emissaries were sent to Byzantium to find and purchase both scientific and philosophical works, and over the course of the next two centuries or so a great many such works began to circulate within the Islamic world.[2]

Many of those who actually undertook these translations were Christians. The greatest translator of them all was Ḥunayn ibn Isḥāq (809/193–873/260), a Nestorian Christian from al-Ḥīra who had studied at Gundeshapur, and who, according to Fakhry, translated numerous works into Arabic, but many other figures were also involved, including not only Nestorian Christians but also Monophysites and others.[3] The translations were sometimes undertaken directly from the Greek, but in many cases the Greek works were translated from already existing translations into other languages such as Syriac, and it was this which partly gave rise to some of the celebrated confusions concerning the authorship of some philosophical works, especially the so-called *Theology of Aristotle*, which was not by Aristotle at all and whose real author is unknown.[4] The real influences on this work were Neoplatonic, and the misattribution of its authorship goes a considerable way towards explaining how it was that many medieval Islamic thinkers thought of Aristotle as far more sympathetic to many of their ideas than his authentic works would have suggested.

According to one Muslim author it was Aristotle himself who provided the inspiration for the establishment of the *bayt al-ḥikma* by appearing to al-Ma'mūn in a dream.[5] Be that as it may, al-Ma'mūn personally seems to have been genuinely interested in religious and intellectual questions, and as well as his sponsorship of the translation venture, he also hosted a number of debates or discussions of religious questions, involving representatives of different religious communities, which were conspicuous for their atmosphere of openness and honesty. In this, as indeed also with the promotion of the translation movement, al-Ma'mūn was not a complete pioneer, as his predecessors al-Manṣūr (754/136–775/158) and Hārūn al-Rashīd (786/170–809/193) had made a start at translation, and the third 'Abbasid caliph, al-Mahdī (775/158–785/169), had engaged in a religious debate with the head of the Nestorian church in Iraq, the Catholicos Timothy, probably in 781/165.[6] But it was al-Ma'mūn who took the process even further, engaging in discussions with representatives of a wide range of religious traditions, including not only Christians but also, for example, Manichaeans.[7]

There are records of participation in these discussions by two important Christian thinkers, the Melkite (i.e. Greek Orthodox) Theodore Abū Qurra, and the Nestorian ʻAbd al-Masīḥ al-Kindī, though the evidence for the involvement of the former is rather stronger than that of the latter since al-Kindī's *Apology* has for some time been a focus of modern scholarly controversy concerning its authenticity.[8]

Abū Qurra became the Greek Orthodox bishop of Harran in northern Syria in 799/183, and he was therefore a representative of the same church and tradition as John of Damascus, whose disciple he in effect was, since he studied at the monastery of Mar Sabas in Palestine to which John had retired.[9] His debate with the caliph al-Ma'mūn probably took place in 829/214, and summaries can be found in the works of Guillaume and Sweetman, but there is as yet no full English translation of the discussion available.[10] A number of different themes were discussed, including such as whether or not circumcision is necessary and whether or not human beings have free will, but the theme which is discussed in by far the greatest detail is the status of Jesus, and in particular whether or not he is co-equal with God. In discussing this theme, Abū Qurra is able to quote from the Qur'ān, and one of the Muslim participants in the debate, Saʻsaʻa ibn Khālid of Basra, is able to quote from the New Testament, and although agreement is reached that Jesus is the word of God and a spirit from God, as is stated in the Qur'ān (4: 171), disagreement breaks out concerning any suggestion that Jesus is anything other than created. What is remarkable about the debate, however, is the fact that when a certain acrimony begins to become evident in the proceedings as one of the Muslim participants, Muḥammad ibn ʻAbd Allāh al-Hāshimī, protests at one of Abū Qurra's assertions, the caliph himself says to the bishop:

> This is a court of justice and equity: none shall be wronged therein. So advance your arguments and answer without fear, for there is none here who will not speak well of you . . . Let everyone speak who has the wisdom to demonstrate the truth of his religion.[11]

The *Apology* of Al-Kindī is a rather different kind of document: according to the account studied by Muir, whose authenticity we have already noted as being suspect to several modern scholars, but which is accepted as authentic by G. Le Troupeau in the second edition of the *Encyclopaedia of Islam*, al-Kindī was a Nestorian Christian of Arab descent (his name being derived from the distinguished pre-Islamic tribe of Kinda), who, possibly around 820/205, was invited by ʻAbd Allāh al-Hāshimī, a scholar at the court of al-Ma'mūn, to convert to Islam. This was not, in other words, a public debate in quite the same style as that involving Abū Qurra, but it nevertheless, if authentic, provides an example of the kind of discussions which were going on at the time. Not only does al-Kindī decline al-Hāshimī's invitation, he also goes on to outline in fairly devastating style his reasons for not so, and in the course of this he launches a number of harsh attacks on different aspects of Islam. These include his suggesting that Muḥammad should not be seen as a prophet, since he did not predict the future, he did not perform miracles, and a number of incidents in his life, involving the use of violence in Holy War and also his treatment of women, throw a somewhat negative light on his character; and that the Qur'ān's claim to be the word of God is also questionable in the light of its barbaric teaching about women and about Holy War, and the fact that its text has not been authentically transmitted and preserved.

Al-Kindī's work may thus be described as offensive in both senses of the word, and it is the nature of some of the attacks in the *Apology* which has caused some scholars to conclude that the work is in fact a later one. But a better explanation of how it was possible for the work to come into existence is perhaps provided by Muir: 'The freedom of our Author's treatment of Islam would have been permitted at none but the most latitudinarian court.'[12].

The age of al-Ma'mūn thus represents what may perhaps be called an early example of dialogue between Christians and Muslims, where representatives of each community were enabled to outline the principles and practices of their faith with a remarkable degree of candour and honesty, after being given assurances of having the freedom to do so with no threat to themselves or to their community. Political power, it is true, rested firmly and clearly with the caliph, and the representatives of other religious communities were thus to some extent vulnerable, but they do not seem to have been inhibited and the discussions do seem to serve as an early example of mutual education and edification.

The interchanges between the two communities continued too. During the ninth/third century the school of philosophy in Alexandria migrated to the city of Harran in northern Syria, and from there, at the start of the tenth/fourth century, it migrated to Baghdad, the capital of the Islamic Empire and also the home of the *bayt al-ḥikma*. Given the closeness of Baghdad to Gundeshapur, the other major centre of Hellenistic philosophy at that time, it was not long before Baghdad's school of philosophy acquired the reputation of being the pre-eminent centre of philosophical enquiry of the day. During the tenth/fourth century the headship of the school passed from a Christian, the

Nestorian Yūḥannā ibn Ḥaylān (d. between 908/297 and 932/320), to a Muslim, al-Fārābī (c. 870/256–950/339), and then back again to a Christian, the Monophysite Yaḥyā ibn 'Adī (893/280–974/363). This is surely another interesting example of interaction between Christians and Muslims in that period.[13]

In this era, then, Christians and Muslims interacted on different levels, and in some areas, as is relatively well known, Christians exerted considerable influence on Muslims, particularly with respect to their translation of Greek philosophical and scientific works. What is less well known, however, is that influence also went the other way, and this can be seen in, for example, the increasing use of the Arabic language by Christians in the Islamic world in this period, and also in the translation of the Bible into Arabic. The oldest known Christian theological work written in Arabic, the so-called *On the Triune Nature of God*, was probably composed around 755/138, in the milieu of the Melkite/Greek Orthodox monasteries of Palestine, with which John of Damascus and Theodore Abū Qurra were associated.[14] And Abū Qurra himself has been described as 'the first theologian whose name we know who wrote regularly in Arabic', on the basis of the twenty or so works of his which were originally written in Arabic and which are known today and have been published.[15] Abū Qurra also wrote in Syriac and in Greek, but the volume of his Arabic writing is symptomatic of a significant cultural and linguistic change.

As regards the translation of the Bible into Arabic, we know that the Hebrew Bible/Old Testament was translated into Judaeo-Arabic (i.e. Arabic in Hebrew characters) by Saadya Gaon (882/269–942/330).[16] The situation with regard to the New Testament, however, was rather more complex, with translations being made at different stages and in different places from Greek, Syriac, Coptic and Latin. The earliest extant manuscript, which came originally from the monastery of Saint Sabas but is now in the Vatican Library, may have come from the eighth/second century, but is more likely to have come from the ninth/third century, and today contains the Pauline Epistles and some portions of the Gospels, which were translated from Syriac. Several other manuscripts can be reliably dated to the ninth/third century, including one which contains the four Gospel accounts, and which was translated from Greek probably at the monastery of Saint Sabas, and there is one account, in Ibn al-Nadīm, of a translation of both the Torah and the Gospel being made from the Hebrew and the Greek in the time of al-Ma'mūn, but this may not be a reliable account. Only in the mid thirteenth/seventh century, however, was an attempt made to produce a more standardised version of at least the Gospels, by Ḥibat Allāh ibn al-'Assāl in Alexandria.[17]

Far more significant for the religious life of the Christian communities under Islamic rule, however, was of course the language of the liturgy, Greek, Syriac and Coptic, with Arabic only beginning to be used there considerably later. In Egypt, for example, it was in the twelfth/sixth century, in response to an exhortation from the Coptic patriarch Gabriel II, that priests began to explain the Lord's Prayer in Arabic, and in the following two centuries Coptic liturgical books begin to have Arabic translations alongside the Coptic words.[18] Slowly though this process advanced, however, it does testify to the fact that in this period influences flowed both ways – from Christian to Muslim, and from Muslim to Christian.

DEVELOPING MUTUAL PERCEPTIONS

At the same time as all these contacts and exchanges were going on, however, paradoxically perhaps, a rather harsher note was beginning to enter into the mutual perceptions of Christians and Muslims. To some extent this can already be seen in the *Apology* of al-Kindī which we have already looked at, but what is probably exceptional in the time of al-Ma'mūn begins to become more widespread, and even normative, not long afterwards.

This can be seen firstly in Byzantine Christian writings, which begin to become more overtly polemical and antagonistic in the late ninth/third century. In part, of course, this development needs to be seen in the context of the on-going military confrontation between the Byzantine Empire on the one hand and the 'Abbāsid Empire and its successor-states on the other, centred around the boundary between Asia Minor and Syria, but given that this conflict was not new some other factor must explain the increasingly acrimonious nature of much Byzantine literature about Islam.

The new tone may be seen first in the writings of the Byzantine historian Theophanes the Confessor, whose work chronicles world events from 284CE to 813/197. As part of this, of course, he treats the coming of Islam, and on this, like John of Damascus, he states that Islam is a heresy, but he adds some further detail which is new, and which has a rather different flavour from John's writings. The genesis of Islam, Theophanes writes, is that Muḥammad had epilepsy, and because of this he had some problems with his wife Khadīja, who had raised him from a modest estate by marrying him. He then travelled to Palestine and Egypt, where he met Jews and Christians, and where he was helped by a heretical Christian monk to put his religious knowledge to good use by claiming to be an apostle. The message of Islam, according to Theophanes, includes references to a sensual paradise, which is obtained by anyone who kills or is killed by an enemy, a call to *jihād*, military warfare, and an invitation to intemperate living, though it is acknowledged that it also includes a recommendation to help the oppressed.

On this basis Muḥammad is described as 'the chief and false prophet of the Saracens', and a further scurrilous note is provided by the suggestion that some Jews believed in him as Messiah and therefore embraced Islam; later, however, they saw him eating camel-meat and realised their mistake, but they were unable to leave the Muslim community so they told Muḥammad false information about Christianity in order to provoke him against the Christians.[19]

The tendency begun by Theophanes was carried even further by Nicetas of Byzantium, who in the middle of the ninth/third century was invited by Emperor Michael III (842/227–867/253) to formulate replies to two letters which he had received from Muslims, possibly from the caliph al-Mutawakkil. Nicetas's replies sought to defend his Christian faith, to answer Muslim objections to Christian convictions about Jesus, and to challenge Muslim assertions about the excellence of the Muslim faith and claims that Islam was the only true religion; they therefore include polemical attacks on Islam and declarations of readiness to take up arms if the opportunity arises, which makes clear the extent to which they should be seen as possessing an element of religious propaganda in an atmosphere of religious confrontation.

Nicetas's principal work was his 'Refutation of the Book Fabricated by the Arab Muḥammad'. As the title makes clear, it is a work which is primarily intended to undermine the Qur'ān; it begins, however, with a defence of the Trinity before it proceeds to refute the Muslim scripture, which is described as 'a lying and pernicious book' which is 'of odious and demoniac origin'. It is a book 'built without art and deprived of consistency', and is 'disconnected, . . . [and] . . . does not proceed from a wise and straight thought'. Muḥammad himself is described as an impudent impostor, and Nicetas breaks new ground in subjecting Muḥammad to a kind of psychoanalysis, suggesting that he was obsessed with securing recognition for his mission and persuading people to accept the divine origin of his mission; he was therefore prepared to do anything to achieve this end. Islam is thus fundamentally idolatry, and despite the claim that it led the Arabs to worship God, in fact it led them to worship Satan; its so-called revelation comes from the Devil, and those who hear it are led to worship the Devil.

During the course of the work Muḥammad is described as an assassin, and it is also suggested that he had at some stage been a follower of Manichaeism, which according to Nicetas explains his attacks on the idea of the deity of Jesus. In short, Muḥammad was an ignorant charlatan who succeeded by imposture in seducing the ignorant barbarian Arabs into accepting a gross, blaspheming, idolatrous, demoniac religion, which is full of futile errors, intellectual enormities, doctrinal errors and moral aberrations.[20]

Nicetas's works thus display a number of new features: firstly, he evidently possessed a considerable knowledge of the complete text of the Qur'ān, as he was able to review its contents in some detail, and examine Suras Two to Eighteen particularly closely, but it is unlikely that he knew any Arabic and he must therefore have been reliant on a translation, though Khoury suggests that he did his own translation; secondly, though, he introduced a considerable element of bile into the discussion, with a lot of ferocity evident. But it is here that the importance of context must once again be emphasised: his Greek Orthodox forebears as writers on Islam, John of Damascus and Theodore Abū Qurra, lived under Islamic rule and had long and regular contacts with Muslims. Nicetas, however, lived behind the frontiers in Byzantium, and Muslims could therefore only be conceived as enemies. Moreover, the emperor who commissioned him to write, Michael III, undertook a number of important military campaigns in Asia Minor, culminating in a great victory in 863/249 which was a turning-point in the struggle between Byzantium and the Arabs:

> From the time of the first inroads made by the Arabs up to the victory of Leo III at Constantinople, Byzantium had had to struggle for mere survival; then for more than a century it had been occupied with an arduous defensive war; but now, after the victory of 863, the tide turned and there began the era of Byzantine attack in Asia, an offensive which opened slowly but which for the second half of the tenth century moved forwards with ever increasing celerity.[21]

Later Byzantine accounts of Islam in the main reproduce much of Nicetas's argument and also much of his tone, especially the ones which commemorate those who have died in military campaigns against the Muslims, who are described as martyrs.[22] It would not be true to say that all Byzantine literature adopted this approach, though, since some writers adopted a more irenic tone and were prepared to acknowledge at least some common ground between Christian and Muslim, including recognition of a common allegiance to monotheism.

One representative of this point of view is Emperor Leo III (717/99–741/123): in his reply to a letter from the caliph 'Umar ibn 'Abd al-'Azīz (717/99–720/101) requesting an exposition of the Christian faith, Leo affirmed that Christians and Muslims believe in the same God, and that both communities are alike in some of the issues which they face. As examples of this he suggests, firstly, the problem of divisions, given that, in his opinion the Muslim community is equally as divided as the Christian one; and secondly, issues arising from worship practices, given that the Christian use of symbols such as the cross should not surprise Muslims who turn towards the Ka'ba in Mecca because of its association with Abraham. Leo also tried to explain the Christian use of icons, saying that there was no reverence given to the objects themselves, but that they had educational and emotional significance. The fact that this correspondence, if authentic, took place in the decade before the prohibition of icons in Leo's Edict of 726/108 is surely significant.[23]

Several centuries later, Emperor Manuel I (1143/538–1180/576) entered into controversy with the patriarch of his day when he insisted that converts from Islam should not be compelled to anathematise the God of Muḥammad, since this seemed to imply that Christians and Muslims did not believe in the same God. Meyendorff comments that this incident illustrates clearly the existence in Byzantium of two views on Islam, one extreme and 'closed', and the other more moderate.[24]

Considerable diversity of opinion about Christianity among Muslims also begins to become evident in this period.[25] In part, as with Byzantine perceptions of Islam, this results from increasing knowledge about the faith of the other community, but such knowledge did not always result in greater tolerance or sympathy. In some cases, indeed, quite the opposite seems to have been the result, but once again the context within which more polemical attitudes emerged needs to be kept firmly in mind.

Two recent articles, one by a Jewish scholar and the other by a Muslim scholar, make this very clear. Hava Lazarus-Yafeh, of the Hebrew University of Jerusalem, emphasises what might be called the tripartite nature of Muslim polemic against Christianity:

> Muslim authors apparently borrowed earlier Jewish polemical attitudes towards Christianity, but gave them a more elaborate, comprehensive expression, which in its turn reinfluenced medieval Jewish authors, who shared many basic values and concepts with Islam. When dealing with the medieval triangle of the three monotheistic religions, we must remember that they can be regrouped differently when looked upon from a variant historical angle: In addition to the traditional model of the usual two *dhimmī* ('protected') religions (Judaism and Christianity) under the rule of Islam, we should also view Judaism and Islam as the

two halakhic, rationalistic, religions, less inclined to symbolism – in contrast to Christianity.[26]

Even more importantly, Abdelmajid Charfi, of the University of Tunis, insists that medieval Muslim polemic must be located firmly in the social context of relationships between different communities. He suggests that six factors need to be kept in mind when seeking to explain the development of polemic: the need to balance demographic factors, given that Muslims in this period were still numerically only a small minority of the population of the Empire as a whole; the need to integrate converts to Islam without adopting a syncretistic approach; the concurrent theological elaboration of Islam, which was not a separate endeavour from the production of polemical literature, given that many individuals were involved in both processes; the Muslim community's research about its roots, which included the search for Biblical references to Muḥammad's message, in order to promote its authentication and legitimation; the need for a solution to social antagonism, which arose particularly in times of economic stagnation, and where the role of polemical literature such as that from the pen of al-Jāḥiẓ was to justify the repression of Christians; and the defence of Islamic civilisation against other civilisations. All these aspects of the contemporary context, Charfi suggests, go some way towards explaining some of the rancour and venom which is evident in some medieval Muslim writing about Christianity, and of course many similar factors, as we have already seen in Chapter 1, need to be kept in mind when looking at some of the early Christian writings against the Jews.[27]

In order to illustrate something of the diversity of Islamic thought about Christianity in the medieval period in a little more detail, the contrasting views which evolved in the two main schools of *kalām* (Islamic Theology) will be examined. This is an important aspect of Islam to keep in mind because, while it is well known that there are four schools of Sunnī *fiqh* law/jurisprudence in Islam, it is less well known that there are two schools of Sunnī *kalām*, the Ash'arī and the Māturīdī; and just as the schools of law, while not differing over the primacy of the main foundations of their discipline – Qur'ān and Ḥadīth – nevertheless do differ substantially over many secondary matters, so too the schools of theology, while not differing over such fundamental items of belief as *tawhīd* (the unity of God) and *nubuwwa* (prophecy), do differ over many other items of doctrine, including how they view Christianity.[28]

Abū'l-Ḥasan al-Ash'arī (874/260–936/324), who gave his name to the Ash'arī school of *kalām*, spent most of his life in Iraq, where he was closely involved in the theological disputes of the day involving the

Mu'tazila, the school of systematising or rationalising theologians, who were particularly insistent firstly on the absolute unity of God, which led them to deny any claim that the Qur'ān was uncreated, and secondly on the primacy of justice among the attributes of God, which led them to insist on the reality of human choice and free will. Al-Ash'arī had originally been a member of the Mu'tazila, but as a result of a dream in the month of Ramaḍān in the year 913/300 he rejected his Mu'tazilī beliefs. The school of thought which traced its ancestry back to him became the dominant one of Sunnī Islam, including a figure of such towering importance as al-Ghazālī (1058/450–1111/505) among its supporters, and it remains dominant in the Western end of the Muslim world today.

Abū Manṣūr al-Māturīdī (?873/261–944/333), who gave his name to the Māturīdī school of *kalām*, spent most of his life in central Asia, in the region of Samarqand in what is today Uzbekistan. Very little is known of his biography, but his theological opinions evidently became well established in central Asia in the succeeding centuries, and from there they became more widely disseminated through the agency of some of the great Turkish dynasties of the Islamic world such as the Seljuks and the Ottomans. Generally speaking, Māturīdī opinion is located somewhere between those of the Ash'arīs and those of the Mu'tazila, so that, for example, a greater role is given to reason by the Māturīdīs than the Ash'arīs, and the former are also more hospitable to claims that human beings do possess autonomy and free-will. Only some time after al-Māturīdī himself can we properly speak of a Māturīdī school of thought, but once it had emerged it became widely-influential in Central Asia and other parts of the Muslim world in which the Turkish peoples were significant players.[29]

Al-Ash'arī himself wrote two works on Christianity, but they are not extant and we know no more than their titles.[30] There is an important reference to Christianity in one of his works, however, a letter which he wrote around 910/297 to the people of Derbend on the Caspian Sea in response to a request for a statement of his beliefs: in it he suggests that the fundamental error of the Christians is not, as was suggested by most Muslims of the day, that they have developed erroneous ideas about Jesus, but simply that they have rejected the prophethood of Muḥammad. If they were to accept Muḥammad, in other words, they would then perceive the truth about Jesus.[31]

If we know little of the opinions on Christianity of al-Ash'arī himself, much more detail is available from a couple of generations later, from the writings of an important Ash'arī theologian, al-Bāqillānī (d. 1013/403). He is perhaps best known for his definitive study on the

I'jāz (inimitability) of the Qur'ān, but for our purposes his *Kitāb al-tamhīd* (Book of Introduction), which has been described as 'the first complete systematic treatise of [Ash'arī] *kalām* known',[32] is more important as it contains one chapter which is specifically devoted to Christianity. As well as being well known for the sharpness of his tongue, as used in arguments against the Shī'a and others, al-Bāqillānī had also taken part in an embassy to Byzantium during which he responded to being forced to enter the emperor's presence through a low door, in order to demonstrate his humility, by entering backwards.[33] It should not surprise us, therefore, if the tone of his treatment of Christianity is rather acerbic, as he systematically rejects Christian arguments about the nature of God, the Trinity, the divinity of Christ, and the incarnation.

Al-Bāqillānī begins his critique by suggesting that it is inappropriate to call God a substance (*jawhar*), as some Christians have done, since this is to be guilty of anthropomorphism, of making God in the image of humanity, and God is utterly incomparable. Even more inappropriate, he suggests, then to argue that God has three hypostases (*aqānīm*), but if Christians are going to introduce this element of plurality, why limit the number to three – why not add others to make the total up to four, or fourteen? Here it is significant that as an Ash'arī, al-Bāqillānī believes that God has eternal attributes, but these are seven or eight in number. And the idea of there being two natures in Christ is also rejected, not least because of the different understandings of this which are evident among Chalcedonian, Monophysite and Nestorian Christians, of which al-Bāqillānī shows himself to be well aware; this idea, he says, is illogical and impossible, since the universal cannot be combined with the particular, or the eternal with the temporal; incarnation is rejected since this would render the divine temporal, and therefore liable to change and decay.[34]

As regards the Māturīdī school, we do have a text from al-Māturīdī himself, a section devoted to Christianity from his major theological work, the *Kitāb al-tawḥīd* (The Book of the Unity of God).[35] This differs from much other Muslim literature about Christianity in that it does not refer to the Qur'ān at all, it has only the briefest of references to the Trinity, and it focuses almost entirely on refuting the claim that Jesus is divine and the Son of God. Not only that but al-Māturīdī's discussion of Christianity is not set apart in a separate chapter, but is rather one element of his section on prophecy or apostleship, so that the Christians here fulfil the function of being a kind of partner in discussion of this theme. In the same way materialists and dualists provide the foil for his discussion of the existence and characteristics of God, which precedes the section on prophecy, and the Mu'tazila are the partners for the discussion of divine and human action, which comes afterwards. As Thomas explains:

> The comparatively brief refutation of Christianity comes at the end of Part 3, on apostleship. Its function here is to enforce the preceding positive arguments in this part by showing that the claim that Christ is any more than a human messenger is unsustainable no matter what reasoning is advanced in its favour. By demonstrating that a rival teaching about the messenger Jesus is incompatible with reason and logic, the refutation strengthens the case for saying that the Islamic perception of how revealed knowledge is transmitted is compatible with the rational arguments presented in Parts 1 and 2, and so can be relied upon to provide a secure base for the exposition of faith that follows in Parts 4 and 5.[36]

Al-Māturīdī thus argues that none of the evidence which Christians have traditionally produced in favour of their claim that Jesus may be described as Son of God actually works: miracles, for example, are no proof, because Moses also performed miracles, and he is not described as 'Son'; neither is the specific miracle of reviving the dead, because Ezekiel also did that, nor Jesus's ascension into heaven, for Elijah also ascended. Jesus must, therefore, al-Māturīdī suggests, be a created being and thus in some sense a subordinate or derivative one.

This is no more positive as a treatment of Christian convictions than the work of al-Bāqillānī which we have already examined, but its place within al-Māturīdī's work as a whole and the reliance on reasoned argument without explicit Qur'ānic quotation do suggest that the approach is rather different from that of many Muslim polemicists. An article by a Turkish professor, Hanifi Özcan, elaborates on this thesis in an interesting way: al-Māturīdī's view of religion, he suggests, is actually a pluralistic one, even if it is a limited pluralism in that it refers only to a pluralism of the divine-revealed religions. Professor Özcan quotes from al-Māturīdī's *Ta'wīlāt* (Interpretations of the Qur'ān), to the effect that:

> Religion is to believe in the unity of God. The religion of all the Prophets is one and the same religion. All the Prophets invite human beings to belief in the unity of God, the knowledge of God's unity, and to the worship only of the One God . . .

He also draws a contrast between the existence of one religion and many *sharī'a*s, and suggests that al-Māturīdī's views may be a helpful stage along the way for the evolution of some kind of Muslim acceptance of religious pluralism in the modern world.[37]

It is probably something of an overstatement to suggest that this is what al-Māturīdī himself had in mind, but given the overall approach of al-Māturīdī, and the way in which his treatment of Christianity is fitted into the elaboration of his theological system, it may be true that it is somewhat easier for someone from the Māturīdī school of *kalām* to engage seriously with Christianity than for someone who is an Ash'arī. This may in part be explained by the fact that al-Māturīdī, living as he did in central Asia, was working out his theology in a context where Christians were a small minority and where many of the factors outlined by Professor Charfi above as to some extent explaining the development of anti-Christian polemic in the more central parts of the Muslim world, where Christians made up a far larger proportion of the population, did not therefore apply. However, it is very suggestive that in the late twentieth/early fifteenth century it is one of the regions of the Muslim world most substantially influenced by Māturīdī *kalām*, namely Turkey, that there has been the greatest readiness both to study Christianity and to allow Christianity to be taught in universities by Christian professors.[38] Other factors, such as the fact that Turkey was never colonised by outside powers, also need to be kept in mind in explaining this phenomenon, but the Māturīdī tradition may have provided a useful theoretical foundation for these developments.

We have taken as our examples of developing mutual perceptions different Byzantine perceptions of Islam, and the different perceptions of Christianity found in the two main schools of *kalām* in the Muslim world. There are, of course, many other interesting examples which could usefully have been investigated. One of the most interesting, which merits at least a brief reference, is the correspondence which took place, indirectly at least, between two significant figures of the later medieval period, Paul of Antioch, the Melkite/Greek Orthodox Bishop of Sidon during the twelfth/sixth century, and the great Muslim thinker Ibn Taimiyya (1263/661–1328/728).[39]

Paul lived in the era of the Byzantine emperor Manuel I, whom we discussed above as an exponent of a relatively positive Byzantine attitude towards Islam. In the Middle East, however, by his time, a new factor had entered the politics of the area, namely the coming of the Crusaders from Western Europe (which will be looked at in more detail in the next chapter), and in the time of Paul's episcopate Sidon was under Crusader control. In this context, Paul composed, probably some time between 1140/535 and 1180/576, a *Letter to a Muslim*, which he claimed was a response to a question put to him by a Muslim friend in Sidon concerning the opinion of Christians about Muḥammad. This was almost certainly a literary device, but be that as it may, the *Letter* became widely circulated among the Christian communities of the Middle East, and succeeded in provoking (though that is probably too strong a word) replies later from two Muslims, Aḥmad ibn Idrīs al-Qarāfī (d. 1285/684), and Ibn Taimiyya.

Paul's *Letter* is notable for its courtesy and its irenic tone, which distinguishes it from much of the rest of medieval Christian literature about Islam, and for its attempt to address the opinions and way of thinking of contemporary Muslims. The Qur'ān is thus utilised positively, particularly through its positive references to Christians, and Muhammad too is regarded positively:

> Paul did not accuse the Prophet of being an imposter or liar or warrior who waged wars and used the sword, accusations made by a number of earlier Christian writers. He recognized that Muḥammad had a religious mission. However, this mission, he argued, was not universal and hence did not include Christians who had already received a superior message, namely the law of Christ. Muḥammad was sent, he said, to the ignorant Arabs who were living in darkness and who had never received a prophet before him.[40]

Paul's *Letter* underwent a considerable amount of expansion and editing after his time, and although al-Qarāfī responded to the original shorter version, it was the expanded version, which had been produced in clerical circles in Cyprus, which was sent to Ibn Taimiyya in 1317/717. As an influential preacher in Damascus, he had already been involved in Christian–Muslim discussion through his *al-risāla al-qubrusiyya* (Cyprus letter), probably written between 1299/699 and 1303/733, which was a letter to Sirjwas the king of Cyprus, asking him to treat Muslim prisoners of war there well.[41] This work foreshadows Ibn Taimiyya's response to Paul's *Letter* in much of its structure and argumentation, but the later work is much more substantial in size, running to around a thousand pages in length.

Entitled *Al-jawāb al-ṣaḥīḥ li-man baddala dīn al-masīḥ* (The Correct Answer to those who Changed the Religion of Jesus), this work has been described by T. Michel as 'a work whose length and scope have never been equalled in Muslim critiques of the Christian religion and whose depth of insight into the issues that separate Christianity and Islam sets it among the masterpieces of Muslim polemic against Christianity.'[42] At the heart of the work is the fundamental suggestion that: 'The difference between Islam and Christianity . . . is that in Islam whenever innovations have appeared

God always raised up those who opposed the innovators and those upholding the sunna, whereas in Christianity the innovators triumphed and those holding the religion of Christ became a scattered few.'[43] Islam, in other words, has been preserved from corruption, while Christianity has succumbed to it, through the corruption of its religious texts, the introduction of new religious practices, and innovations such as the doctrine of the Trinity.

Michel suggests that Ibn Taimiyya probably wrote the work primarily for the Muslim community, in order to warn his fellow-Muslims against falling into the same error. Large sections of the work are therefore devoted to ideas which Ibn Taimiyya reckoned to be influential among his Muslim contemporaries and which threatened to corrupt them, such as *waḥdat al-wujūd* (the unity of existence), philosophy, Sufism, the *kalām* of the Mu'tazilī and Ash'arī theologians, and extreme Shi'ism. But the fact that not only the composition of such an influential work, but also to a considerable extent its form, is shaped by a work of Christian apologetic, is an interesting example of at least a measure of interaction between the two communities.

MUSLIM TREATMENT OF CHRISTIANS II

As well as witnessing some interesting examples of interchange between Christians and Muslims, the ninth/third century also witnessed, paradoxically, significant change with respect to the question of the legal position of other faith communities within the Muslim world. We have seen already how the Covenant of 'Umar, even if it adopted a rather more restrictive policy than the Constitution of Medina with reference to the position of non-Muslims within an Islamic state, nevertheless was in many respects relatively liberal with reference to Christian and Jewish religious practice. The ninth/third century, however, saw a rather subtle change of tone and emphasis, which may be seen in the laws passed by the caliph al-Mutawakkil in the year 850/235. It is worthwhile to quote the laws, as recorded by the historian al-Ṭabarī, in full:

> In the year (235/850), al-Mutawakkil gave orders that the Christians and the *dhimmīs* in general be required to wear honey-colored hoods (*ṭaylasān*) and girdles (*zunnār*); to ride on saddles with wooden stirrups and with two balls attached to the rear; to attach two buttons to the conical caps (*qalansuwa*) of those who wear them and to wear caps of a different color from those worn by the Muslims; to attach two patches to their slaves' clothing, of a different color from that of the garment to which they are attached, one in front on the chest, the other at the back, each

> patch four fingers in length, and both of them honey-colored. Those of them who wear turbans were to wear honey-colored turbans. If their women went out and appeared in public, they were only to appear with honey-colored head scarves. He gave orders that their slaves were to wear girdles, and he forbade them to wear belts (*minṭaqa*). He gave orders to destroy their churches which were newly built and to take the tenth part of their houses. If the place was large enough, it was to be made into a mosque; if it was not suitable for a mosque, it was to be made an open space. He ordered that wooden images of devils should be nailed to the doors of their houses to distinguish them from the houses of the Muslims. He forbade their employment in government offices and on official business where they would have authority over the Muslims. He forbade that their children attend Muslim schools or that any Muslim should teach them. He forbade the display of crosses on their Palm Sundays and Jewish rites in the streets. He ordered that their graves be made level with the ground so that they should not resemble the graves of the Muslims.[44]

Interesting features of these laws are, firstly, the importance which was evidently attached to dress – it is interesting to see the extent to which later medieval laws in the West concerning the Jews mirrored some of the details of these laws;[45] and, secondly, the attention which the laws devote to the social and educational position of Christians. In this they correspond to the polemical tract of al-Jāḥiẓ (c. 776/160–869/255), *al-radd 'alā'l-naṣārā* (The Refutation of the Christians), which is as much an attack on the social position of Christians as it is on their system of belief.[46] In short it could reasonably be said that the spirit which these laws represent is a spirit which sought to make it manifestly clear that Christians and Jews were to be seen as second-class citizens within the Islamic world, to be manifestly lower than Muslims in terms of prestige and social position. It is important to remember, however, that this situation bears many similarities to the position of non-Christians in the Roman Empire once Christianity became the official religion of the Empire in the fourth century, when they became disadvantaged in a number of ways, not least financial.

There is thus a certain irony in the fact that while on one level Christians were exerting considerable influence on the Muslim community through their role as translators in this period, on another level they were beginning to be more explicitly disadvantaged in Islamic society. Theoretical debate about this has continued subsequently, however, with a more pragmatic approach being seen in, for example, the work of the great political thinker al-Mawardī (974/364–1058/450), in his *Al-aḥkām al-ṣulṭāniyya* (The Laws of Governance), and a more antagonistic approach being evident in some of the writings of Ibn Taimiyya, especially his *Ma'salat al-kanā'is* (The Question of the Churches).[47]

In any discussion of this theme, it is extremely important that a sense of proportion is kept. Some modern Jews and Christians insist on judging the medieval world of Islam according to modern Western criteria, forgetting that the United Nations Declaration of Human Rights had not been compiled at the time. The strictures of the Jewish writer who publishes under the pseudonym Bat Ye'or (Daughter of the Nile) are thus not justified.[48] By medieval standards, the Muslim treatment of Jews and Christians was relatively tolerant and liberal, though it was clearly, by modern standards, still discriminatory to some extent. Comparisons can only fairly be made with other medieval societies, and on this basis the Muslim world scores extremely well.

CONVERSION TO ISLAM

It is often remarked that the Middle East is the home of three of the world's great monotheistic religions: Judaism, Christianity and Islam. What is often forgotten, however, is that during the course of Middle Eastern history, the majority of the population of the region has changed its religious allegiance. Judaism was never the religion of anything but a small minority of the population of the region as a whole. Later, for several centuries, Christianity was the numerically dominant faith. And today, Islam is the religion of the overwhelming majority of the people of the Middle East, even if Judaism and Christianity both remain significant presences in certain parts of the region, for different reasons. The process of this transition, whereby the majority of the population somehow shifted its religious allegiance, is an extremely interesting one, and it is important that we devote some attention to it now.

Conversion to Islam has been the focus of a number of interesting academic studies in recent years. In 1972–3, a seminar arranged at the School of Oriental and African Studies in London was devoted to the theme, which was investigated on a global level and with a timescale that stretched up until today; from that conference came the volume edited by the Israeli scholar Nehemiah Levtzion, under the title *Conversion to Islam*.[49] In 1973, a conference held in Los Angeles for the award of the fourth Giorgio della Vida Medal, to Gustave von Grunebaum, was devoted to the theme of 'Islam and Cultural Change in the Middle Ages'. Although conversion is only one element among many in the process of cultural change, several of the papers delivered at the conference did devote some attention to it, looking in particular at the relationship between Arabisation and Islamisation in such places as Egypt, Syria and Spain, and including some reference to India as well as the central Islamic lands.[50] In 1979 the American scholar Richard Bulliet devoted a lively monograph specifically to the subject of conversion, with particular reference to the medieval world, and focusing on the central part of the Islamic world.[51] And more recently, a conference was held in 1986 at the University of Toronto entitled 'Conversion and Continuity: Indigenous Christian Communities in Medieval Islamic Lands'; again this concentrated on the Middle East and Spain, but it did carry the story forward to the eighteenth/twelfth century.[52] How, when, and why, therefore, did people in the Middle East convert from Christianity to Islam?

One feature of this process which these scholarly researches make very clear is that it took place at different rates and had different stages in different countries, so that there was considerable regional variation. It is this fact, of course, which is partly responsible for the different demographic balances in different parts of the Middle East today, whereby in some parts of the Arab world such as north Africa, Christianity has disappeared almost completely but in other regions, such as the Lebanon, Christian churches remain a significant presence.

In order to investigate the process of conversion today, it is possible to conduct interviews and to use some of the other tools of anthropological investigation in order to ascertain motives for and processes in conversion. For the more distant past, however, this is not possible, necessitating reliance on historical and other literary sources. Bulliet's methodology, in this context, is an imaginative one, since the main body of material which he used consists of the great biographical dictionaries which were produced in the medieval Islamic world at different stages, the medieval equivalent of today's 'Who's Who' volumes. He focused in particular on the names of the individuals in the dictionaries; these were entered on a computer, and a detailed analysis was undertaken of when the first Islamic names, such as Muḥammad, appear. Bulliet's thesis is essentially that the appearance of such specifically Islamic names probably represents the appearance of the first generation of born-Muslims; in other words it signifies that it was probably the generation before these individuals which converted to Islam, because while the converts themselves probably did not change their names, they probably did give Islamic names to their children.

Bulliet does not downplay the weaknesses of this methodology. In particular, the fundamental assumption about it being the children of converts who first bear Islamic names is not proven, since names are not necessarily a foolproof guide. And perhaps most importantly the people who appear in the biographical dictionaries are not necessarily representative; by definition they tend to be members of an élite. But despite these weaknesses, which tend to result in a slight exaggeration in the percentage of the population which had become Muslim at any one time, Bulliet's research is extremely valuable in providing a plausible interpretation of the process of conversion as a whole, and also in providing comparative data concerning the rate at which the process proceeded in different parts of the Islamic world.

Bulliet's research makes the obvious point, first of all, that conversion was a gradual rather than a sudden process. The Middle East was not transformed from a situation in which Christianity was the religion of the majority of the population to a situation in which Islam, overnight, became the majority faith. The process was gradual, and it also proceeded in fits and starts. Secondly, Bulliet suggests that different stages can be discerned so that in any particular context first a few innovators, or trendsetters, convert, then the process accelerates so that the majority of the population joins in the process, and then there are a few of what he calls the 'laggards', who remain attached to the earlier faith. Many centuries may therefore be involved, but on the strength of this interpretation, with the help of his computer, Bulliet was able to produce a series of graphs to demonstrate the rate at which conversion took place in different parts of the medieval Islamic world.

If we move from west to east, what we therefore find is that in North Africa the process of conversion began relatively early and was certainly completed very early. One of the great centres of the early Christian church, which produced such significant figures as Tertullian (d. c. 220), Cyprian (d. 258), and Augustine (d. 430), was almost completely Muslim by the twelfth/sixth century. North Africa therefore serves as one of the most dramatic examples of the process of conversion from Christianity to Islam, with an interesting letter from Gregory VII, the Pope from 1073/466–1085/478, demonstrating that even by his time Christians had become a small minority in the region.[53]

Three reasons can be suggested for the rapidity with which this process took place. Firstly, with respect to the nature of the Islamic community in North Africa, it is important to note that in the field of the *sharī'a* (Islamic law), it was the Mālikī school which became dominant. This is significant because for this school it was above all else the example of the Muslim community in Medina which provided the model for later Islamic practice, and given that Christians did not have a significant presence there some of the pronouncements of Mālikī *fiqh* (jurisprudence) tended to be rather harsher in their attitude towards Christians than those of other schools such as the Ḥanafī.[54]

The second and third factors relate more to the nature of the Christian church in North Africa, for one of the important facts about this church in the era before the coming of Islam was that it was deeply divided, particularly by the Donatist schism.[55] Augustine in the fourth and fifth centuries had fought against the Donatists, as had many of his successors as bishops of Hippo (Carthage), and the bitterness and mistrust which some of their methods created did much to leave a legacy of disunity. Thirdly, and not unrelated to this point, much of the North African church was very definitely a Roman church, as opposed to an indigenous church; the church, in other words, was the church of the governing classes, of Rome's representatives in North Africa, rather than of the local populace themselves, and for this reason the church's structures in the area seem to have been severely weakened when Roman rule itself collapsed in the aftermath of the Vandal invasions in 429.[56]

In Egypt, by contrast, although there were certain similarities between the process there and what was happening in North Africa, the pace of conversion was rather different, to the extent that today, in the form of the Coptic church, there still remains a substantial Christian minority in the country, which possibly makes up as much as ten or even fifteen per cent of the population.[57] Large-scale conversion to Islam in Egypt began during the eighth/second century, and was very much linked with economic hardship. Oppressive taxation led to a whole series of revolts in different regions of Egypt between 725/107 and 832/217, and these were crushed by the local governors and, in the end, the caliph al-Ma'mūn himself, who visited the province in 832/217. Conversion was in part a mechanism for escaping from the burden of this taxation, especially in the Nile Delta, the northern part of Egypt, and I. M. Lapidus comments:

> Coptic resistance to taxation by force of arms was broken. The despair which followed these crushing defeats seems finally to have set in train the movement of mass conversions to Islam . . . We may say that the defeat of the rebellion broke the backbone of mass Coptic allegiance to Christianity . . .[58]

Once begun, the process of conversion continued gradually, with the pace of conversion very much affected by the policies of the different dynasties which ruled Egypt. An outburst of fairly savage persecution occurred in the time of the Fatimid ruler al-Ḥākim (996/386–1021/

411), and on several other occasions during the course of medieval history there were a number of instances of riots against Christians in Egypt over such things as new church-building and the influence which Christians continued to exert in the government administration. At certain periods, indeed, Christians more or less dominated this aspect of Egyptian life, and on occasion it is clear that this provoked considerable resentment.[59]

The result of this was that perhaps as early as the tenth/fourth century the majority of the population of Egypt was Muslim, but the Christian church survived, and remains a significant feature within Egypt, perhaps for two main reasons: firstly the church had succeeded in establishing its local roots – the word 'Coptic' as used today with reference to the church is in origin simply the Greek word for 'Egyptian'; and secondly the church managed to retain a remarkable degree of unity, with the vast majority of Egypt's Christian population being members of the Coptic Orthodox Church until modern times, when a number of Western churches established a presence in Egypt.

Moving eastwards and northwards to Syria (understood in the sense of Greater Syria, in other words what is today Syria, Lebanon, Jordan and Palestine/Israel), here the process of conversion to Islam took place rather more slowly than in Egypt, so that even by the year 1300/700, according to Kamal Salibi, Islam was still not the religion of the majority of the population. Given the importance of the relative unity of the church in Egypt in ensuring its survival this may seem surprising, since Syrian Christianity was far more divided, with a number of Christian churches, both Chalcedonian and non-Chalcedonian, represented. But if Syrian Christianity was divided so too was Syrian Islam, with the presence of both Sunnī and Imāmī Shīʿī Muslims and also a number of offshoots from both groups such as the Druzes. It is perhaps this fact, together with the geographical fragmentation of Greater Syria (which itself goes some way toward explaining its religious diversity) which explains Christian survival even despite Christian disunity. Today, therefore, the population of the modern nation of Syria is roughly 10 per cent Christian, and in the Lebanon, as defined by its 1923/1341 boundaries, Christians made up the majority of the population at that time and are today perhaps 45 per cent of the population.[60]

Further east, in Iraq and Iran, there is one major historical difference between these areas and those we have examined already, namely that here Christianity had never been the dominant religion: in the days of the Sassanian Empire, as we have seen, Christians, particularly those belonging to the Nestorian church, were a significant and influential minority, but Christianity was never either the state religion or the religion of the majority of the population. In Islamic times conversion began fairly early, and probably proceeded more quickly in Iran than in any of the more westerly provinces simply because the demise of the Sassanian Empire left Zoroastrianism without any equivalent to the Byzantine emperor to serve as a powerful external sponsor, or even protector, of the community. While it is probable, therefore, that Islam became the religion of the majority of the population in Iran relatively early, possibly as early as the start of the ninth/third century, it is not clear to what extent this involved the conversion of Christians rather than Zoroastrians.[61]

A complicating factor in this region towards the end of the medieval period was the coming of the Mongols from Central Asia, as at one stage there was a not completely unrealistic expectation among the Christians of south-west Asia that the Mongols would convert to Christianity. One of the wives of the Mongol emperor Hulagu (1256/654–1265/663) was a Christian, and there was a considerable Nestorian influence on many of the Mongol rulers.[62] But in the end the Mongols converted to Islam, and the enthusiasm with which some Christians had greeted the Mongol conquerors was not forgotten by later generations of Muslims.[63]

In both Iraq and Iran the process of conversion to Islam even today has not run its full course, and both countries still retain not insignificant Christian minorities within their borders. Perhaps some 4 per cent of the population of Iraq today is Christian, mostly belonging to a number of Catholic churches, as illustrated most powerfully in recent decades by the person of Tariq Aziz, the former Foreign Minister, who became Deputy Prime Minister of Iraq in 1991/1411. He is a member of the Chaldaean Church, the element of the ancient Nestorian Church (or sometimes called the Assyrian Church) which submitted to papal authority in 1553/960; and some 1 per cent of the population of Iran is Christian, with the overwhelming majority being Armenian Orthodox.[64]

The other geographical area which was a major centre of early Christianity, to the extent that three of Paul's letters in the New Testament, to the Galatians, Ephesians and Colossians, were written to churches within its borders, is Turkey. Today, however, it has a tiny Christian presence, limited almost to its capital city and some of its border areas. The process of conversion to Islam here, however, has taken a very different course from that in the areas examined so far, because of the very different history of the region. Firstly, Turkey, or Asia Minor as it was then known, did not come under Islamic control in the first wave of Islamic expansion but remained a province of the Byzantine Empire until the eleventh/fifth century when, as a result of the battle of Manzikert (1071/463) the heartland of the province came under the rule of the Seljuk Turks; and secondly, even after the Islamic conquest of the region, the relatively tolerant policies towards religious minorities pursued by the different Turkish dynasties, and in particular the Ottoman rulers, meant that while conversion to Islam certainly took place, substantial religious minorities remained present in what is today Turkey until well into the twentieth/fourteenth century.[65] It was only in the aftermath of World War I, in fact, when international negotiations concerning borders and the fate of the former territories of the Ottoman Empire resulted in the creation of the modern nation of Turkey, that a substantial transfer of population took place between Turkey and Greece, which resulted in the virtual disappearance of any Christian presence in the Asian part of Turkey. The majority of Turks in the Ottoman Empire had always been Muslim, the Turks being one of the peoples of the world who have been most united in their religious allegiance. But it is important to remember that even in the heyday of the Ottoman Empire, Turks were numerically less than half of the population, and even with other Muslims among the empire's diverse population, Muslims probably made up only some two thirds of its population as a whole.[66]

NOTES

1. See I. R. Netton, *Allah Transcendent*, London: Curzon Press, 1989, esp. pp. 13–15.
2. F. Rosenthal, *The Classical Heritage in Islam*, London: Routledge and Kegan Paul, 1975. M. Fakhry, *A Short Introduction to Islamic Philosophy, Theology and Mysticism*, Oxford: Oneworld, 1997, pp. 135–7, lists the major philosophical works translated into Arabic in this period.
3. M. Fakhry, *A History of Islamic Philosophy*, 2nd edn, Columbia University Press, 1983, pp. 12–14, and D. Gutas, *Greek Thought, Arabic Culture*, London: Routledge, 1998, esp. pp. 131–45.
4. Fakhry, *History*, pp. 19–27, and Netton, *Allah Transcendent*, pp. 12–13.
5. Fakhry, *History*, p. 12.
6. See A. Mingana, 'The Apology of Timothy the Patriarch before the Caliph Mahdi', in *Bulletin of the John Rylands Library*, 12 (1928), pp. 137–298, and R. Caspar, 'Les versions arabes du Dialogue entre le Catholicos Timothée I et le calife al-Mahdi', in *Islamochristiana*, 3 1977, pp. 107–75.
7. A. Guillaume, 'Theodore Abu Qurra as Apologist', in *Muslim World*, 15 (1925), p. 46.
8. On Abū Qurra, see S. Griffith, 'Reflections on the Biography of Theodore Abū Qurrah', in *Parole de l'Orient*, 18 (1993), pp. 143–70, esp. pp. 153–8, and A-Th. Khoury, *Les Théologiens Byzantins et l'Islam*, Louvain: Nauwelaerts, 1969, Chapter 3; on al-Kindī, see W. Muir, *The Apology of al-Kindy*, London: Society for Promoting Christian Knowledge, 1887; N. A. Newman (ed.), *The Early Christian–Muslim Dialogue: a Collec-*

tion of Documents from the First Three Islamic Centuries, Hatfield PA: Interdisciplinary Biblical Research Institute, 1993, pp. 355–545; and G. Tartar, *Dialogue islamo-chrétien sous le calife al-Ma'mūn 813–834, les épitres d'al-Hashimī et d'al-Kindī*, unpublished PhD thesis, University of Strasbourg, 1977.

9. Griffith, 'Reflections. . .', p. 150.
10. Guillaume, 'Theodore Abu Quarra. . .', pp. 46–51, and J. W. Sweetman, *Islam and Christian Theology*, Part I, vol. I, London: Lutterworth Press, 1945, p. 68.
11. Guillaume, 'Theodore Abu Qurra. . .', p. 46.
12. Muir, *The Apology of al-Kindy*, p. 27.
13. See I. R. Netton, *Al-Fārābī and his School*, London: Routledge, 1992, pp. 1–11, and J. L. Kraemer, *Humanism in the Renaissance of Islam*, Brill: Leiden, 2nd edn, 1992, pp. 75–7 and 104–7.
14. See S. K. Samir, 'The Earliest Arab Apology for Christianity (c. 750)' in S. K. Samir and J. S. Nielsen (eds), *Christian Arabic Apologetics during the Abbasid Period (750–1258)*, Leiden: Brill, 1994, pp. 57–114, and S.H. Griffith, 'The View of Islam from the Monasteries of Palestine in the Early 'Abbāsid Period' in *Islam and Christian–Muslim Relations*, 7 (1996), pp. 9–28, esp. pp. 10–12.
15. Griffith, 'Reflections. . . p. 13.
16. J. Blau, 'Saadya Gaon's Pentateuch Translation and the Stabilization of Mediaeval Judaeo-Arabic Culture' in J. Krasovec (ed.), *Interpretation of the Bible*, Sheffield Academic Press, 1998, pp. 393–8. See also H. Lazarus-Yafeh, *Intertwined Worlds: Medieval Islam and Bible Criticism*, Princeton University Press, 1992, Chapter 5.
17. B. M. Metzger, *The Early Versions of the New Testament: their Origin, Transmission and Limitations*, Oxford University Press, 1977, pp. 257–68, esp. pp. 259–62.
18. O. F. A. Meinardus, *Christian Egypt, Ancient and Modern*, Cairo: French Institute of Oriental Archaeology, 1965, p. 108.
19. See Khoury, *Les Théologiens Byzantins*, Chapter 4.
20. Ibid., Chapter 5. See also J. Meyendorff, 'Byzantine Views of Islam' in *Dumbarton Oaks Papers*, 18 (1964), pp. 113–32, esp. pp. 121–3 and 127–8.
21. G. Ostrogorsky, *History of the Byzantine State*, 3rd edn, Rutgers University Press, 1969, p. 227.
22. See Khoury, *Les Théologiens Byzantins*, Chapters 6 to 8, and Meyendorff, 'Byzantine Views of Islam', pp. 123–5 and 129–30.
23. See Khoury, *Les Théologiens Byzantins*, Chapter 9; Meyendorff, 'Byzantine Views of Islam pp. 125–7; A. Jeffery, 'Ghevond's Text of the Correspondence between Umar II and Leo III' in *Harvard Theological Review*, 37 (1944), pp. 269–332; and J-M. Gaudeul, 'The Correspondence between Leo and 'Umar: 'Umar's Letter Re-Discovered?' in *Islamochristiana*, 10 (1984), pp. 109–57.
24. Meyendorff, 'Byzantine Views of Islam', pp. 124–5. See also C. L. Hanson, 'Manuel I Comnenus and the "God of Muḥammad": a Study in Byzantine Ecclesiastical Politics' in J. V. Tolan (ed.), *Medieval Christian Perceptions of Islam*, New York and London: Garland, 1996, pp. 55–82.
25. For further detail of this, see my *Muslim Perceptions of Christianity*, London: Grey Seal, 1996, Chapter 2. See also the various studies of D. R. Thomas, especially his *Anti-Christian Polemic in Early Islam: Abū 'Īsā*

al-Warrāq's 'Against the Trinity', Cambridge University Press, 1992, and his forthcoming study of the same author's work on the Incarnation.

26. H. Lazarus-Yafeh, 'Some Neglected Aspects of Medieval Muslim Polemics against Christianity' in *Harvard Theological Review*, 89 (1996), p. 84.
27. A. Charfi, 'La fonction historique de la polémique islamochrétienne à l'époque abbasside', in S. K. Samir and J. S. Nielsen (eds), *Christian Arabic Apologetics during the Abbasid Period (750–1258)*, Leiden: Brill, 1994, pp. 44–56.
28. I am grateful to Professor Aref Nayed of the Pontifical Institute for Arab and Islamic Studies in Rome for his suggestion that I investigate this topic, and to Dr. David Thomas of the Centre for the Study of Islam and Christian–Muslim Relations in Birmingham for his help in obtaining material for the following paragraphs.
29. For the biographies and main opinions of both figures, see W. M. Watt, *The Formative Period of Islamic Thought*, Edinburgh University Press, 1973, pp. 303–16; for details of the founders of the two schools and of their later development, see R. Caspar, *A Historical Introduction to Islamic Theology*, Rome: Pontifical Institute of Arabic and Islamic Studies, 1998, Chapter 8.
30. R.J. McCarthy, *The Theology of al-Ash'ari*, Beirut: Imprimerie Catholique, 1953, p. 227, Nos. 84 and 86.
31. The *Risala ila ahl-thaghr bi bab al-abwab*, ed. Qiwameddin (sic), in Ilahiyat Fakültesi Mecmuasi, 8 (1928), pp. 80–108.
32. Caspar, *Islamic Theology*, p. 214.
33. W. Z. Haddad, 'A Tenth-Century Speculative Theologian's Refutation of the Basic Doctrines of Christianity: al-Bāqillānī (d. AD 1013)', in Y. Y. Haddad and W. Z. Haddad, (eds), *Christian–Muslim Encounters*, Gainesville: University Press of Florida, 1995, p. 85.
34. See ibid., pp. 82–94, esp. pp. 86–91, and A. Abel, 'Le Chapitre sur le Christianisme dans le "Tamhid" d'al-Baqillani', in *Études d'Orientalisme Dédiées á la Mémoire de Lévi-Provencal*, Paris: Maisonneuve et Larose, 1962, pp. 1–11.
35. D. Thomas, 'Abū Manṣūr al-Māturīdī on the Divinity of Jesus Christ', in *Islamochristiana*, 23 (1997), pp. 43–64.
36. Ibid., pp. 48–9.
37. H. Özcan, 'Abū Manṣūr al-Māturīdī's Religious Pluralism', in *Islamochristiana*, 23 (1997), pp. 65–80; the quotation comes from p. 72.
38. As an example of the former see A. Aslan, *Religious Pluralism in Christian and Islamic Philosophy*, London: Curzon, 1998; and for the latter see T. Michel, 'Teaching the Christian Faith in the Faculties of Theology of Turkey', in *Encounter: Documents for Muslim-Christian Understanding*, (Rome: Pontifical Institute of Arabic and Islamic Studies), No. 164 (April 1990), pp. 1–9.
39. See P. Khoury, *Paul d'Antioche*, Beirut: Imprimerie Catholique, 1964; T. Michel, *A Muslim Theologian's Response to Christianity: Ibn Taymiyya's Al-Jawab al-Sahih*, Delmar NY: Caravan Books, 1984; and M. H. Siddiqi, 'Muslim and Byzantine Christian Relations: Letter of Paul of Antioch and Ibn Taymīyah's Response', in *Greek Orthodox Theological Review*, 31 (1986), pp. 33–45.
40. Siddiqi, 'Muslim and Byzantine Christian Relations', pp. 34–5.
41. Michel, 'Teaching the Christian Faith', pp. 73–8.

42. Ibid., p. vii.
43. Ibid., p. 125.
44. Al-Ṭabarī, *Ta'rīkh* (History), vol. iii, pp. 1389–90, translated in B. Lewis, *Islam*, vol. II, New York: Harper and Row, 1974, pp. 224–5.
45. F. E. Peters, in his *Judaism, Christianity, Islam: the Classical Texts and their Interpretation*, Vol II, Princeton University Press, 1990, tellingly juxtaposes, on pp. 380–2, a translation of the Covenant of 'Umar and the decree of the Fourth Lateran Council of 1215/612 concerning the dress required of Jews and Muslims in Christian provinces.
46. See Goddard, *Muslim Perceptions of Christianity*, pp. 32–3, and also the comment of Charfi, 'La fonction historique', pp. 53–4.
47. See W. Z. Haddad, '*Ahl al-dhimma* in an Islamic State: the Teaching of Abū al-Ḥasan al-Mawardī's *Al-aḥkām al-sulṭāniyya*', in *Islam and Christian–Muslim Relations*, 7 (1996), pp. 169–80; B. O'Keefe, 'Aḥmad ibn Taimiyya, *Mas'alat al-Kanā'is* (The Question of the Churches)', in *Islamochristiana*, 22 (1996), pp. 53–78, and Michel, *A Muslim Theologian: Response to Christians . . .*, pp. 78–83.
48. Bat Ye'or, *The Dhimmi: Jews and Christians under Islam*, New Jersey: Associated University Presses, 1985, and *The Decline of Eastern Christianity under Islam: from Jihad to Dhimmitude, Seventh to Twentieth Century*, New Jersey: Fairleigh Dickinson University Press, 1996.
49. N. Levtzion (ed.), *Conversion to Islam*, New York: Holmes and Meier, 1979.
50. S. Vryonis Jr (ed.), *Islam and Cultural Change in the Middle Ages*, Wiesbaden: Harrassowitz, 1975.
51. R. Bulliet, *Conversion to Islam in the Medieval Period*, Harvard University Press, 1979.
52. M. Gervers and R. J. Bikhazi (eds), *Conversion and Continuity: Indigenous Christian Communities in Islamic Lands – Eighth to Eighteenth Centuries*, Toronto: Pontifical Institute of Medieval Studies, 1990.
53. See C. Courtois, 'Grégoire VII et l'Afrique du Nord: Remarques sur les Communautés Chrétiennes d'Afrique au Xie siècle', in *Revue Historique*, 195 (1945), pp. 97–122 and 193–226; and M. Talbi, 'Le Christianisme Maghrébin de la Conquête Musulmane à sa Disparition: une Tentative d'Explication' in Gervers and Bikhazi, *Conversion and Continuity*, pp. 313–51.
54. M. Speight, 'The place of Christians in Ninth Century North Africa, according to Muslim sources', in *Islamochristiana*, 4 (1978), pp. 47–65. See also A. Fattal, *Le Statut Légal des non-Musulmans en pays d'Islam*, Beirut: Imprimerie Catholique, 1958, p. 164.
55. W. H. C. Frend, *The Donatist Church*, Oxford University Press, 1952.
56. J. Cuoq, *L'Église d'Afrique du Nord du IIe au XIIe siècle*, Paris: Centurion, 1984.
57. M. Brett, 'The Spread of Islam in Egypt and North Africa' in Brett (ed.), *Northern Africa: Islam and Modernization*, London: Cass, 1973, pp. 1–12; and Bulliet, *Conversion to Islam, Chapter 8.*
58. I. M. Lapidus, 'The Conversion of Egypt to Islam' in *Israel Oriental Studies*, 2 (1972), p. 257.
59. S. K. Samir, 'The Role of Christians in the Fāṭimid Government Services of Egypt to the Reign of al-Ḥāfiẓ', in *Medieval Encounters*, 2 (1996), pp. 177–92, Y. Lev, 'Persecutions and Conversion to Islam in Eleventh-Century Egypt', in *Asian and African Studies*, 22 (1988), pp. 73–91,

and D. P. Little, 'Coptic Conversion to Islam under the Baḥrī Mamlūks, 692–755/1293–1353', in *Bulletin of the School of Oriental and African Studies*, 39 (1976), pp. 552–69. See also a number of studies by M. Perlmann concerning anti-Christian polemical literature in Egypt in the Mamluk period.

60. R. M. Haddad, *Syrian Christians in Muslim Society: an Interpretation*, Westport: Greenwood, 1970, and K. Salibi, *A House of Many Mansions*, London: I. B. Tauris, 1989.
61. Iran is the major focus of Bulliet's study, *Conversion to Islam in the Medieval Period*, especially chapters 3 to 6; Iraq is discussed in Chapter 7.
62. R. W. Southern, *Western Views of Islam in the Middle Ages*, Harvard University Press, 1962, p. 65.
63. Ibid., pp. 69, 74.
64. R. B. Betts, *Christians in the Arab East*, 2nd edn, London: SPCK, 1978, and N. Horner, *Rediscovering Christianity where it First Began*, Beirut: Near East Council of Churches, 1973.
65. K. Karpat, 'Ottoman Views and Policies towards the Orthodox Christian Church', in *Greek Orthodox Theological Review*, 31 (1986), pp. 131–55, and B. Braude and B.Lewis (eds), *Christians and Jews in the Ottoman Empire*, 2 vols, New York: Holmes and Meier, 1982.
66. See S. J. Shaw and E. K. Shaw, *History of the Ottoman Empire and Modern Turkey*, vol. II, Cambridge University Press, 1977, p. 240, which gives the breakdown of the population of the Empire by religious allegiance at the end of the nineteenth/thirteenth century. On the history of conversion in what is now Turkey see S. Vryonis, *The Decline of Medieval Hellenism in Asia Minor and the Process of Islamization from the Eleventh through the Fifteenth Century*, University of California Press, 1971, and V. Ménage, 'The Islamization of Anatolia', in Levtzion, (ed.) *Conversion to Islam*, Chapter 4.

5

The Medieval Period II: Confrontation or Interaction in the West?

WESTERN CHRISTIAN REACTIONS TO THE COMING OF ISLAM

In Chapter 1 we have already seen how Western and Eastern Christianity were developing differently even before the coming of Islam: the different languages which they used, Latin and Greek respectively, the different intellectual contexts within which they developed, especially as regards their interaction with Hellenistic philosophy, and the particular experiences of Augustine (354–430) in the West all contributed to the two branches of Christendom coming to focus on different themes and developing different preoccupations. As regards the central focus of their theology, East and West came to concentrate respectively on divinisation and redemption.

At the time of the coming of Islam, East and West also had different experiences of Islam: as we have seen, it was Eastern Christians who first encountered Islam and who therefore formulated the initial Christian interpretations of, and responses to, Islam. Several decades passed before there was any lasting encounter between Muslims and Western Christians, since although there were minor Muslim military campaigns in north Africa in the 640s/20s, lasting conquest was only attempted in the 660s/40s, with Kairouan being established as the main centre of Muslim power in 670/50. Even then, despite the dashing march of 'Uqba ibn Nāfi' to the Atlantic Ocean in 680/60, the Muslim position remained vulnerable until 697/78, when Carthage fell, and even after that there were several significant Berber revolts which threatened Muslim control.[1]

Even before the coming of Islam, however, the church in north Africa had become somewhat detached from the church in Western Europe, not least as a result of the Vandal invasion of 429, and the majority of Western Christians did not become particularly aware of Islam until the next stage of Muslim expansion, which came with the Muslim invasion of Spain in 711/92. The Berber general Ṭāriq, who gave his name to Gibraltar (*Jabal*/Mountain of Ṭāriq), crossed from Africa with some 7,000 men, and a decisive defeat of the Visigothic army in the summer of the same year led, as in Iran, to the almost complete collapse of the kingdom. The capital, Toledo, surrendered without offering any resistance, and within three years virtually the whole of the Iberian Peninsula apart from the mountains in the far north came under Islamic rule.[2]

Nor did the Muslim armies stop there. As early as 714/96 raiders crossed the Pyrenees into the south of France, and for two or three decades from 720/102 the town of Narbonne was under Muslim control. The furthest point which the raiders reached was near the town of Tours, a mere 125 miles/200 kilometres south-west of Paris, where in 732/114 they were defeated by a Frankish army under Charles Martel.[3]

As a result of these military campaigns, Western Europe as a whole certainly became aware of the coming of Islam. In 731/113, the Venerable Bede in his *History of the English Church and People,* which was composed in the monastery in Jarrow in the north-east of England, wrote:

> In the year of our Lord 729, two comets appeared around the sun, striking terror into all who saw them. One comet rose early and preceded the sun, while the other followed the setting sun at evening, seeming to portend awful calamity to east and west alike. One comet was the precursor of day and the other of night, to indicate that mankind was menaced by evils at both times. They appeared in the month of January, and remained visible for about a fortnight, bearing their fiery trails northward as though to set the welkin aflame. At this time, a swarm of Saracens ravaged Gaul with horrible slaughter, but after a brief interval in that country they paid the penalty of their wickedness.[4]

Bede's interpretation of the coming of Islam was fairly matter-of-fact: he saw it basically as being explained by the references in the Book of Genesis to the coming of the descendants of Ishmael, similarly to the way in which the first Eastern Christians to encounter Islam had explained it. And if the Muslims were a threat, the language used to describe the threat was little different from that used later of, for example, the Vikings, whose raids disrupted north-west European life so severely during the ninth/third and tenth/fourth centuries.[5]

After the battle of Tours, the Muslim raids in France became restricted to Provence and the southern coast lands, and as Frankish power became consolidated, the Frankish kings opened diplomatic communication with the 'Abbasid Empire in the East: a Frankish embassy was sent to Baghdad by King Pepin in 765/148, and Charlemagne, who was crowned Holy Roman Emperor in 800/184, exchanged gifts with the 'Abbasid caliph in Baghdad, Hārūn al-Rashīd (786/170–809/193), who, among other things, sent Charlemagne an elephant.[6] By this time relations between the Christian and Muslim worlds were complicated, firstly by the fact that from 756/138 a separate Umayyad caliphate had been established in Spain, so that Hārūn's keenness to cultivate good relations with the Franks may therefore in part be explained by his desire to solicit their support against the Umayyads; and secondly by the fact that disputes among the Muslims in Spain led one group of Muslim princes, in 777/160, to appeal to Charlemagne for help against some of their Muslim rivals. His response was positive, and he marched into Spain in order to support them, with some success, but during his return to France the rearguard of his army was ambushed and slaughtered. It was this incident which gave rise, centuries later, to the composition of the epic poem *The Song of Roland*, about the heroism of the leader of the rearguard as he was attacked by the Saracens, but it is important to note that in history, if not in epic, the attackers were actually not Muslims at all, but Basques.

It was in Spain during the ninth/third century that the set of circumstances unfolded which were to bring into being a distinctively Western response to Islam, which has proved remarkably persistent, lasting even to the present day. This peculiarly negative view of Islam has its origin in the movement known as the Spanish Martyrs' Movement, which during the decade between 850/235 and 860/246 formulated what might be called an apocalyptic vision of Islam.

Southern outlines clearly the circumstances in which this view emerged: the Christians of Cordoba, the capital of the Umayyad caliphate in Spain, were, like Christians elsewhere in the world of Islam, tolerated and protected, yet also in some ways disadvantaged. They could worship, and their lives were not endangered, but they had to pay the *jizya*, a special tribute to their rulers, and there were considerable restrictions on public manifestations of worship. The Christians of Cordoba suffered other disadvantages, however, particularly that they were isolated from the rest of the Christian world, and ignorant of Latin learning, both Christian and secular, even to the extent of not knowing Augustine's *City of God*. They also lived in the capital city of the Umayyad caliphate, in the midst of a brilliant and flourishing civilisation, and this evidently exercised a considerable seductive power over them.[7]

It was in this context of Islam being perceived as a threat to the Christians of the city that two Cordoban Christians, a priest, Eulogius, and a layman, Paul Alvarus, became convinced that Islam was the precursor of the coming of the Antichrist. They reached this conclusion on the basis of their reading of the Bible, for like the earliest Eastern Christians in their first attempts to interpret the coming of Islam, Eulogius and Paul looked to the Bible as their primary source of guidance. But the parts of the Bible which they thought provided that guidance were very different from those which the Eastern Christians had used. In particular Eulogius and Paul Alvarus looked to the apocalyptic literature of the Bible, the book of Daniel in the Old Testament and parts of the Gospel accounts and the Book of Revelation in the New Testament in order to interpret the coming of Islam.

They thus seized on passages such as Daniel 7, which refers to a vision or dream of Daniel in which he saw four beasts, the first like a lion, the second like a bear, the third like a leopard, and the fourth which has no animal given to describe it, but which is terrible, dreadful and strong, and has ten horns (verse 7). When Daniel seeks the meaning of the vision, he is told that the four beasts represent four kings who will arise (verse 17), and the main stream of Christian interpretation of this is that it refers to the Empires of Babylon, Persia, Greece (i.e. Alexander the Great and his successors), and Rome, and the special attention given to the fourth beast is connected with the fact that it was in Roman times that Jesus lived. This was not how Eulogius and Paul Alvarus interpreted the chapter, however, for in their view the fourth beast meant something different. In a modern English translation of the Bible, the Revised Standard Version/Common Bible, the discussion of the fourth beast goes as follows:

> Then I desired to know the truth concerning the fourth beast, which was different from all the rest, exceedingly terrible, with its teeth of iron and claws of bronze; and which devoured and broke in pieces, and stamped the residue with its feet . . . He [the interpreter of the vision] said: 'As for the fourth beast, there shall come a fourth kingdom on earth, which shall be different from all the kingdoms, and it shall devour the whole earth, and trample it down, and break it to pieces. As for the ten horns, out of this kingdom ten kings shall arise, and another shall arise after them; he shall be different from the former ones, and shall put down three kings. He shall speak words against the Most High, and shall wear out the saints of the Most High, and shall think to change the times and the law; and they shall be given into his hand for a time, two times, and half a time. But the court shall sit in judgement, and his dominion shall be taken away, to be consumed and destroyed to the end. And the kingdom and the dominion and the greatness of the kingdoms under the whole heaven shall be given to the people of the saints of the Most High; their kingdom shall be an everlasting kingdom, and all dominions shall serve and obey them.' (Daniel 7: 19, 23–7)

To Eulogius and Paul Alvarus, what was being described here was their own situation, being worn out as the saints of the Most High by a force which was taking over the whole earth, putting down the empires of Greeks, Franks and Goths, speaking against the Most High through its scripture, the Qur'ān, and setting up its own calendar and legal system. But this was not going to last for ever, because this force would last only for a time, two times and half a time, and if a time was taken to mean the Biblical idea of 'three score years and ten', this meant 245 years; and if Islam came into existence, or began its calendar in 622, this meant that it was about to run its course, and the end of its period of influence and the vindication of the saints was imminent.

Other apocalyptic passages from the New Testament, such as Mark 13, with its references to desolation in Jerusalem, and Revelation 13, with its picture of the beast arising and persecuting and oppressing the people of God, were interpreted as confirming this interpretation of the current situation in Cordoba. A life of Muḥammad, which was in circulation at the time in Spain, calculated that Muḥammad had died in the year 666 of the Spanish calendar (cf. Revelation 13: 18), and since this was the number of the beast, it was taken to be a clear pointer that Muḥammad was to be identified as the Antichrist. Eulogius therefore concluded that the end of all things was near.

This way of thinking is not unique in human history. Many examples of millennialist convictions can be found, in most of the world's religious traditions.[8] But what is unusual about what happened in Cordoba was the response of some Christians to this conviction, which was to seek to arouse fellow-Christians from their spiritual lethargy and infatuation with certain aspects of Arabic culture by public demonstrations of piety. These took the form either of publicly insulting Muḥammad or of publicly calling on Muslim officials to convert to Christianity, both of which actions were prohibited to Christians under Islamic law, and both of which were therefore extremely provocative to the Muslim leadership. Some of the individuals who undertook these actions succeeded in their ambition, were executed, and were considered by their co-religionists as martyrs; not only that, but a number of Muslims were indeed sufficiently impressed by their devotion and willingness to die for their faith that they were converted to Christianity, and some of them were in turn executed and considered to have been martyred. But after some time the Muslim authorities reacted to the movement by threatening to execute all Christians indiscriminately if they continued their acts of provocation, and in response to this, and to the fact that the end did not come, the movement petered out.

Some fifty individual Christians, both male and female, were executed by the authorities in the decade between 850/235 and 860/246, among them Eulogius, who was decapitated in 859/245. A number of recent studies have investigated the so-called Spanish Martyrs' Movement from a number of different perspectives, some more historical, some theological, some missiological, and some more anthropological.[9] R. W. Southern's comment on Alvarus and Eulogius remains as apt as ever, however: 'Their distress of mind and the urgent duty they felt to rouse their fellows to a sense of their danger and mission gives dignity to a system which intellectually has nothing to recommend it.'[10] But he added: 'Whatever else may be said of all this, it was the first rigidly coherent and comprehensive view of Islam, related to contemporary circumstances, to be developed in the West.'[11] And as such it was a view which was to prove extremely influential and remarkably tenacious in the West in the medieval period and beyond.

THE CRUSADES

One of the most important legacies of the very negative judgement on Islam which emerged in Spain in the ninth/third century was the subsequent rise, towards the end of the eleventh/fifth century, of what has to be called a movement of militant Christianity. The supporters of this movement, the Crusades, were convinced that they had a religious obligation to take up the cross, literally, in order to recapture the Holy Land – the land in which Jesus had lived and taught – from the infidel Muslim, in order to facilitate or expedite the return of Christ.

Recent Western scholarship has emphasised the wide range of motives held by the Crusaders, which included fairly crudely material ones such as the desire to travel, the wish to acquire booty or land, and the simple longing for fame and glory. But there is no denying that in the minds of most of the participants there was a considerable measure of religious motivation, including the longing to make the pilgrimage to the Holy Land as well as the desire to secure eternal salvation, and at least in the early years the whole movement was suffused with an air of apocalyptic expectation.

The course of the crusading movement was briefly this: in 1095/488 Pope Urban II preached the Crusade at Clermont in France. In doing so he was in part responding to an appeal for help from the Byzantine emperor Alexius I (1081/474–1118/512), since Byzantium was still reeling from its defeat by the Seljuk Turks in 1071/463 at the battle of Manzikert and the loss of most of its Asian territory. But Urban also added another element to the Crusaders' task, namely the liberation of Jerusalem, declaring that whoever participated in this task with pure motivation would be released from any penance which had been required of them earlier. To the diplomatic aim of helping the Byzantines was thus added a more specifically religious one, recovering the Holy City in order to facilitate pilgrimage.

The response to the Pope's call, however, was perhaps rather greater than he had expected. A number of princes from many regions of Europe decided to take up the cross, and itinerant preachers such as Peter the Hermit (c. 1050/442–1115/509) succeeded in arousing widespread popular enthusiasm for the venture:

> It was an age of visions: and Peter was thought to be a visionary. Medieval man was convinced that the Second Coming was at hand. He must repent while yet there was time and must go out and do good. The Church taught that sin could be expiated by pilgrimage and prophecies declared that the Holy Land must be recovered for the faith before Christ could come again. Further, to ignorant minds the distinction between Jerusalem and the New Jerusalem was not very clearly defined. Many of Peter's hearers believed that he was promising to lead them out of their present miseries to the land flowing with milk and honey of which the scriptures spoke. The journey would be hard; there were the legions of Antichrist to be overcome. But the goal was Jerusalem the golden.[12]

The appearance of a shower of meteorites in the sky earlier in 1095/488 also added to the atmosphere of expectation and enthusiasm.

In 1096/489, therefore, five armies, together numbering perhaps 50–60,000 men, set off from different parts of Western Europe to Jerusalem, with the intention of assembling at Constantinople. They had been preceded, however, by perhaps 20,000 men and women who had been inspired by the preaching of Peter the Hermit and who made up the so-called People's Expedition.[13] This expedition ended ignominiously in the autumn of 1096/489, with the loss of many thousands of lives, but the main body of the First Crusade enjoyed spectacular success, crossing into Asia Minor in 1097/490, capturing the city of Antioch in Syria after a nine-month-long siege in the summer of 1098/491, and then successfully capturing Jerusalem on 15 July 1099/22 Sha'bān 492. The governor of the city and some of his defeated garrison were given a safe-conduct out of the city, but other members of the garrison, the entire civilian Muslim population of the city, and the entire Jewish community, which had fled to its chief synagogue, were massacred. Perhaps 40,000 Muslims were massacred by the Crusaders in two days, and one eye-witness, Raymond of Aguilers, wrote that when he went to visit the Temple area of Jerusalem he had to pick his way through corpses and blood which reached up to his knees.[14]

Most of the Christian population of the city had been expelled from the city beforehand by the governor, who feared treachery, but some had remained, particularly the priests of the different Eastern churches who officiated at the liturgy in the Church of the Holy Sepulchre. The Crusaders expelled them from the church, however, thus making clear their intention that Jerusalem was to become not only a Christian city but also a Western or Latin Christian city. Runciman comments on the events which followed the Crusaders' capture of the city as follows:

> The massacre at Jerusalem profoundly impressed all the world. No one can say how many victims it involved; but it emptied Jerusalem of its Moslem and Jewish inhabitants. Many even of the Christians were horrified by what had been done; and amongst the Moslems, who had been ready hitherto to accept the Franks as another factor in the tangled politics of the time, there was henceforward a clear determination that the Franks must be driven out. It was this bloodthirsty proof of Christian fanaticism that recreated the fanaticism of Islam. When, later, wiser Latins in the East sought to find some basis on which Christian and Moslem could work together, the memory of the massacre stood always in their way.[15]

Whatever its legacy, the capture of Jerusalem in 1099/492 was undoubtedly an astounding military feat. For the Crusaders to have marched several thousand miles from north-western Europe, endured considerable hardship during a number of sieges in Syria, and then to achieve their goal of reconquering Jerusalem was, if nothing else, a great tribute to their tenacity. Having achieved their ambition, however, the Crusaders had to retain what they had conquered, and very quickly a number of difficulties emerged which would make that ambition hard to realise. Prominent among these were divisions among their leaders, as a result of both differences of national background and individual ambition, the climate, which was very different from what most Crusaders were used to and which therefore caused a high mortality rate, and the difficult issue of how to relate to the local population, Jewish, Eastern Christian, and Muslim. Some Crusaders sought to pursue a policy of zealous separatism, but others were ready to inter-marry with the local population, a policy which always ran the risk of assimilation.

Fights therefore broke out among the Crusaders, with alliances being formed between some Crusaders and some locals against other Crusaders and other locals. In the pleasing aphorism of J. T. Addison, 'Most of the time nobody was fighting, and at no time was everybody fighting.'[16] But even if fighting was not constant, the Crusaders experienced a more or less constant war of attrition as regards their supplies, and were in constant need of numerical reinforcement. In addition, the four crusading states which were established in the aftermath of the First Crusade – the County of Edessa, the Principality of Antioch, the County of Tripoli, and the Kingdom of Jerusalem – with the exception of the first, were all coastal states, vulnerable to pressure from the Muslim states further inland, and what had made the conquest of the coastal areas so relatively easy was Muslim disunity and the absence of any real control of the coast by the inland states, based at Aleppo and Damascus. Attempts were made by the Crusaders to take over those cities, but they never succeeded: an opportunity to take possession of Aleppo in 1127/521, during a period of chaos in the city arising partly from the activities of the Assassins, a small but deadly extreme Shīʿī Muslim sect, was squandered by rivalry between the Prince of Antioch and the Count of Edessa, and an attempt to take advantage of a similarly unsettled situation in Damascus in 1129/523 failed because of some Crusaders' preference for booty over systematic campaigning.[17]

The tide therefore began to turn against the Crusaders. In 1144/539 the Turkish amir Zengi captured Edessa, depriving the Crusaders of the one inland city they had managed to control. In response to this a Second Crusade was preached in Europe, with Bernard of Clairvaux calling for people to take up the cross at Vézélay in Burgundy in 1146/540. For modern Christian sensibilities it may seem paradoxical to learn of Bernard, the contemplative mystic with his great stress on God's infinite love and mercy, and the author of such famous Christian hymns about Jesus as 'O sacred head sore wounded', 'Jesus, thou joy of loving hearts', and 'Jesus, the very thought of thee', preaching the Crusade, but it is important to remember that in the view of the day crusading was itself understood as being an act of love, and this view at least makes Bernard's involvement intellectually consistent.[18] It is also significant that Runciman is able to preface every chapter of his three-volume *History of the Crusades* with a Biblical quotation, which shows the extent to which the whole programme of the Crusades could be seen as compatible with scriptural teaching.

Bernard's preaching secured the participation in the Second Crusade of both King Louis VII of France (1137/531–1180/576) and the German emperor Conrad III (1138/532–1152/547), but Conrad lost nine-tenths of his men in Asia Minor, and the Crusade's attack on Damascus in 1148/543 failed. And in 1154/549, when Damascus was annexed by Nūr al-dīn, the son of Zengi and ruler of Aleppo, the crusading states' eastern frontier for the first time bordered onto a single and united Muslim state.

In 1187/583 real disaster for the Crusaders ensued, when the Kurd Ṣalāḥ al-dīn (Saladin), who had united Syria and Egypt under his rule, invaded Palestine and crushed the Crusaders' army at the battle of Hattin (or Ḥiṭṭīn), near the Sea of Galilee. Ṣalāḥ al-dīn was chivalrous in victory, offering Guy de Lusignan, the king of Jerusalem, a goblet of rose-water, iced with snow from Mount Hermon, when he surrendered.[19] But he was not so kind to some others such as Raymond of Châtillon, who was considered guilty of treachery and whom he therefore decapitated himself, and the members of the Military Orders, the Templars and the Hospitallers, who were all slain except for the Grand Master of the Temple.

Over the next few months Ṣalāḥ al-dīn gradually extended his control over most of Palestine, and in October 1187/Rajab 583 Jerusalem surrendered. Runciman comments:

> The victors were correct and humane. Where the Franks, eighty-eight years before, had waded through the blood of their victims, not a building now was looted, not a person injured. By Saladin's orders guards patrolled the streets and the gates, preventing any outrage on the Christians.[20]

The cross which had been placed on top of the Dome of the Rock was removed, however, and Muslim worship was restored in that building and also in the al-Aqṣā mosque, but Christian pilgrimage to the Church of the Holy Sepulchre continued to be permitted, on payment of a fee. Of the whole of the Kingdom of Jerusalem, only Tyre remained in Crusader hands.

Again a Crusade was preached in Europe: this time the kings of France, Germany and England promised to take part, but the German Emperor Frederick Barbarossa (1152/547–1190/1586) drowned in Asia Minor, and Philip II (Augustus) of France (1180/576–1223/620) and Richard I (the Lionheart) of England (1189/585–1199/595) quarrelled; and although Richard seized Cyprus from the Byzantines, and Acre and several other coastal ports were reconquered from the Muslims, little else was achieved.

During the course of the next century, the tide of power ebbed backwards and forwards to some extent. In 1229/626, the Holy Roman Emperor Frederick II (1211/608–1250/648), who was also the ruler of Sicily, succeeded in negotiating the return of Jerusalem and Bethlehem to Crusader control, with the Dome of the Rock and the al-Aqṣā mosque remaining in Muslim hands. Frederick himself entered Jerusalem, even visiting the Muslim places of worship, but the arrangement made by him lasted for only ten years and then Muslim control over the city was re-established. The coming of the Mongols from central Asia raised Crusader hopes of relief from Muslim pressure, but the defeat of their Syrian invasion by the Mamluks at 'Ain Jalūt (The Spring of Goliath) near Nazareth in 1260/658 meant that there was no relief and eventually, in 1291/690, Acre, the last crusading outpost in Palestine, fell to the Mamluks. One small Christian enclave, at Gibelet, known in ancient times as Byblos, and today as Jubail (in the Lebanon), held out till 1302/701, but its fall represented the end of any crusading presence in Asia.

The real centre of crusading action had in fact already moved elsewhere. In 1204/600, encouraged by the Venetians, the Fourth Crusade had not gone to Palestine at all but had instead sacked Constantinople, the capital of the Eastern Christian Empire:

> The sack of Constantinople is unparalleled in history. For nine centuries the great city had been the capital of Christian civilization . . . But the Frenchmen and the Flemings were filled with a lust for destruction . . . Neither monasteries nor churches nor libraries were spared . . . Wounded women and children lay dying in the streets. For three days the ghastly scenes of pillage and bloodshed continued, till the huge and beautiful city was a shambles. Even the Saracens would have been more merciful, cried the historian Nicetas, and with truth.[21]

Then the Fifth Crusade, of 1217/614 to 1221/618, opened a new military front in Egypt, capturing Damietta in 1219/616, but they were compelled to withdraw two years later. The Sixth Crusade, in 1249–50/647–8, under the leadership of King Louis IX (the Pious) of France (1226/623–1270/669), adopted the same approach and was compelled to surrender and pay a ransom in order to be released. And in 1270/668 Louis launched another Crusade, this time to Tunis, but this too was defeated, with Louis himself dying just outside Tunis. North Africa was the focus of several Crusades over the succeeding centuries, with Holy Roman Emperor Charles V (1519/925–1556/963) leading one against Tunis in 1535/942, but increasingly, from the thirteenth/seventh century onwards, the Crusades began to become campaigns either for the expansion of Christendom in such places as Spain and the Baltic, or for the consolidation of Christendom against internal heretics such as the Cathars in France and later the Hussites in Bohemia.[22]

Stephen Runciman's conclusion on the whole crusading movement puts the whole movement into perspective:

> The triumphs of the Crusade were the triumphs of faith. But faith without wisdom is a dangerous thing . . . In the long sequence of interaction and fusion between Orient and Occident out of which our civilization has grown, the Crusades were a tragic and destructive episode . . . There was so much courage and so little honour, so much devotion and so little understanding. High ideals were besmirched by cruelty and greed, enterprise and endurance by a blind and narrow self-righteousness; and the Holy War itself was nothing more than a long act of intolerance in the name of God, which is the sin against the Holy Ghost.[23]

What is absolutely clear is that even modern Westerners continue to see the Crusades as positive examples of heroic and self-sacrificial enthusiasm for a good cause, as seen in the tendency of some British politicians at the end of the second millennium of Christian history to talk of crusades to do such noble things as eradicate poverty, raise educational standards and the like. The Muslim perception of the movement is utterly different, to the extent that the editors of the modern reference work, *The Encyclopaedia of Religion*, concluded that for the Crusades, uniquely, it was necessary to have two articles, one written on the Christian perspective and the other on the Muslim perspective.[24]

Contemporary Muslim reactions varied from puzzlement to horror. Amin Maalouf, a Lebanese journalist, in his account of Arab reactions to the Crusades, tells of how, according to the Frankish chronicler Radulph of Caen, the Crusaders resorted to cannibalism after their capture of Ma'arrat al-Nu'mān in Syria in 1098/492, the report reading: 'our troops boiled pagan adults in cooking-pots; they impaled children on spits and devoured them grilled'.[25] The commanders of the expedition themselves referred to this incident in a letter to the Pope in the following year, stating: 'A terrible famine racked the army in Ma'arra, and placed it in the cruel necessity of feeding itself upon the bodies of the Saracens.'[26] This account served as an introduction to a recent BBC television series on the Crusades, and was referred to in the first paragraph of the accompanying book to illustrate what was almost the motto of the series and the book, the saying of the eleventh-fifth-century poet Abū' l-'Alā' al-Ma'arrī (973/363–1057/449), who happened to come from Ma'arrat al-Nu'mān, though he died over half a century before the Crusaders arrived:

> The world is divided into two sects:
> Those with religion but no brains
> And those with brains but no religion.[27]

Some time later, in the account of the times by Usāma ibn Munqidh (1095/488–1188/584), the ruler of the neighbouring town of Shaizar, who was born in the same year that the Crusade was first proclaimed, a considerable element of astonishment is evident as he describes some of the actions of the Crusaders. In particular Usāma is horrified by two examples of Frankish medicine: in the first, a knight who has an abscess on his leg dies on the spot when a Frankish doctor resorts to amputation with an axe, and in the second, a woman suffering from some kind of mental disorder dies when an incision is made in her head and salt is rubbed in the exposed skull bone. He is also appalled by two examples of Frankish justice, one in which a dispute is settled by a duel and the other in which a case is settled by the ordeal of water, where an accused man is thrown with his arms bound into a cask of holy water, on the assumption that if he were guilty the water would not accept him. Usāma records that: 'This man did his best to sink when they dropped him into the water, but he could not do it. So he had to submit to their sentence against him.'[28] Usāma is also fair-minded enough to tell of two other instances, involving the treatment of infection and scrofula, where Frankish medicine worked, but in neither of these instances were the Islamic alternatives life-threatening.[29]

The Crusades have therefore left a powerful legacy of mistrust in the Arab world and throughout the Muslim world, and the crusading era is not forgotten. The exploits of Ṣalāḥ al-dīn still recounted, for example, in the cafés of Damascus, and the Arabic term used for 'Crusader', *Ṣalībī*, literally 'Crosser' or one who bears the cross, serves to reinforce the already well-established Muslim suspicion of the symbol of the Cross, going back to its use as a symbol of Byzantine power.

More sober historical judgements suggest that the legacy of the Crusades can be seen in six different aspects: among Muslims the Crusades firstly left a lasting suspicion of Western Christians, as we have already seen; they also helped to provoke the revival of Muslim expansion, with Runciman commenting wryly:

> The Crusades were launched to save Eastern Christendom from the Moslems. When they ended the whole of Eastern Christendom was under Moslem rule. When Pope Urban preached his great sermon at Clermont the Turks seemed about to threaten the Bosphorus. When Pope Pius II preached the last Crusade the Turks were crossing the Danube.[30]

Thirdly, the Crusades resulted, paradoxically, in producing among Muslims a greater emphasis on Jerusalem as the third Holy Place of Islam. Among Christians, the Crusades contributed to a worsening of the position of Christians under Muslim rule, given that they were increasingly distrusted as a potential fifth column; at the same time they also furthered the course of the involvement of the Western Church in the Middle East, as seen in the decision of the Maronite Church in the Lebanon in 1180/576 to submit to papal authority in Rome; and they also contributed, to some extent, to the development of contacts on different levels between the Muslim world and Western Europe.[31]

ALTERNATIVE PERCEPTIONS OF ISLAM

So far, we have looked at the rather negative perceptions of Islam which grew up in Western Europe during the medieval period, which began with the Spanish Martyrs' Movement, and remained the fundamental substratum of most Western Christian perceptions of Islam during these centuries, thus forming part of the background to the Crusades. It would not be true to say, however, that these had the field all to themselves – there were other views which emerged in the second half of the Middle Ages, and to these we now turn.

Prior to the early years of the twelfth/sixth century, Western Europe had what R. W. Southern suggests might almost be called a fantasy view of Islam: '[T]he productions of this time . . . belong less to the history of Western thought about Islam than to the history of the Western imagination.'[32] Muḥammad himself, for example, was presented as an epileptic who was sexually licentious and used the permission of sexual licence to undermine Christendom. He was a magician who had destroyed the Christian church in Africa, and he had been killed by pigs during one of his fits. And Muslims, as portrayed in *The Song of Roland* and other *chansons de geste* literature, were idolaters who worshipped the three gods of Mahound, Apollyon, and Termagent (i.e. Muḥammad, Apollo, and a divinity whose identity is not at all clear).[33]

Much of this material was based on earlier Byzantine polemical literature such as that of Nicetas, which we have examined above, with a fair amount of speculative material added in the Western context, but during the twelfth/sixth century the ignorance which the earlier views essentially express begins to be supplemented by something much more reasonable. Just to take three examples of those referred to by Southern, somewhere between 1106/499 and 1110/503, Petrus Alfonsi, a Spanish Jew who had converted to Christianity, composed a Dialogue between a Christian and a Jew which Southern describes as 'the earliest account of Mahomet and his religion which has any objective value' and 'the account and criticism of the Moslem faith . . . [which] . . . is by far the best informed and most rational statement of the case in the twelfth century, and one of the best in the whole Middle Ages.'[34] N. Daniel wrote that 'it is careful to separate the factual element from the critical', and he adds that it is this feature which distinguishes the work from the *Apology* of al-Kindī.[35] Then in around 1120/514 William of Malmesbury observed that Islam was not idolatrous and pagan but monotheistic, and also that Muḥammad was regarded not as God in Islam but as the prophet of God. Finally, in Germany, sometime between 1143/538 and 1146/541, the chronicler Otto of Freising observed that the Muslims worship one God, and that they respect Christ and his apostles, and that they are therefore wrong in only one thing, namely in their denial that Jesus Christ is God or the Son of God and in their veneration of Muḥammad as the prophet of the supreme God.[36]

By far the greatest contribution to this reappraisal of Islam, however, was inspired by Peter the Venerable (c. 1092/485–1156/551), the abbot of the great monastery of Cluny in Burgundy. Peter was a friend of Bernard of Clairvaux, yet had a rather different understanding of Christianity from Bernard, and one of the many ways in which this manifested itself was in his approach to Islam. Out of loyalty he did not oppose the Crusades, but he did propose an alternative, namely to study the religion of Islam comprehensively and from its own sources. This involved undertaking a comprehensive translation programme in order to make Muslim material accessible, and Peter was heavily involved in setting this up, although much of the work was done in Spain, especially in Toledo. In 1142/536 Peter himself travelled to Spain, and Kritzeck called this a 'momentous event in the intellectual history of Europe'.[37]

A number of works were translated as part of this project, including one on Islamic traditions from Adam to the Umayyad caliph Yazīd I, two on Muḥammad, and al-Kindī's *Apology*. By far the most important, however, was the first translation of the Qur'ān into Latin, which was undertaken by Robert of Ketton and was completed in either June or July 1143/Dhu'l-Ḥijja 537. We know the date fairly precisely because the manuscript interestingly gives the date of completion according to four dating systems, 'the year of our Lord 1143, the year of Alexander 1403, the year of the Hijrah 537, the year of the Persians 511', and this enables the calculation to be made that it was completed between 16 June, the start of Persian year 511, and 15 July, the start of the Muslim year 538.[38] This was 'a landmark in Islamic Studies. With this translation, the West had for the first time an instrument for the serious study of Islam.'[39]

Peter himself then wrote two works on Islam, the *Summa totius heresis Saracenorum* (The Summary of the Entire Heresy of the Saracens), and the *Liber contra sectam sive heresim Saracenorum*

(The Refutation of the Sect or Heresy of the Saracens). Peter himself originally envisaged writing only the first of the two, which simply summarised Islamic doctrine, but when no-one else was willing to use his compendium to produce any refutation of Islamic doctrine, he himself produced a work of that kind. As the titles of the two works indicate clearly, like John of Damascus Peter essentially concluded that Islam should be regarded as a Christian heresy.

In the first of the two works he therefore described Islam, outlining Islamic teaching concerning God, Christ, the Last Judgement, Muḥammad (where Peter made his most serious error, suggesting that Muḥammad's claim to prophethood postdated the first battles in which he was involved, so that it was the result of his desire for political power over his people), the Qur'ān and its sources (Peter suggests that Satan sent a Nestorian monk Sergius and then Jewish influences became important later), Heaven, Hell, Moral Precepts, and the Spread of Islam. On the basis of this description Peter then explains his view that Islam should be seen as a Christian heresy, indeed as the summation of Christian heresies, yet also close to paganism in that it denies the sacramental system of the Christian church. He also suggests that Islam should be seen as part of a satanic scheme to harm the Christian church, so that the position of Muḥammad is somewhere between that of Arius and that of the Antichrist, seeking as he did to eradicate faith in the incarnate God, but whereas Arius and Porphyry attempted to do that and failed, Muḥammad succeeded, and Peter has no answer to the question of why he was allowed to succeed. This work has some errors in it, and some weaknesses, and Kritzeck comments that it has a rather superior tone, demonstrates fits of impatience, and contains frankly derogative adjectives, but nevertheless it marks a tremendous advance over what went before.[40]

It is clear that Peter took as the precedent for his works the patristic Christian model of the apologists and polemicists against the Christian heresies of that era. The task was thus to remedy the ignorance of his co-religionists and then refute the elements of Islam which Christians considered to be false, but Peter's views concerning how the second of those tasks was to be undertaken was unique to his age. Early on in his Refutation, he wrote:

> It seems strange, and perhaps it really is, that I, a man so very distant from you in place, speaking a different language, having a state of life separate from yours, a stranger to your customs and life, write from the far parts of the West to men who inhabit the lands of the East and South, and that I attack, by my utterance, those whom I have never seen, whom I shall perhaps never see.

> But I do not attack you, as some of us often do, by arms, but by words, not by force, but by reason; not in hatred, but in love.[41]

The last sentence in particular of that statement of intent displays a very novel approach to the Muslims, and the two authorities for this attitude, he suggested, were Christ's love and human reason. Both the Bible and the Qur'ān are quoted in support of his approach: the quotation from the Bible is 1 Peter 3: 15, 'Always be prepared to make a defence to anyone who calls you to account for the faith that is in you, yet do it with gentleness and reverence', and the Qur'ānic quotations are 3: 18–19, 3: 61, and 29: 46, all of which could be interpreted as discouraging conversation with non-Muslims, but Peter asks Muslims to give him a fair hearing.[42] He hopes, therefore, that what he describes as the 'close combat' which will take place will be carried out 'with peace . . . not with fury; with reason, not with madness; with tranquillity, not with iniquity'.[43]

During the course of the book, on several occasions, Peter makes it clear that he is calling Muslims to salvation: 'Loving, I write to you; writing, I invite you to salvation.'[44] 'Hear, therefore, for the time is nigh, to what you have consecrated your souls, your bodies, and your death. Hear whether you have placed your hope in a safe place, whether you have believed in a salutary doctrine, or in a true prophet and messenger of God.'[45] He then discusses the Muslim accusation that the Christian scriptures, both Old and New Testaments, have been corrupted, demanding proof for the accusations, and the question of Muḥammad's claim to prophethood, which he discusses by comparing his career with the career of Moses and many other Old Testament prophets; he also draws a contrast between Muḥammad's constant repetitions of his claims to prophethood and the humility of Amos and John the Baptist concerning their status.[46] The Qur'ān is rejected. Peter's work is thus by no means anything other than a refutation, but Kritzeck suggests that it at least demonstrates fundamental goodwill, as seen in Peter's readiness to share openly his disagreements with his fellow Christians, his willingness to employ Islamic terminology, and his recognition of the similarities between Christianity and Islam.[47]

The work of Peter the Venerable thus broke new ground in setting out a more reasoned approach to Islam, not least through using its own sources rather than those which were the products of the hyperactive imagination of some earlier Western Christian writers. It thus laid the foundation for the work of such later figures as Roger Bacon (c. 1214/611–1292/691) who, in a treatise composed between 1266/664 and 1268/666 for Pope Clement IV, argued that in recent history Christendom had been misguided in its aims, which were more concerned with domination than with conversion, and had relied on inadequate methods; preaching, he suggested, was the only way to realise the expansion of Christendom in the future, and to that end languages had to be learnt, other beliefs had to be studied, and arguments had to be formulated in order to refute them. Bacon tried, without success, to motivate the Pope to encourage the learning of languages, but he himself produced an interesting scheme of six types of unbelief, each dominated by a different ultimate concern – pleasure, riches, honour, power, fame, or happiness in a future life – with Islam, he suggested, primarily seeking pleasure. He also formulated a programme for responding to these systems of unbelief: neither war nor miracles suffices, he suggests, so reliance must be placed on philosophy, and here the irony is that the Muslims are better equipped than the Christians. Bacon thus breaks new ground in attributing to Islam a positive role in world history, seeing it as part of an upward movement towards unity and articulateness, rather than as an example of a falling away from truth and a preparation for the coming of the Antichrist.[48]

In the next century, in 1312/712, plans were made to establish the schools of languages called for by Bacon by the Council of Vienne: at the instigation of Raymond Lull (c. 1235/632–1316/716) schools of Arabic, Greek, Hebrew and Syriac were to be set up at Paris, Oxford, Bologna, Avignon, and Salamanca, but the plan never really came to anything.[49] Southern suggests that the decade from 1450/854–1460/864, which witnessed the fall of Constantinople to the Ottoman Turks in 1453/857, also witnessed a flowering of optimism concerning the possibility of some kind of positive interaction with Islam, as seen especially in the writings of John of Segovia and Nicholas of Cusa who sought some kind of conference with Islam in order to address the outstanding issues between Christians and Muslims. In its day this idea came to nothing, but as we shall see later, it did at least serve as a useful precedent for interesting later developments.[50]

Peter the Venerable's achievement in producing a more subtle and reasoned interpretation of Islam certainly did not come to dominate Western Christian thinking, the main stream of which continued to be governed by a more antagonistic and apocalyptic model, but it did provide an alternative view which was influential in some circles at some stages, and it did therefore have some later influence.

THE TRANSMISSION OF KNOWLEDGE FROM THE ISLAMIC WORLD TO THE WEST

As has already been hinted above, one of the ironies of medieval Western history is that at the same time as the Crusades, with Peter the Hermit, Bernard of Clairvaux and others preaching a message which was fundamentally against Islam, in some parts of Europe the era was one of lively cultural and intellectual exchange between Muslims and Christians. In some respects, indeed, the twelfth/sixth century in somewhere like Spain was a kind of mirror image of the ninth/third century in Baghdad, with an active translation movement making accessible works of philosophy and science to a new audience. Whereas in Baghdad, however, the translations were from Greek and Syriac into Arabic, in Spain they were from Arabic into Latin.

R. W. Southern draws an interesting comparison between the levels of culture and learning in the medieval West and the world of Islam around the year 1000/390. He looks at two figures: the Christian Gerbert of Aurillac, born in France around 940/328, and the first Frenchman to be Pope (as Silvester II, from 999/389 until his death in 1003/393), and Ibn Sīnā/Avicenna, who was born in 979/369 in Bukhara and died in 1037/428. Both figures, Southern observes, were men of affairs who possessed passionate intellectual curiosity. In terms of the scholarly resources which were available to them, however, the contrast is staggering: the monastery and cathedral libraries accessible to Gerbert would have made available to him Porphyry's *Introduction* to Aristotle's logic and Boethius's translations and summaries of some of its parts, Boethius's handbooks on arithmetic, music, geometry, and astronomy, and some fragments of Greek medical knowledge. Ibn Sīnā, by contrast, had studied Porphyry's *Introduction* and other parts of logic, Euclid's Geometry, Ptolemy's *Almagest*, a whole library of Greek medicine, and some Indian arithmetic, as well as Muslim law, by the age of sixteen. Southern comments: 'Even if we allow for some element of exaggeration in the recollections of this youthful prodigy, the general picture of his resources is certainly not exaggerated: the boy had at hand riches undreamt of at this time in western Europe.'[51] Ibn Sīnā also described the library of the Sultan of Bukhara, which had many rooms, each devoted to the study of a particular subject – language, poetry, law, logic, medicine and so on – and with a catalogue. There was no equivalent of this in Western Europe for something like half a millennium, until the end of the Middle Ages.[52]

In 1000/390, then, Europe was backward intellectually, politically weak and divided, and socially and economically primitive compared with the Muslim world. It is this fact, of course, which goes some way to explaining the fantastic interpretations of Islam that we have seen circulating in the West. In the eleventh/fifth century, and even more in the twelfth/sixth century, however, this imbalance begins to change, and it does so through the transmission of Greek thought to the West from the world of Islam.

There were two main locations in which this process took place; firstly Spain, and secondly Sicily. Spain was geographically part of Europe and was Latin-speaking, yet large parts of it were under Islamic rule, with most of the population still being Christian, and it was therefore on the frontier of the Christian and Muslim worlds. The Christian *Reconquista* began after 1002/392, when the Umayyad caliphate of Cordoba began to fragment, and in 1085/478 Toledo was captured by King Alfonso VI of Leon (1072/464–1109/502).[53] It was in this setting that much of the translation from Arabic to Latin took place, and once works had been translated into that language they were able to circulate widely throughout Western Europe. We have seen how Peter the Venerable, in his attempt to obtain Islamic sources about Islam, himself travelled to Toledo in 1142/536, and there he met scholars such as Robert of Ketton and Herman of Dalmatia who were active in providing translations for him, which were later assembled together as the so-called Toledan Collection.[54] And it was the Archbishop of Toledo, Raimundo, who occupied the see from 1125/519 to 1151/546, who seems to have been instrumental in organising the school.[55]

The other prime location for the translation movement was Sicily. Conquered by Muslim invaders from Tunis from 827/212, who took over control from the Byzantines, Sicily also served as a base for raids on Italy, with Rome itself being threatened in 846/231. But from the middle of the tenth/fourth century disputes broke out between different local rulers, and this gave the opportunity for Norman raiders from northern Europe to reconquer the island, which was accomplished between 1060/452 and 1072/464, when the last Arab stronghold, Palermo, was taken.[56]

In the years that followed, especially under Roger II (1111/504–1154/549), Sicily functioned as a kind of cultural melting-pot, with court documents being issued in Latin, Greek and Arabic. Islamic culture still exerted a substantial influence, as seen in the fact that the great Arab geographer al-Idrīsī (1100/493–1166/561) worked at his court, but there was also considerable Greek influence too.[57] Towards the end of the twelfth/sixth century, the line of Norman rulers came to an end, and Sicily was incorporated into the Holy Roman Empire. As a result of this, in the thirteenth/seventh century it was ruled by Frederick II (1215/612–1250/648); he and Roger II were described as 'the two baptized sultans of Sicily' because of the continuing influence of Islamic culture under their rule.[58]

In the process of transmission of knowledge from the Muslim world to Western Europe the role of Spain was undoubtedly greater than that of Sicily, but perhaps the most important individual translator in

Toledo, Gerard of Cremona 1114/508–1187/583, who translated over eighty works from Arabic to Latin, began his interest in translation in Italy.[59]

The works which were translated into Latin in these two centres included works of logic and philosophy, and works on science, medicine, astronomy, geography, mathematics, physics, and politics. As well as the works of important Islamic figures such as al-Fārābī, Ibn Sīnā, al-Ghazālī and Ibn Rushd, the works of Greek authors such as Aristotle, Ptolemy, Euclid, Galen and Hippocrates became accessible.[60] There was also a considerable literary impact, though this has sometimes been exaggerated. As regards literature of this type, we have seen already the importance of a work like *The Song of Roland* in influencing popular perceptions of Islam, and other literature of the *chansons de geste* type also fulfilled this function. Another example of a story which underwent a considerable amount of revision in the course of its transmission down the generations was the story of El Cid, a name which is derived from the Arabic *al-sayyid* (the lord), and was given to Rodrigo Diaz de Viva, a Castilian noble who quarrelled with his king, Alfonso VI, around 1081/474, offered his services to the Muslim ruler of Saragossa, and ended up as independent ruler of Valencia. Watt comments that despite his association with Muslim rulers at various points, later accounts of El Cid present him as an example of Christian heroism against the Muslims.[61] There is also the possibility that some of the ideals of romantic courtly love were transmitted from Muslim Spain across the Pyrenees to the troubadours of Provence.[62]

What is more certain, however, is that in at least two respects one institutional and one intellectual in the wider sense, Islamic culture had a major impact on late medieval Europe. Firstly, Islamic influence was crucial for the establishment in Western Europe of a new kind of institution, beginning in the twelfth/sixth century, namely the university. The idea of the university in the modern sense, that is, a place of learning where students congregate to study a variety of subjects under a variety of teachers, is generally recognised as being an Islamic innovation, going back to the establishment of al-Azhar in Cairo in 969/358. Earlier institutions of learning such as those of the ancient Greeks tended to be centred on individual teachers, and it is therefore the idea of an institution with different faculties which represents the Islamic contribution towards the emergence of the university as a distinct institution.

Five Western European universities trace their origins to the years before 1200/596, and their locations, when put alongside the dates of their foundation, provide some evidence that the idea developed in those parts of Europe nearest to the world of Islam and then spread northwards from there. They are Bologna and Salerno in Italy, famous respectively for law and medicine, Montpellier and Paris in France, and Oxford in England. As with the question of the extent of the influence of Islamic models on the poetry of the troubadours, so with the universities the detail of exactly how much and in what ways Islamic institutions were influential is not absolutely clear, but in two large books George Makdisi has shown that there is considerable influence in at least some respects. He gives a number of examples: the fact that we still talk of professors holding the 'Chair' of their subject is based on the traditional Islamic pattern of teaching where the professor sits on a chair and the students sit around him. The term 'academic circles' has the same origin, since the students sat in a circle around their professor. Terms such as having 'fellows', 'reading' a subject, and obtaining 'degrees', can all be traced back to Islamic concepts, Makdisi suggests, the precedents being respectively the Arabic terms *aṣḥāb* (companions, as of the prophet Muḥammad), *qara'a* (reading aloud the Qur'ān), and *ijāza* (licence to teach).[63] And practices such as delivering inaugural lectures, wearing academic robes, obtaining doctorates by defending a thesis, and even the idea of academic freedom are also modelled on Islamic custom.[64] In his first book Makdisi lists eighteen parallels of terminology which indicate at least some influence of Islamic institutions on western ones.[65] And Islamic influence was certainly discernible in the foundation of the first deliberately planned university, that of Naples, founded by Frederick II (1215/612–1250/648), in 1224/621.[66]

Makdisi is careful not to overstate his case, noting, for example, that in the legal sense of a corporation, Western universities owe nothing to the world of Islam because such a concept does not exist in Islamic law; the original meaning of the word *universitas* was thus simply community or guild. It is therefore the colleges, as they evolved first in Paris and then in universities like Oxford and Cambridge, which are based on the Islamic model of the *waqf* (charitable endowment), and show the real traces of Islamic influence.[67] And carrying the story forwards to the modern development of universities, Makdisi concludes:

> From 'borrower' in the Middle Ages, the West became 'lender' in modern times, lending to Islam what the latter had long forgotten as its own home-grown product when it borrowed the university system replete with Islamic elements. Thus not only have East and West 'met'; they have acted, reacted and interacted, in the past, as in the present, and, with mutual under-

standing and goodwill, may well continue to do so far into the future with benefit to both sides.[68]

The other undoubted aspect of major Islamic influence on medieval Western Europe is its impact on the wider intellectual renaissance which began in the twelfth/sixth century and gathered pace thereafter. This was in part a legacy of the translation movement, especially in Spain, which we have already looked at in connection with Peter the Venerable's efforts to gather more accurate information about Islam, but it was more particularly a result of the translations which were made of works in the field of philosophy, both original Greek works and Islamic commentaries on them.

It was through the medium of Spain, therefore, that Western Europe became aware once again of many of the works of Aristotle, and also of the contribution to philosophical thinking of such great Islamic thinkers as al-Fārābī (870/256–950/339), Ibn Sīnā (979/369–1037/428), and Ibn Rushd (1126/520–1198/595). Ironically, because of a coincidence involving which of his works were translated, al-Ghazālī (1058/450–1111/505), who was known in the Muslim world as a vigorous opponent of philosophy on the strength of his *tahāfut al-falāsifa* (The Incoherence of the Philosophers), in the West gained a reputation as a philosopher because of his *maqāṣid al-falāsifa* (The Aims of the Philosophers), in which he summarised the views of the philosophers so scrupulously fairly that Westerners simply assumed that he must have been one himself.[69]

The translations, once made in Spain by such figures as John of Seville and Dominic Gundisalvus between 1130/524 and 1153/548, Gerard of Cremona between 1160/555 and 1187/583, and Mark of Toledo between 1200/596 and 1230/627, began to cause considerable intellectual ferment in Europe as a whole.[70] Perhaps most provocative of controversy was the work of Ibn Rushd. Cordoba, where Ibn Rushd was born, was in the early years of the twelfth/sixth century a city which exemplified what was later called *convivencia* (co-existence).[71] Cordoba was also the birthplace of the great Jewish philosopher Moses Maimonides in 1135/529. But the coming to power of the Almohad dynasty (the *Muwaḥiddūn*, literally Unitarians), in the 1140s/540s, threatened this tolerance: Maimonides, as a young boy, was taken to Morocco by his father, and he and his family were obliged to convert outwardly to Islam, and Ibn Rushd too found himself under suspicion because of some of his philosophical views. Towards the end of his life, after 1195/591, indeed, he was obliged to appear before a tribunal in Cordoba; there his doctrine was anathematised, and edicts were issued that his philosophical works should be burnt rather than studied, and although these edicts were repealed shortly before his death they testify to the extent to which Ibn Rushd's views were suspect to some Muslims.

The main reason for this was his enthusiasm for Aristotle. He was accused by a later Spanish Muslim philosopher, Ibn Sab'īn (d. 1270/669), of agreeing with Aristotle even if he had heard him saying that someone can be sitting and standing at the same time; and it was certainly under Aristotle's influence that he suggested that the physical matter of the universe was eternal, a view which challenged any idea of creation *ex nihilo*, and that after death, rather than enjoying bodily resurrection, the human intellect would be absorbed into the Active Intellect. Ibn Rushd, in other words, was here suggesting that philosophy and reason had equal authority with revelation and scripture, and this was not acceptable to the majority of his co-religionists.

When Ibn Rushd's works were translated into other languages, not surprisingly controversy also followed. Maimonides followed Ibn Rushd's views closely in many respects, and when after his death his works were translated into Hebrew, some Jewish scholars in the south of France sought to prevent the study of his works, arguing that they were a threat to Judaism and to rabbinical learning. And when they were translated into Latin, they also caused a controversy which was centred on the University of Paris in the 1260s/660s. There Siger of Brabant (1240/637–1281/680) put forward many of Ibn Rushd's opinions, acquiring a reputation as an Averroist (Averroes being the Latin name for Ibn Rushd) 'who would not compromise Aristotelian teachings for the sake of Christian doctrine'.[72] He thus argued for the eternity of the world and the unity of the human intellect, but he was opposed in this by perhaps the greatest Christian theologian of the medieval – or indeed any – age, Thomas Aquinas (c. 1225/622–1274/672), who while greatly admiring Aristotle also insisted that there was a supernatural world beyond creation which could be known only by revelation and not by reason alone. Aquinas therefore insisted on the reality of the individual intellect, and on the primacy of revelation over reason, of grace over nature. Some of Siger's works were condemned in 1270/669, and there was a much more comprehensive condemnation in 1277/676; some of Aquinas's opinions were also condemned in that year, but in 1323/723 Aquinas was canonised and the condemnations of his views were withdrawn.[73]

Aquinas thus demonstrates both the extent and the limitations of Islamic influence on European Christian thinking in the thirteenth/seventh century. Himself born in southern Italy, at Roccasecca, near Naples, he studied liberal arts at the new University of Naples before moving to Paris to study theology. There, at around the age of thirty, he composed a short work which encapsulates many of the fundamental ideas which he elaborated in much more detail in later works. The *De ente et essentia* (On Being and Essence) begins as follows:

> Because a small error at the outset ends by being great, according to the Philosopher in *On the Heavens* 1, and because being and essence are what intellect first conceives, as Avicenna says in the beginning of his *Metaphysics*, therefore, lest ignorance of them give occasion for error, and in order to lay open the difficulty concerning them, it should be said what 'essence' and 'being' mean, how they are found in different things, and how they are related to logical intentions, namely, genus, species and difference.[74]

In his first sentence, therefore, Aquinas refers explicitly to two figures who are for him authoritative – Aristotle ('the Philosopher'), and the Islamic philosopher Ibn Sīnā (whose Latin name was Avicenna). Some of the fundamental building blocks of Aquinas's thought are therefore quite openly based on Greek and Islamic thought. On the other hand Aquinas argued powerfully against other aspects of both Greek and Islamic philosophy, particularly some aspects of Aristotle's thought as mediated by Ibn Rushd, and he also composed, between 1261/659 and 1264/662, the *Summa contra Gentiles* (Summary against the Gentiles), a four-volume work whose purpose was to make the truth of the Catholic faith manifest to those who did not hold it. He had Muslims particularly in mind here, since the work was written primarily for fellow-members of the Dominican order who were active in the Muslim world, and it stands, therefore, very much in the tradition of the apologetic works of Peter the Venerable.[75]

Aquinas's work therefore enjoys a kind of ambivalent relationship with Islamic thought, but even if Western Christian thought reacted against, as well as absorbed, Islamic ideas, the extent of Islamic influence cannot be denied. This can be seen in other fields such as mathematics, and also in the vocabulary of many European languages: not for nothing are the numerals which are used today in the West known as Arabic numerals, since they were transmitted to Europe from the world of Islam, even if their origin actually lies even further to the East, in India; and the use of the zero sign in particular made possible huge advances in numerical calculations as compared with what was possible in the Roman place value system.[76] And it is reckoned that some 600 words in the English language derive from Arabic, including scientific and military words, and words referring to luxury or food items.[77]

It was because of all this influence that the Italian poet Dante (1265/663–1321/721), in his *Divine Comedy*, a work which was itself, according to one scholar's theory, influenced by Islamic models, particularly the *risālat al-ghufrān* (Epistle of Pardon) of Abū'l-'Alā' al-Ma'arrī, placed three Muslim figures in Limbo, the uppermost circle of Hell, among the unbaptised but virtuous pagans.[78] There, along with figures from the Old Testament – Abel, Noah, Moses, David, Abraham, Israel, Rachel and others – and many of the great figures of classical antiquity – Electra, Hector, Aeneas, Caesar, Camilla, Penthesilia, Latinus, Lavinia, Brutus, Marcia, Cornelia, Julia and Lucrece – is Saladin; and then in the philosophic band, alongside Aristotle, Socrates, Plato, Diogenes, Thales, Zeno, Democritus, Empedocles, Anaxagoras, Heraclitus, Dioscorides, Tully, Orpheus, Linus, Seneca, Euclid, Ptolemy, Galen and Hippocrates, are Avicenna and Averroes.[79] Muḥammad, it is true, with his cousin and son-in-law 'Alī, is much lower in Hell, among the Sowers of Discord, but so too is Absalom, because of his treachery against his father David.[80]

It was in the same spirit of pointing to the unity of knowledge that, in art, Michelangelo (1475/880–1564/971), on the ceiling of the Sistine Chapel in Rome, located among the figures who are presented as prophesying the coming of Christ (alongside many figures from the Old Testament), a Persian Sibyl, along with an Erythraean Sibyl, a Cumaean Sibyl, and a Libyan Sibyl.[81] For the same reason too, Raphael (1483/888–1520/926), in his *The School of Athens*, alongside the Greek masters, puts not only Zoroaster, who was at least a contemporary of most of the other figures portrayed, engaged in discussion with Ptolemy and Euclid, but also Averroes (Ibn Rushd), looking eagerly over the shoulder of Pythagoras, and the only non-ancient figure in the whole picture.[82] Therefore, for all the violence and antagonism between Western Christendom and the world of Islam in the Middle Ages on some levels and in some regions, on other levels and in other places there was a much more positive and mutually beneficial interaction.

NOTES

1. F. Gabrieli, *Muḥammad and the Conquests of Islam*, London: Weidenfeld and Nicolson, 1968, pp. 180–8.
2. Ibid., pp. 189–95.
3. Ibid., pp. 199–201.
4. Bede, *A History of the English Church and People*, 2nd edn, London: Penguin, 1965, pp. 324–5.
5. R. W. Southern, *Western Views of Islam in the Middle Ages*, Harvard University Press, 1962, pp. 16–18.
6. Einhard, *The Life of Charlemagne*, London: Penguin, 1969, p. 70.
7. Southern, *Western Views of Islam*, pp. 19–21.
8. See F. Bowie (ed.), *The Coming Deliverer: Millennial Themes in World*

Religions, Cardiff: University of Wales Press, 1997, and J. J. Collins, B. McGinn, and S. J. Stein, (eds), *Encyclopaedia of Apocalypticism*, 3 vols, London: Cassell, 1998.

9. A. Cutler, 'The Ninth-Century Spanish Martyrs' Movement and the Origins of Western Christian Missions to the Muslims', in *Muslim World*, 55 (1965), pp. 321–39; J. Waltz, 'The Significance of the Voluntary Martyrs of Ninth-Century Cordoba', in *Muslim World*, 60 (1970), pp. 143–59 and 226–36; N. Daniel, *The Arabs and Medieval Europe*, 2nd edn, London: Longman, 1979, Chapter 2; K. B. Wolf, *Christian Martyrs in Muslim Spain*, Cambridge University Press, 1988; and J. A. Coope, *The Martyrs of Cordoba: Community and Family Conflict in an Age of Mass Conversion*, University of Nebraska Press, 1995.
10. Southern, *Western Views of Islam*, p. 24.
11. Ibid., p. 25.
12. S. Runciman, *A History of the Crusades*, vol. I (The First Crusade), Cambridge University Press, 1951, p. 115.
13. Ibid., pp. 121–33.
14. See K. Armstrong, *Holy War: the Crusades and their Impact on Today's World*, 2nd ed., London: Macmillan, 1992, pp. 178–9; C. Hillenbrand, *The Crusades: Islamic Perspectives*, Edinburgh University Press, 1999, pp. 63–6; A. Maalouf, *The Crusades through Arab Eyes*, London: al-Saqi, 1984, pp. 50–1; F. Gabrieli (ed.), *Arab Historians of the Crusades*, London: Routledge and Kegan Paul, 1969, pp. 10–11; and Runciman, *A History of the Crusades*, vol. I, pp. 286–7.
15. Runciman, *A History of the Crusades*, vol. I, p. 287.
16. J. T. Addison, *The Christian Approach to the Muslim: a Historical Study*, Columbia University Press, 1942, p. 34.
17. S. Runciman, *A History of the Crusades*, vol. II (The Kingdom of Jerusalem), Cambridge University Press, 1952, pp. 178–81.
18. J. Riley-Smith, 'Crusading as an Act of Love', in *History*, 65 (1980), pp. 177–92.
19. Runciman, *A History of the Crusades*, vol. II, p. 459.
20. Ibid., p. 466.
21. S. Runciman, *A History of the Crusades*, vol. III (The Kingdom of Acre), Cambridge University Press, 1954, p. 123.
22. See J. Riley-Smith (ed.), *The Atlas of the Crusades*, London: Times Books, 1991, esp. pp. 67–79, and B. Hamilton, *The Crusades*, Stroud: Sutton, 1998, esp. pp. 65–74.
23. Runciman, *A History of the Crusades*, vol. III, p. 480.
24. M. Eliade (ed.), *The Encyclopaedia of Religion*, London: Macmillan, 1987.
25. A. Maalouf, *The Crusades though Arab Eyes*, London: al-Saqi, 1984, p. 39.
26. Ibid.
27. T. Jones and A. Ereira, *Crusades*, London: BBC Books, 1994, p. 9.
28. Usāma ibn Munqidh, *Memoirs of an Arab-Syrian Gentleman*, tr. P. K. Hitti, Columbia University Press, 1927, pp. 161–70, esp. pp. 162 and 167–8. For the views of Usāma and other contemporary Muslim writers, see W. Z. Haddad, 'The Crusaders through Muslim Eyes', in *Muslim World*, 73 (1983), pp. 234–52.
29. Usāma ibn Munqidh, *Memoirs of an Arab-Syrian Gentleman*, pp. 162–3.

30. Runciman, *A History of the Crusades*, vol. III, p. 469.
31. See K. M. Setton (ed.), *A History of the Crusades*, 6 vols, University of Wisconsin Press, esp. vol. III (The Fourteenth and Fifteenth Centuries), 2nd ed, 1975, Chapter 18, and vol.V (The Impact of the Crusades on the Near East), 1985, Chapters 2 and 10; and P. K. Hitti, 'The Impact of the Crusades on Eastern Christianity', in S. A. Hanna (ed.), *Medieval and Middle Eastern Studies in Honour of A. S. Atiyah*, Leiden: Brill, 1972, pp. 211–17.
32. R. W. Southern, *Western Views of Islam in the Middle Ages*, Harvard University Press, 1962, p. 29.
33. See N. Daniel, *Heroes and Saracens*, Edinburgh University Press, 1984, pp. 142–5 for some suggestions about the identity of the three deities.
34. Southern, *Western Views of Islam*, p. 35.
35. N. Daniel, *Islam and the West: the Making of an Image*, 2nd edn, Oxford: Oneworld, 1993, p. 23.
36. Southern, *Western Views of Islam*, pp. 35–6.
37. J. Kritzeck, *Peter the Venerable and Islam*, Princeton University Press, 1964, p. 14.
38. See J. Kritzeck, 'Robert of Ketton's Translation of the Qur'ān' in *Islamic Quarterly*, 2 (1955), pp. 310–11.
39. Southern, *Western Views of Islam*, p. 37.
40. Kritzeck, *Peter the Venerable*, esp. pp. 116 and 150–2.
41. Ibid., p. 161.
42. Ibid., pp. 165–72.
43. Ibid., p. 186.
44. Ibid., p. 162.
45. Ibid., p. 187.
46. Ibid., pp. 189–90.
47. Ibid., pp. 196–7.
48. See Southern, *Western Views of Islam*, pp. 56–61.
49. Ibid., pp. 72–3.
50. Ibid., pp. 84–103, esp. pp. 85–94. See also N. Rescher, 'Nicholas of Cusa on the Qur'ān', in *Muslim World*, 55 (1965), pp. 195–202, and J. E. Biechler, 'Nicholas of Cusa and Muḥammad: a Fifteenth-Century Encounter', in *Downside Review*, 101 (1983), pp. 50–9.
51. Southern, *Western Views of Islam*, p. 11.
52. Ibid.
53. See W. M. Watt and P. Cachia, *A History of Islamic Spain*, Edinburgh University Press, 1965, and H. Kennedy, *Muslim Spain and Portugal*, London: Longman, 1996.
54. See Kritzeck, *Peter the Venerable*, pp. 73–112.
55. Ibid., pp. 51–69.
56. See J. J. Norwich, *The Normans in the South, 1016–1130*, London: Longmans, 1967.
57. See A. Ahmad, *A History of Islamic Sicily*, Edinburgh University Press, 1975, pp. 58 and 63–4.
58. See J. J. Norwich, *The Kingdom in the Sun, 1130–1194*, London: Faber, 1970; Ahmad, *A History of Islamic Sicily*, pp. 82–7; and J. P. Dolan, 'Medieval Christian Tolerance and the Muslim World', in *Muslim World*, 51 (1961), pp. 180–7.
59. Ahmad, *A History of Islamic Sicily*, p. 88.
60. See J. Puig, 'The Transmission and Reception of Arabic Philosophy in

Christian Spain (until 1200)', in C. E. Butterworth and B. A. Kessel (eds), *The Introduction of Arabic Philosophy into Europe*, Leiden: Brill, 1994, pp. 7–30; G. F. Hourani, 'The Medieval Translations from Arabic to Latin made in Spain', in *Muslim World*, 62 (1972), pp. 97–114; F. Gabrieli, 'The Transmission of Learning and Literary Influences to Western Europe', in P. M. Holt, A. K. S. Lambton, and B. Lewis (eds), *The Cambridge History of Islam*, vol. II, Cambridge University Press, 1970, pp. 851–89; N. Daniel, *The Arabs and Medieval Europe*, 2nd edn, London: Longmans, 1979; and W. M. Watt, *The Influence of Islam on Medieval Europe*, Edinburgh University Press, 1972.

61. Watt and Cachia, *A History of Islamic Spain*, pp. 93–4.
62. Ibid., pp. 159–61, and Watt, *Influence of Islam*, pp. 27–8.
63. See G. Makdisi, *The Rise of Colleges: Institutions of Learning in Islam and the West*, Edinburgh University Press, 1981, pp. 92, 141, and 140 respectively.
64. Ibid., pp. 154–9, 157–9, 151–2, and G. Makdisi, *The Rise of Humanism in Classical Islam and the Christian West*, Edinburgh University Press, 1990, pp. 30–3 and 37–8 respectively.
65. Makdisi, *The Rise of Colleges*, pp. 287–8.
66. G. D. Newby, 'The Foundation of the University of Naples: Typological Parallels with Arab Institutions of Higher Learning', in *Medieval Encounters*, 3 (1997), pp. 173–83.
67. Makdisi, *The Rise of the Colleges*, pp. 224–9.
68. Ibid., p. 291.
69. D. Burrell, *Freedom and Creation in Three Traditions*, University of Notre Dame Press, 1993, p. 189, n. 16.
70. See the list of translations given in Hourani, 'Medieval Translations' pp. 109–13.
71. V. B. Mann, T. F. Glick, and J. D. Dodds (eds), *Convivencia: Jews, Muslims, and Christians in Medieval Spain*, New York: George Braziller, 1992.
72. D. Luscombe, *Medieval Thought*, Oxford University Press, 1997, p. 110.
73. F. C. Copleston, *Aquinas*, London: Penguin, 1955, p. 243.
74. Thomas Aquinas, *Selected Writings*, (tr. R. McInerny), London: Penguin, 1998, pp. 30–1.
75. See N. Kretzmann and E. Stump (eds), *The Cambridge Companion to Aquinas*, Cambridge University Press, 1993, especially Chapter 3, D. B. Burrell, 'Aquinas and Islamic and Jewish thinkers'; and J. Waltz, 'Muḥammad and the Muslims in St. Thomas Aquinas', in *Muslim World*, 66 (1976), pp. 81–95.
76. See Watt, *Influence of Islam*, pp. 33–4 and 64; S. H. Nasr, *Islamic Science*, London: World of Islam Festival Trust, 1976, pp. 77–9; and H. R. Turner, *Science in Medieval Islam*, University of Texas Press, 1997, pp. 45–6.
77. Watt, *Influence of Islam*, pp. 85–92, and R. Devereux, 'The Arabic Contribution to English' in *Islamic Quarterly*, 28 (1984), pp. 165–78.
78. The thesis of M. A. Palacios, *La escatologia musulmana en la Divina Comedia*, published in Madrid in 1919, is discussed in Gabrieli, 'The Transmission of Learning', pp. 878–81. See also S. M. Toorawa, 'Muḥammad, Muslims, and Islamophiles in Dante's *Commedia*', in *Muslim World*, 82 (1992), pp. 133–43.

79. Dante, *The Divine Comedy*, (tr. D. L. Sayers), vol. I (Hell), London: Penguin, 1949, pp. 92–5.
80. Ibid., pp. 246–7, and 250.
81. G. L. Hersey, *High Renaissance Art in St. Peter's and the Vatican*, University of Chicago Press, 1993, pp. 198–204.
82. M. Hall (ed.), *Raphael's School of Athens*, Cambridge University Press, 1997, pp. 154–8.

6

The Changing Balance of Power: Mission and Imperialism?

THE GROWTH OF EUROPEAN POWER

It is commonly stated that the last decade of the fifteenth century/the years either side of AH 900 represented a crucial change in the balance of power between the Christian and Muslim worlds. In 1492/897, the last Muslim state in Spain, the Nasrid kingdom of Granada, fell to Ferdinand and Isabella, the so-called 'Catholic monarchs'. The same year witnessed the European discovery of the Americas on behalf of the Spanish crown by Christopher Columbus, but perhaps even more significant for Christian–Muslim relations was Vasco da Gama's sailing round the Cape of Good Hope and into the Indian Ocean on behalf of the Portugese in 1497/903. This made possible for the first time direct contact between Europe and Asia, without the need for European travellers and traders to pass through the Muslim world en route for Asia, and brought about a very important psychological change: whereas previously Europe had felt itself to be surrounded by the Muslim world, increasingly, as European travellers voyaged further and further across the oceans, that situation was reversed, and the Muslim world began to feel increasingly surrounded by European influence.

Significant as the events of that decade are with hindsight, however, they did not necessarily appear quite so significant at the time. The Crusades, which have sometimes been described as the first stage of European expansion, had of course ultimately failed in their bid to secure control of Palestine.[1] And at the same time as the voyages of discovery were being launched from Western European ports, Eastern Europe was feeling increasingly vulnerable to Muslim expansion of a more traditional kind, namely conquest by the land armies of the Ottoman Turks. In 1354/755 Ottoman armies had crossed into Europe for the first time. In 1361/762 Edirne (Adrianople) surrendered, and in 1389/79, in a battle which continues to have very important resonances today, Serbian Prince Lazar met Ottoman Sultan Murad I (1360/761–1389/791) at the battle of Kosovo (or Kosovo Polje), a few miles to the north-west of Pristina. A recent historian of Kosovo, Noel Malcolm, comments on the battle as follows:

> The few things that are known with real certainty about this battle can be stated in very few words. The fighting was intense,

> and there were heavy losses on both sides. Both Lazar and Murat were killed. At the end of the battle the Turks were left in possession of the field . . . Everything else about the battle of Kosovo is uncertain: who took part, how large the armies were, what the order of battle was, what the key turning-points in the fighting may have been, how and when Lazar and Murat met their deaths, and whether, in the end, it should be characterized as a victory or a draw.[2]

Whatever the immediate result of the battle, however, there is little doubt about its long-term legacy. On the one hand

> the Turks . . . had indeed lost a vast number of troops, but they had many more in the east and were able in the following years to return and raid, and continue their successful push into the Balkans. The Serbs were left with too few men to resist successfully, and although they did not lose the battle, they lost the war over the next two to three years because they could no longer resist the Turks effectively; and their losses at Kosovo were, of course, the main reason why they had so few men left to defend Serbia.[3]

A Christian counter-attack involving Crusaders from all over Western Europe under the command of King Sigismund of Hungary was defeated at the battle of Nicopolis on the Danube in 1396/798, and the Ottomans eventually went on to become masters of the Balkans.

On the other hand, a powerful myth about the battle developed among the Serbs, which remains influential today:

> A feeling of despair permeated Lazar's lands after the prince's death and, conscious of the need to combat pessimism in Serbia and create hope for a bright future, the monastic authors of the day wrote eulogies and sermons in praise of Lazar in which they interpreted the events of the time for their own contemporaries. They portrayed Lazar as God's favoured servant and the Serbian people as the chosen people of the New Testament – the 'new Israel'. Like the Hebrews in Babylonian captivity they would be led out of slavery to freedom. According to accounts in epics, Lazar dreamed on the eve of the battle that he was offered either a heavenly or an earthly kingdom, and being a man of his time, he chose the heavenly one.[4]

Lazar himself therefore came to be regarded as a martyr, and in later Serbian thought the view emerged that the whole Serb people were also to be seen as martyrs.[5] In this respect comparisons can perhaps be drawn between the self-image of many Serbs and that of many Iranians, who as Shīʿī Muslims have also sometimes been affected by a cult of martyrdom.[6]

The Byzantine Empire by this time had become a shadow of its former self. Decimated, as we have seen, by the Fourth Crusade, it had at least managed to throw off Latin rule in 1261/659, but since then it had become, sandwiched as it was between Ottoman territories in Europe and Ottoman territories in Asia, virtually a vassal-state of the Ottoman Sultans; and in 1453/857 Constantinople itself was finally taken by Sultan Mehmed (Muḥammad) II (1451/855–1481/886).[7] Ottoman expansion did not stop there, either, for the advance into south-eastern Europe continued, with Vienna being besieged in 1529/936, Hungary coming under Ottoman control during the 1540s/950s, and Vienna being besieged again in 1683/1094.[8]

So it was not at all clear, in, say, 1495/900 that the balance of power was shifting away from Muslim states and towards Christian ones, and it was in this context that the great figures of the Reformation in Europe formulated their views of Islam. In Germany Martin Luther (1483/888–1546/953) 'looked forward to the probability that Christendom would be engulfed in Islam. He wrote to strengthen the faith of those Christians who might find themselves in this condition.'[9] Building on the ideas of John Wycliffe, in a sense a precursor of the Reformation,

> Luther wrote as if he were a man in the twilight of Christendom before the long night, and, as he looked into the future, he asked whether Mahomet and his followers were the final Antichrist. Like Joachim of Fiore, he answered No. Islam was too gross and irrational for this mighty role: the true and final, subtle and insidious Antichrist must come from within the Church; he was none other than the Pope himself. This had been the picture also of Joachim and of much late medieval apocalyptic, though Luther added thereto his own theological hostility. For him and them, Christendom was caught in the grip of an external and an even more formidable internal enemy. To succeed against the external enemy, it must first renounce the internal enemy. Till this time there could be no counsel but to suffer. So too Wycliffe had said.[10]

The French Reformer John Calvin (1509/915–1564/971) too basically 'followed the stereotypes of his time in remarking on the Turks and their religion'.[11] For modern Christian sensibilities there is thus a rather ominous note in one of his sermons, in which he says:

> When the Turks put their Muḥammad in the place of God's Son, and when they do not recognize that God is manifested in the flesh, which is one of the principle articles of our faith, then they are guilty of perversities and are leading so many people astray that they deserve to be put to death.[12]

Other statements of Calvin, it should be noted, are more tolerant than this, and the views of other Reformers who worked in Switzerland were not quite so negative about Islam as those of Calvin.[13]

During the sixteenth/tenth century, even if Europe continued to be threatened by the Turks on land, the balance of power did shift at sea, as symbolised by the battle of Lepanto, in the Gulf of Corinth, in 1571/979, where the Ottoman fleet was destroyed by an alliance of Spain, Venice and Genoa. At the same time European involvement in trading activities became more significant, with, for example, an English consulate being established in Aleppo in Syria, at the western end of the old Silk Route, in 1580/988 and the English Levant Company being set up in the following year. Sir Thomas Roe, whom we have already seen in the Introduction, conducting an embassy to the court of the Great Moghul at Ajmir in 1614/1023, was also ambassador to the Ottoman Empire between 1621/1030 and 1628/1037, and by the end of the seventeenth/eleventh century a quarter of all England's overseas trade was conducted with the Ottoman Empire.[14]

One of the major incentives for the voyages of discovery in Asia, which involved so much competition between different European powers, was the search for spices; as well as giving food taste they also help to make poorly preserved food palatable.[15] Therefore, when Ferdinand Magellan (?1480/885–1521/927) reached the Moloccan spice islands by sailing westwards from Spain, round Cape Horn and across the Pacific Ocean, thereby becoming the first man to circumnavigate the earth, a new point of encounter between Christian and Muslim was opened up. Islam, which had been spreading eastwards for many centuries, now met Christianity spreading westwards, with the encounter most graphically illustrated in the Philippine islands, named after King Philip II of Spain (1556/963–1598/1007) and today the only nation in Asia whose population is mainly Christian, but with a significant Muslim minority established in the south of the islands, in Mindanao. Here we see clearly, therefore, the emergence of a new situation where Christian–Muslim encounter ceases to be a Mediterranean phenomenon and becomes a global one, with new frontiers emerging in both Africa and Asia. Some time earlier, however, a new and rather different Western Christian approach towards Islam had been beginning to emerge, and to this we now turn.

THE ESTABLISHMENT OF CHRISTIAN MISSIONS

In its early centuries Christianity had been, of necessity, a missionary religion, relying on preaching and example to persuade people to join the Christian community. When Constantine converted to Christianity and made it the official state religion of the Roman Empire, mission in the early sense faltered as the faith came to be identified rather closely with the Roman state. It did not cease completely, however, with missions continuing beyond the frontiers, both among the Germanic tribes north of the Roman frontier (for example, the work of Ulfilas [c. 311–c. 381] among the Goths), and to the east of the Roman Empire, in Sassanian Persia and beyond, where Nestorian missionaries were particularly active, reaching as far as China within a few years of the death of Muḥammad.[16]

When Islam appeared, however, Eastern Christians do not seem to have entertained any idea of undertaking any missionary activity among Muslims. In the case of those Christians who found themselves living under Muslim rule, this was partly due to the generally positive initial reaction which they had towards the coming of Islam, as outlined above in Chapter 3, and partly due to the legal position they found themselves in under Islam as it became more firmly established: according to this they were allowed to worship relatively freely but they were not permitted to try to persuade Muslims to become Christians. In the case of the Christians of the Byzantine Empire it was more due to their close identification of church and state, and to the situation of military confrontation which existed on the frontier with the Islamic world in Asia Minor; Orthodox missions were sent to the Slavs, most famously under two brothers, Cyril (or Constantine) (826/211–869/255) and Methodius (c. 815/199–885/272), with huge consequences for the expansion of the Orthodox world, especially when Kiev became Christian in 988/378, but there were no comparable missions to Muslims, any delegations sent in that direction being primarily diplomatic in intent.

It was among Western Christians, therefore, that any idea of Christian mission to Muslims seems to have begun, though quite when the idea emerged is a cause of some dispute. It has been suggested, for example, that the Spanish Martyrs' Movement should be understood as being in part a missionary movement.[17] There is also a correspondence between an anonymous 'monk of France' and a Muslim scholar at the court of al-Muqtadir of Saragossa (1046/438–1081/474), which has been described as being in some way an early example of Christian mission, although it is in fact closer in style to the correspondence between al-Hāshimī and al-Kindī in the time of al-Ma'mūn.[18]

It is really only with the emergence of the Mendicant (literally 'begging') orders in the thirteenth/seventh century, therefore, that we encounter Christians undertaking missions to Muslims, using 'mission' in the sense in which the word was used in the early Christian centuries and has become generally understood in more recent centuries.[19]

The key figure in the transition to this new approach was Francis of Assisi (1182/578–1226/623). The son of a wealthy textile merchant, during a pilgrimage to Rome in 1205/601 he had a vision in which he was commissioned to rebuild a church near Assisi. In order to do this he sold his own goods and also some of his father's, for which he was disowned by his father, but Francis persisted in his task, and in 1209/605 he established the Franciscan order, vowed to poverty, preaching and caring for the poor. Francis was not only concerned for his homeland, however; he was also concerned for the Muslim world, but his approach was to be very different from that of his crusading contemporaries. Attempts to get to Syria in 1212/609 and Morocco in 1214/611 were frustrated, by the weather and by illness respectively, but the third attempt, in 1219/616, succeeded: Francis and some twelve companions sailed to Acre and then on to Damietta in Egypt, which was at that time being besieged by the army of the Fifth Crusade.

Francis's encounter with the realities of a crusading army, however, seems to have been something of a shock: instead of heroes imbued with Christian virtue and dedicated to the service of God under the sign of the cross, he found adventurers and fugitives, whose whole approach was a rather mercenary one. He therefore denounced the Crusade and sought an interview with the Sultan, al-Malik al-Kāmil (1218/615–1238/635), which was granted. Accounts of the interview vary, but it seems that Francis requested the opportunity to undergo the ordeal by fire in order to demonstrate the truth of the Christian faith, in a sense taking up the challenge which had been declined by the Christians of Najrān in 628/7. The sultan denied him this opportunity, however, so Francis was compelled to return to the Crusader camp. But his whole approach at the very least represents a radical alternative to the dominant crusading paradigm of the time, centred as it was on the conviction that military victory might be good for Christendom but did nothing to promote Muslim knowledge of Christ, and the belief that it was better to create Christians than to destroy Muslims. Not for nothing did Francis become known as the 'apostle of love', and not for nothing did Pope John Paul II choose Assisi as the location for the

Day of Prayer for Peace, involving members of different faith communities, in 1986/1407.[20]

Some decades later another figure, Ramon Lull (c. 1232/629–1316/716), took up something of Francis's vision, but directed it in a slightly different way. Lull was born in Majorca, probably just a year or two after its reconquest by the Christians. He became a soldier but in 1263 he had a vision, which led to his conversion, and shortly afterwards, while attending mass on the feast day of St Francis, he resolved to dedicate his life wholly to Christ. He determined to do three things: to write books explaining the Christian faith to those who did not believe in it, to work for the establishment of colleges for the training of Christian missionaries, and to lay down his life as a martyr. These ambitions in a sense symbolise the way in which he combined the legacies of Francis of Assisi and Peter the Venerable, determined as he was to engage in mission to Muslims but on the basis of serious study. He eventually became a third order (i.e. lay) member of the Franciscan order in 1295/694.

Lull had mixed success in realising his ambitions. As regards his desire to produce works explaining the Christian faith, he wrote *The Book of the Gentile and the Three Wise Men*, an allegorical work consisting of a kind of dialogue involving a Jew, a Christian, a Muslim, and a philosopher, in which the three wise men at first work together to persuade the philosopher of the existence of God but then disagree over which of them bears the true religion; throughout the work the spirit is one of fairness and openness, to the extent that the philosopher comes to no decision in the end, and although the Jew's case is perhaps presented less effectively, the Muslim case is presented with some sympathy. As regards the establishment of training colleges, Lull had some success, with a college set up in 1276/675 at Miramar in Majorca to teach thirteen friars; it only lasted for some sixteen years, however, and his attempts to persuade both secular and religious authorities elsewhere to set up similar schools seem to have come to nothing.

Lull himself, however, spent nine years studying Arabic, and in 1291/690, aged almost sixty, he arrived in Tunis to enter into debate with Muslim scholars there. He told them that he had studied the laws of the Christians and now wished to learn about Islam, promising that if it were better he would become Muslim, but his answers to the questions which he was asked were so challenging that his life was threatened and he was forced to flee. He returned in 1307/706, however, and this time adopted a more confrontational approach, declaring in the market-place that the laws of the Christians were true and holy and that the sect of the Moors was false and wrong, which resulted in his being imprisoned. He was released in response to the petition of some European merchants, who took him back to Europe, but he returned once more in 1314/714, and after spending some time working peacefully in Tunis he moved to Bugia, some 100 miles east of Algiers, where, according to some accounts, some provocative comments about Islam resulted in his being stoned to death. His desire for martyrdom may, therefore, have been fulfilled, but there is some doubt about the historicity of these accounts.

Lull is therefore in some ways a paradoxical figure in his attitude towards Islam, influenced on the one hand by Sufi writings which have left their mark on some of his contemplative writings, yet arguing forcefully against other influences from the world of Islam, especially Averroism in Paris in 1297/696. He is sometimes called the 'fool of love', and there is no doubt that his life served as a powerful example for many in future generations.[21]

At the same time the other order of friars, the Order of Preachers (or the Dominicans), founded by the Spaniard Dominic (1170/565–1221/618) in 1216/613, had also become involved with the Muslim world. The origins of this order lay in Dominic's perception of the need to combat heresy, particularly the Albigensian heresy in the south of France, by preaching and teaching, and great stress was therefore laid on learning. There were close links between the order and the new universities of Europe, with Thomas Aquinas being simply the most distinguished Dominican of the thirteenth/seventh century. We have seen already his concern with Islam, as expressed in his composition of the *Summa contra Gentiles*, but other Dominicans were even more intimately involved with Islam. They include Andrew of Longjumeau (d. 1270/668), who studied Arabic in Tunis; William of Tripoli, who, as his name suggests, was born in the East and who is best known for his *De Statu Saracenorum et Mahomete Pseudopropheta eorum et eorum Lege et Fidei* (On the Status of the Saracens and their Pseudo prophet Muḥammad and their Laws and Faith), composed around 1273/672; Raymond of Penaforte (c. 1175/570–c. 1275/674), who was instrumental in setting up schools of Arabic in Tunis and Murcia; and probably most remarkable of all, the Florentine Ricoldo of Montecroce (1243/640–1320/720), who travelled widely in the Middle East between 1289/688 and 1291/690, and was in Baghdad when news arrived of the fall of Acre and the end of the crusading presence in Palestine – he later had to undergo the experience of seeing Christian prisoners in Baghdad, an experience which seems to have left him traumatised.[22]

Many of these figures were also involved in diplomatic missions to the rulers of different parts of the Muslim world and beyond, particularly to the Mongols who for a time in Europe were envisaged as potential allies against the world of Islam. John de Carpini, who was sent by Pope Innocent IV (1243/641–1254/652) to the Mongol court at Karakorum in 1245/643, was a Franciscan friar, as was William of Rubroek, who was sent to the same destination in 1252/650 by King Louis IX of France (1226/623–1270/669). The Dominicans were also involved as Andrew of Longjumeau led an expedition to the Mongol court in 1248/646, and William of Tripoli accompanied Marco Polo on his journey through Syria in 1271/669.[23]

The earliest Christian missions therefore were only to a limited extent missions to Muslims; apart from the individual efforts of Francis and Lull, they were perhaps as much missions to the Muslim world and beyond, and their legacy is seen primarily in such things as the establishment of the Franciscan mission in the Holy Land in 1345/746, which was devoted to the care of the Christian Holy Places, and the development of links with Eastern Christians who were living in the Muslim world. We have already seen how the Maronite church in the Lebanon submitted to papal authority in 1180/576, and in the succeeding centuries further efforts were made to secure the reunification of the Eastern and Western churches, or at least the recognition by Eastern Christians of the supreme spiritual authority of Rome. In many cases this simply resulted in further division within the already deeply divided Eastern churches, and the creation of Uniate churches, which acknowledged Rome but were permitted to retain their own patriarchs and the use of their traditional liturgies in their own languages: we thus see the establishment of Catholic patriarchs for Catholics who left the Nestorian church in 1552/959, the Greek Orthodox church in 1724/1137, the Armenian church in 1740/1153, the Syrian Orthodox church in 1773/1187, and the Coptic church in 1824/1240.[24]

From the sixteenth/tenth century however, the emphasis seems to move back to some extent towards the intentions of Francis and Lull, especially as a result of the activities of some of the new post-Reformation orders. The Vatican published an Arabic Bible in 1583/991, and established a college for the education of Maronite clergy in Rome in the following year. Diplomatic considerations were not irrelevant to many of these activities, however, as in 1535/942 Francis I of France (1515/921–1547/954) concluded an alliance with the Ottoman sultan Sulaimān the Magnificent against the Holy Roman Emperor Charles V (1519/925–1556/963), and from this time relationships with different Muslim powers increasingly became part of the web of rivalry between different European powers.

Thus when, in the early years of the seventeenth/eleventh century, a Carmelite mission was sent by Pope Clement VIII (1592/1000–1605/1013) to Iran, it had three main purposes: to find out about the country, to investigate the prospects for a political alliance with western powers against the Ottomans, and to seize any opportunity to make known the Christian faith. Two missions were eventually despatched, the first in 1604/1013 and the second in 1621/1030, and the report of the first contains a great deal of information about the country. On the second visit, however, the opportunity arose for a theological discussion between the friars and Shah 'Abbās I (1588/996–1629/1038). There was also a third party involved, a small group of English merchants, present in Iran because of the silk trade, with their chaplain, and this made the course of the discussion particularly interesting.

Iran had by this time adopted Shī'ī Islam as its state religion, and the English church had become Protestant: the English chaplain is described in the account as a Lutheran. Four themes were selected for discussion: fasting and good works; the cross and images; free-will and predestination; and authority. Clearly none of these were questions on which the Carmelites and the Anglicans were likely to agree, and this became very clear as the discussion progressed. It seems that the English relied on an interpreter, while the Carmelites were able to converse in Persian – and this gave them something of an advantage as the Shah often asked them for clarification of what the English had said, and on each point the Shah basically agreed with the Carmelites. The first topic, that of fasting, was raised because the Carmelites were fasting, and when the Shah asked the English when they fasted, they replied that God had not commanded people to fast; the Shah and his entourage said that this was a great error. The second point, concerning making the sign of the cross, emerged from the fact that the English had earlier suggested to the Shah that Catholics were idolaters because of their use of images and their making the sign of the cross; the Carmelites defended themselves against this charge by asking the Shah whether his custom of bowing down in prayer made him an idolater, and since the answer was of course that it did not, they had made their point powerfully. Concerning the sign of the cross, there was then a discussion of whether or not Jesus was crucified and raised from the dead, and on this Catholic and Protestant were able to agree. The third focus of discussion was free-will and predestination:

> The king turned to question the Fathers – who were the better, the English or the Roman Christian. The Fathers replied that by its fruit the goodness and quality of the tree are known: that the king should enquire about the things the English did and the examples they gave, and from these he would be able to judge. The Agent of the English rejoined that they were the better Christians, and that they had the right faith. On this the Fathers observed: 'Shah, we do not want to say more to your Highness

> than this, that the English are heretics and of a like sect as the Turks, who deny free-will and say that all the evil men do and the demons do is done of necessity, and they cannot do less, because God so wills: and so they (the English) say that God does everything, whether good or evil.'
>
> Here the grandees of the king looked at each other, and the Shah in particular jumped from his seat (as the saying goes) and began to make a sermon to all present, very earnestly as he detested that theory. He spoke with great gusto, so that the Tatar envoys from Caffa, who were there and who are of the same sect as the Turks, should hear him. After the king finished his arguments, the Father said: 'This is the reason, your Majesty, why the English, who have no consciences nor fear of God, are pirates, rob, slay, destroy, and one cannot rely on their word, because they say that they cannot do anything else, seeing that they have no option.'
>
> The English did not know what reply to make during all this harangue of the Shah, which lasted for the space of more than three-quarters of an hour, during which his Highness brought forward many arguments and examples in opposition to the English who deny free-will, and in particular he said that it was most false . . .[25]

The fourth and final point of discussion concerned the antiquity of the Roman Catholic religion and the primacy of the Roman pontiff. Here too the Shah made clear his preference for the Catholic position, since although the English claimed to be following the primitive Christian religion, their acknowledgement that seventy or eighty years previously the English had accepted the authority of the Roman pontiff clearly indicated that they were now heretics.

The discussion then turned to diplomacy. Here the tone was rather different. The Shah said that the English had not told him falsehoods, had always carried out their promises, and been very useful in his country, but the Catholics had lied: the king of Portugal and Spain had promised to make war on the Turks but had not done so. The Carmelites denied the accusation, saying that Christian princes had made war on the Turks, that it was this which had made possible Persian territorial gains, and the king of Poland was making war against the Turks at that very moment. 'Tell me what the Pope is doing, not what others are doing', said the Shah, and the Carmelites attempted to argue that what the Christian princes did, the Pope also did since he was the head, but the Shah was not satisfied: if the Pope would go to fight against the Turks, he said, the rest of the Christian princes would follow his example. The Carmelites replied that it was, unfortunately, not so, since some people, like the English, do not obey the Pope: 'they are the cause of the Christian Catholic princes not making war on the Turks.'[26] This conversation thus shows clearly not only the diplomatic and political aspects of the mission, but also what we might call the increasing fragmentation of Christian–Muslim relations: it shows a Persian Shīʿī ruler agreeing theologically with the representatives of Catholic Christendom against the English representatives of Protestantism, yet also seeking the best diplomatic alliance for his own political purposes. It thus reflects a situation where it is no longer a case of Christians on one side and Muslims on the other, but some Christians and some Muslims on one side and other Christians and other Muslims on the other.[27]

The fullest shift towards the revival of the vision of Francis and Lull, however, came with the activities of the Jesuits. This order, founded as a brotherhood of seven men by Ignatius Loyola in 1534/940, was formally recognised as The Society of Jesus by Pope Paul III (1534/941–1549/956) in 1540/947. Loyola, a Spaniard and a former soldier, had been on pilgrimage to Jerusalem in 1523/929, and later, with his six colleagues, resolved to pursue a career either in the service of the Holy Land or of the Pope. War prevented the former, so the Jesuits, as they came to be called, became one of the spearheads of the Counter-Reformation, and in the course of the sixteenth/tenth century they became involved in some highly imaginative examples of Christian mission in different parts of the world.

Four names are particularly significant in this connection: Francis Xavier (1505/911–1552/959), one of the original members of Loyola's brotherhood, who worked in south-west India and Japan; Matthew Ricci (1552/959–1610/1019), who worked in China; Jerome Xavier (1549/956–1617/1026), a great-nephew of Francis and the most important for our purposes, who spent the years between 1595/1003 and 1614/1023 at the court of the Moghul emperors Akbar (1556/963–1605/1014) and Jahangir (1605/1014–1627/1037); and in the next century, Robert de Nobili (1577/985–1656/1066), who worked among Hindus in India. These figures are outstanding because of their sensitivity to local culture and religion, their insistence on the importance of learning languages, and their flexibility in seeking to make Christian ideas comprehensible in the local idiom.[28]

The invitation to the Jesuits to send some representatives to the Moghul court came from Emperor Akbar, who on a personal level seems to have been seriously interested in religious questions and on a political level to have been concerned by the divisive effect religion sometimes had on the population of his empire, which was very mixed religiously; Muslims held political power there, but made up less than twenty-five per cent of the population. In 1579/987 he sent a message to the Portugese centre of Goa, suggesting that he would welcome some Jesuits at his court. Three were despatched and made welcome, and engaged in several debates with the emperor and Muslim scholars; most remarkably, Akbar entrusted his second son, Murad, to the Jesuits for education in both the Portugese language and the Christian faith, but two insuperable problems presented themselves – the Christian belief in the divine sonship of Jesus, and the belief which followed from that conviction, namely the Trinity. For all his dissatisfaction with Islam, therefore, Akbar did not feel able to accept these Christian convictions, and the Jesuits returned to Goa in 1583/991.

In 1593/1001 a second mission was sent, again in response to a request from Akbar, but this mission lasted for less than a year before the Jesuits departed. They did so without Akbar's permission, however, and he quickly requested the despatch of other learned men; this time, it was Jerome Xavier who was sent, with two companions, Benedict de Goes, who left in 1603/1011, in order to travel to central Asia, and Emmanuel Pinheiro. Xavier worked hard at learning Persian, and great efforts were made to produce Christian literature in Persian, including a life of Christ and a number of works set out in the form of discussions between a Jesuit, a Muslim and a philosopher, in the tradition of Lull's work. The liturgical ceremonies of the Christian community were also used to embody the principles of Christian belief. But ultimately, any hope of Akbar converting to Christianity came to nothing: his preferred solution to the religious problems of the empire was the establishment of a new religion, the *din-i-ilahi*, (religion of God), which was firmly monotheistic, but included religious practices taken from several religious traditions, and had the emperor himself at its heart as a focus of loyalty.

When Akbar died, the Jesuits had high hopes that his successor Jahangir might convert, and their hopes were raised in 1610/1019, when he ordered his three nephews to be not only instructed in the Christian faith but also baptised. In 1613/1022, however, they apostasised and gave their crucifixes back to the Jesuits, and two years later Xavier and Pinheiro withdrew. Political factors were part of the reason for the difficulties faced by the Jesuits, given that they had set off from the Portugese centre of Goa; they had been careful initially not to send any Portugese to the Moghul court – the three figures who went in 1579/987 were Italian, Spanish and Persian – but the tensions which developed in 1613/1022 did so in the context of war between the Moghuls and the Portugese, and the growing struggle between the English and the Portugese for influence in the Moghul Empire. It was in the following year, 1614/1023, that the embassy of Sir Thomas Roe to the court of the Great Moghul, which we have already looked at, took place.[29]

All of the missionary activity which we have investigated so far has involved Roman Catholic missions. Given that the Reformation took place in the early sixteenth/tenth century it may be somewhat surprising that we have as yet witnessed no Protestant involvement, but Lyle Vander Werff, in his detailed study of Protestant missions to Muslims, suggests that there are four main reasons for this: the conviction that the so-called 'Great Commission' of Matthew 28: 19–20, in which Jesus is recorded as telling his disciples to make disciples of all nations, had been fulfilled by the apostles, the first generation of Christians; the doctrine of divine election, as espoused, for example, by the English in Isfahan, precluded the need for mission; the idea that the task of mission belonged to civil rulers rather than to the church on its own; and the argument that even if the principle was right, the time was not ripe because there were more urgent tasks at hand, such as the struggle against Roman Catholicism.[30]

Only after the emergence in the eighteenth/twelfth century of the Pietist movement, with its stress on the idea of the invisible church – a kind of church within a church separate from the state – and on the necessity of personal salvation through an individual experience of conversion, did these views change. The start of widespread Protestant interest in worldwide mission is generally traced to the preaching of a sermon by a Baptist minister, William Carey, in the Baptist Chapel on Friar Lane in Nottingham in 1792/1206, in which he urged his hearers to 'attempt great things for God and expect great things from God'. The sermon was subsequently published under the title 'An Enquiry into the Obligations of Christians to use Means for the Conversion of the Heathens'; in it, Carey argued that Christians were accountable to God for those who were not Christian, and so they were obliged to act in order to build the church throughout the world. The sermon led directly to the foundation of the Baptist Missionary Society in the same year, and within the next few years several other societies were also established in Britain, including the interdenominational London Missionary Society in 1795/1209, the Anglican Church Missionary Society in 1799/1203, and the British and Foreign Bible Society in 1804/1219. In 1812/1227 the American Board of Foreign Missions was also set up.[31]

Carey himself set off to India in 1793/1207, and died there in 1834/1250; his interest had mostly focused on Hinduism, and he had produced a Sanskrit grammar and translated the Bible into Bengali, Sanskrit and Marathi. As regards mission to Muslims the pioneer among the Protestants was Henry Martyn (1781/1195–1812/1227), a Cambridge graduate who arrived in India in 1806/1221 and during the remaining seven years of his life translated the New Testament into Urdu, and substantially revised the Persian and Arabic translations of the same work. In 1811/1225 Martyn set out from Calcutta to return to England, travelling by boat to Bushire in the Persian Gulf and then overland through Iran and Turkey; he spent almost a year in Shiraz, where he stimulated considerable discussion of religious questions, and the best part of three months in Tabriz, but six weeks later he died in Tokat, near Sivas in Eastern Turkey, in 1812/1227.

Martyn is important for three main reasons: firstly, his translations of the New Testament were of a particularly high standard, the Urdu one especially being influential for many decades; secondly, in contrast to the Jesuits, who sought to, as it were, work from the top down by influencing political leaders, Martyn laid great stress on making contact with ordinary Muslims, something which he was able to do particularly on his travels; and thirdly, while he was willing to enter into debate with Muslim leaders and scholars, to subject the conflicting claims of Christianity and Islam to public discussion, he was somewhat cautious about the usefulness of this approach, and he set himself one important rule in debate, never to attack Islam publicly. In this, as we shall see, he differed from some of his important Protestant successors as missionaries to Muslims, and subsequent events will show clearly the wisdom of Martyn's approach.[32] Part of Martyn's legacy, however, was simply his example, as his life could be interpreted as one of great self-sacrifice, based as it was on a self-proclaimed desire to 'burn out for God', and involving as it did an element of frustrated romance.[33]

THE HEYDAY OF EUROPEAN INFLUENCE

By the time that we reach what modern Western historians sometimes call the long nineteenth/thirteenth century, that is, the period between the French Revolution in 1789/1204 and the outbreak of World War I in 1914/1332, we enter an era in which on the one hand Christian missions are enjoying spectacular growth and success, and on the other hand the changing balance of power between the Christian and Muslim worlds which we looked at earlier also comes to a head in the growth of European imperialism. The nineteenth/thirteenth century has thus been described as seeing the greatest expansion of the Christian church since the era of the first apostles and their missionary journeys in the Roman world, and it also witnessed larger and larger areas of the world coming under the rule of different European powers.

The greatest missionary successes were not in the Muslim world but in the Americas, in some parts of Asia, and in Africa. Vander Werff chronicles the development of Christian (or at least Protestant) missions in the Muslim world, looking at the growth of Christian missions over the course of the nineteenth/thirteenth century in both India and the Middle East. He traces the development of the different approaches adopted by different missionary societies, both European and American, some of which laid great stress on the development of educational or medical institutions as instruments of Christian mission, and some of which concentrated simply on the development of church congregations.

Towards the end of his book, as he moves into the twentieth/fourteenth century, Vander Werff draws an effective contrast between what he calls Anglican and Reformed approaches to mission to Muslims. The figures whom he takes as the supreme representatives of these two traditions are the Englishman Temple Gairdner (1873/1290–1928/1346), who worked mainly with the Anglican Church Missionary Society in Egypt, and the Dutch-American Samuel Zwemer (1867/1283–1952/1371), the founder of the Arabian Mission, that venture of the Reformed Church of America to the heartland of Islam. Both of these figures stressed the importance of learning Arabic in order to be able to communicate the Christian message effectively to educated Muslims by whatever means were available, including newspapers, books and pamphlets, and both sought to arouse greater interest in mission to Muslims among their fellow Christians. Their interpretations of Islam, however, were slightly different, with Gairdner tending towards a more irenical approach, being willing to compare Christianity and Islam, to build on the common ground between them, and to be self-critical in the sense of acknowledging the past failures of his own religious community. He thus saw much good in Islam, particularly in the writings of the Sufis and of al-Ghazālī, and viewed Islam not as the antithesis of Christianity but rather Christianity as a kind of fulfilment of Islam, with Islam as a kind of preparation for Christianity. Zwemer, by contrast, adopted a more confrontational approach, with the Christian task being essentially to preach the gospel to Muslims, since Christianity was the final revelation of God and there could thus be no compromise with Islam as a system since fundamentally it was the antithesis of Christianity. It could be said that Zwemer thus had much sympathy with Muslims, but no sympathy with Islam, and his approach was a much more dialectical one, stressing contrast as opposed to continuity.

The titles of some of their books in a sense illustrate the contrast between their approaches: Gairdner is best known for his *The Reproach of Islam*, the title of which clearly testifies to the element of self-criticism discernible in his approach, since he suggests that the mere existence of Islam is, in a sense, a reproach for past Christian failings.[34] The titles of some of Zwemer's books, by contrast, have a slightly triumphalistic note, such as *The Disintegration of Islam* or *The Cross above the Crescent*, but this tone is supremely illustrated by the title of a book by W. A. Rice, a CMS (Church Missionary Society) missionary in Iran, which was entitled *Crusaders of the Twentieth Century; or the Christian Mission and the Muslim.*[35] Subsequently, the approaches of both of these figures have been influential in different quarters, with Gairdner's views being influential in many denominational Christian missionary societies, and Zwemer's views being more influential in evangelical circles.[36]

The concentration on Protestant missions in this period does not imply that Catholic missions had ceased to be active or had become moribund. Jesuit missions had continued to be active in different parts of the world, but perhaps without some of the imagination and originality which had characterised the pioneering Jesuit figures whom we looked at earlier.[37] In other parts of the world, however, new ventures were emerging, and just to take one example, the pioneering work of the White Fathers in Africa is worthy of note: this society, officially known as 'The Society of Missionaries of Africa', was founded by Cardinal Lavigerie, the French Archbishop of Algiers, in 1868/1285, with the intention of disseminating knowledge of Christianity in the region of the Sahara desert. Early attempts in this direction failed when two groups of missionaries were murdered by Tuareg nomads on the way to Timbuktu, but the society went on to work both in sub-Saharan Africa, especially in east Africa, and in north Africa where it sought to retain a Christian presence.[38] And Africa was also, incidentally, the focus of an interesting Protestant missionary venture to a group in what is now Nigeria, who claimed to be followers of ʿĪsā (Jesus) on the basis of what they read about him in the Qurʾān, and therefore called themselves Isawas.[39]

If the Muslim world was not affected by the activities of Christian missionaries in the nineteenth/thirteenth century as much as some other regions of the world, it was, however, intimately affected by colonialism. A few dates can serve as a simple illustration of this process of European expansion: in 1700/1112 the Muslim world comprised three great states, sometimes called the 'Gunpowder Empires' – the Ottoman Empire in the West, Safavid Iran in the middle, and the Moghul Empire in south Asia. These states covered an area stretching from Algiers and Hungary in the West through to the Bay of Bengal in the East, and there were smaller outlying Muslim states in Morocco, in west Africa, in central Asia and in south-east Asia. Over the course of the next two centuries, however, this situation changed dramatically.

As regards the European frontier of the Ottoman Empire, having threatened Vienna, as we have seen, in 1529/936 and 1683/1094, the Ottomans found themselves in retreat. They had to cede Hungary to Austria under the terms of the Treaty of Carlowitz in 1699/1110, and then the Crimea, whose population was Muslim, to Russia in the Treaty of Kucuk Kaynarca in 1774/1188. From 1757/1170 British expansion in India began to accelerate, following the battle of Plassey, leading ultimately to the extinction of the Moghul dynasty a century or so later, after what the British called the Indian Mutiny in 1857/1273. The events of 1774/1188 were simply the start of Russian expansion in central Asia, which in just over a century reached the southern boundaries of the steppe at the Caucasus and the Elburz mountains. In 1830/1246 the French occupied Algiers, and began their expansion throughout north and west Africa. In 1839/1255 the British occupied Aden. In 1881/1298 the French occupied Tunisia, and in 1882/1299 the British occupied Egypt. The Sudan followed in 1898/1316. In 1907/1325 Iran was divided into British and Russian spheres of influence. The Italians occupied Libya in 1912/1330. In the same year the French declared a Protectorate over Morocco, and the Spanish over Mauritania. Other parts of the Muslim world were also affected, with British as well as French expansion taking place in west Africa, and British and Dutch control being established over south-east Asia, in the Malay States and the Dutch East Indies respectively.

After World War I the process reached its climax: in 1920/1338 the League of Nations established British and French mandates over Iraq and Palestine, and Syria and Lebanon respectively, with the result that between World War I and World War II, only three Muslim countries were completely independent of European control – Afghanistan, Turkey and Saudi Arabia – and even they had all been threatened or influenced in some way at some stage. Afghanistan in 1841/1257 was the scene of a notable British military disaster when the population rebelled against the army which had occupied Kabul two years earlier in the First Afghan War, and only one Briton survived to tell the tale; more recently it has had to endure Soviet occupation between 1979/1399 and 1989/1409. As regards Turkey, plans were made after the defeat of the Ottoman Empire in World War I for its dismemberment and division into Russian, French and Italian spheres of influence, although these plans in the end came to nothing. And in Saudi Arabia in the 1920s/1340s, over a quarter of the state's income of some £210,000 consisted of a British subsidy of £60,000.[40] Even after World War II, as European influence began to retreat and the era of independence began to dawn, the creation of the new state of Israel in the heart of the Middle East in 1948/1367 was perceived by many as being yet another example of Western interference, and caused further resentment in much of the Muslim world.

The Muslim world, then, was heavily influenced by European colonialism and, puzzling though it is to many modern Westerners, it is important to remember that at the time, in the minds of many of those involved in the colonial venture there was a strong religious element in it. 'God has given us Indonesia' was the conviction of Abraham Kuyper, the devout Christian who became prime minister of the Netherlands in 1901/1318. During the war between the United States and Spain for control of the Philippines in 1898/1316, President William McKinley explained his motivation as follows:

> There was nothing left for us to do but to take them all, and to educate the Filipinos, and uplift and civilize and Christianize them, and by God's grace do the very best we could by them, as our fellow-men for whom Christ died.

Cardinal Lavigerie, the founder of the White Fathers, 'was a patriotic Frenchman as well as an ecclesiastical statesman of real stature; it seemed to him that the extension of French influence and Roman Catholic teaching could go forward together . . .'[41] And a particularly telling example of the identification which was sometimes made between imperial policy and religious conviction can be found in the reaction to what was called in Britain the Indian Mutiny: a day of national humiliation was called for by royal proclamation, many of the sermons preached on that day suggested that the mutiny was a divine judgement on Britain for her sins as a nation, and an increasing identification evidently was made between the success of British arms and the cause of God.[42]

MUSLIM RESPONSES

Confronted on the one hand with the growth of European power and imperialism, and on the other with the development of Christian missions, the Muslim world reacted in many different ways. This diversity of response should not surprise us, given, firstly, the size and diversity of the Muslim world, and secondly the time-span over which the different encounters took place. As continents and centuries are involved, it is therefore only natural to find a wide variety of responses and reactions.

At one extreme, one reaction to the growth of European influence was imitation. In the Ottoman Empire, for example, despite the traditional Sunnī Muslim prohibition of portraying in art any living being, Mehmed II (1451/855–1481/886), the conqueror of Constantinople, had his portrait painted by the Italian painter Bellini.[43] The eighteenth/twelfth century saw the emergence of a baroque style of architecture in the Ottoman Empire, exemplified by the Nur-u-Osmaniye (Light of Osman) mosque just to the east of the Grand Bazaar in Istanbul; constructed between 1748/1161 and 1755/1168, it was one of the earliest examples of Ottoman baroque. In the following century in Egypt, in the days of the Khedive Ismā'īl (1863/1280–1879/1296), efforts were made to reconstruct the capital city of Cairo physically, with wide boulevards on a Parisian model, and the opening of an opera house; the first performance, in 1869/1286, was Verdi's *Rigoletto*, and the same composer's *Aïda* premiered there in 1896/1314. Not for nothing was Ismā'īl described by P. J. Vatikiotis as 'the impatient Europeaniser'.[44] And in India, the important educational reformer Sayyid Ahmad Khan (1817/1232–1898/1316), who founded the Muḥammadan Anglo-Oriental College at Aligarh in 1875/1292, wrote during a visit to England in 1869/1286: 'All good things spiritual and worldly, which should be found in man, have been bestowed by the Almighty on Europe, and especially on England.'[45]

Even more important than these examples from the field of culture, is the imitation, by certain parts of the Muslim world, of European models in the fields of government and the state, and the economy. Developments of this kind proceeded at different paces in different regions of the Muslim world, and the extent to which they took deep root depended very much on whether the changes were introduced independently – in other words, of the rulers' own volition – or were rather introduced under European tutelage. They went furthest in the Ottoman Empire, where some sultans, albeit in some cases with European encouragement, were convinced of the urgent need to modernise and transform the structures of the empire: the Tanzīmāt (Reorganisations) of the nineteenth/thirteenth century resulted in fundamental change in many aspects of the Empire's life, including movement in the direction of constitutionalism, democracy, and even religious freedom, including the freedom to convert from Islam to other religions.[46] Change also took deep root in India, but here it did so under British tutelage, which gave it a rather ambivalent status in the eyes of many. In many other parts of the Muslim world, notably Iran, the process of change had very little impact at all during the nineteenth/thirteenth century.

At the other extreme, another reaction to the growth of European influence was a strong rejection of it, in the form of *jihād*, or military struggle. This sometimes meant organised opposition to the spread of European rule, but it also sometimes involved resistance by other means to the activities of Christian missionaries. Thus in the course of the nineteenth/thirteenth century, across the Muslim world, resistance leaders emerged who fought the attempts of the British, French, Russians and Dutch to expand the areas under their control. Examples of these include ʿAbd al-Qādir (1808/1223–1883/1300) in Algeria, who defied the French for some twenty years before his defeat by them in 1847/1263; the Sanūsī Sufi order, which resisted both French expansion in West and Central Africa and the Italian occupation of Libya in the early years of the twentieth/fourteenth century, under Sayyid Aḥmad al-Sharīf (head of the order from 1902/1320 to 1933/1352) and Sayyid Muḥammad Idrīs, who eventually became the king of Libya from its independence in 1951/1371 until 1969/1380; the opposition to French and British influence in Egypt led by Colonel Aḥmad Urabi in 1881/1298–1882/1299; the Tobacco Protest in Iran in 1891/1308, when popular protest against the granting of a monopoly in the trading of tobacco to a British merchant by Shah Nāṣir al-Dīn (1848/1264–1896/1313) culminated in the Shah's assassination; the resistance to Russian expansion in the Caucasus region organised by the Naqshbandi Imam Shamil for some twenty-five years until his defeat in 1859/1275; the opposition to British rule, as well as Sikh rule, initiated by Sayyid Aḥmad Barelvi (1786/1200–1831/1246) in India; and the long struggle against Dutch expansion in the sultanate of Aceh, in northern Sumatra, which lasted from 1873/1290 to 1908/1326.[47]

Behind several of these movements, particularly those of Urabi in Egypt and the Iranian protest movement of 1896/1313, lay the ideas and personality of Jamāl al-dīn al-Afghānī (1838/1254–1897/1314). Many details of his life, including where he was born and where he was educated, are not clear, but he spent much of it seeking to alert his fellow-Muslims to the threat facing the Muslim world, especially from the British, whom he described as 'the enemy of the Muslims', and to persuade Muslim rulers to resist European encroachment more vigorously. He constantly referred to the idea of 'Islam at risk', and he also clashed with Sayyid Ahmad Khan, whom we have referred to already, over his policy of seeking to imitate Western styles of education.[48]

Between the two extremes of these political reactions there were of course many intermediate positions, with many gradations. Sayyid Ahmad Khan, as well as imitating Western educational models, took up a kind of mediating intellectual stance, whereby some Western ideas, particularly some Western scholarship, could be taken up and used by Muslims to re-examine both their own Islamic tradition and their views of other traditions, including Christianity. This was not to be done uncritically, however, but selectively, so that the best of Western scholarship could be used but the worst could be rejected.[49]

In the Middle East a similar view was elaborated by Muḥammad 'Abduh (1849/1265–1905/1323), a figure who, like Sayyid Ahmad Khan, is commonly described as an 'Islamic modernist', on the basis of his willingness to countenance the expression of Islamic doctrine in ways different from the traditional ones in order to take account of modern knowledge. His work *al-islām wa'l-naṣrāniyya* (Islam and Christianity) was an attempt at a comparative analysis of the two religions, whose essential purpose was to redress the balance against a number of attacks which had been made on Islam either by Western writers or by Middle Eastern Christians. Each faith, according to 'Abduh, had a number of fundamental principles, and two in particular, he suggested, made Islam in some sense superior to Christianity: its greater rationality, with no belief in miracles and no demand for faith in the impossible, and its greater tolerance both towards those outside its community and towards dissent within.[50] The fact that 'Abduh became the Chief Mufti (Legal Interpreter) of Egypt in 1899/1317, and his involvement in the administrative council (the governing body) of al-Azhar, the ancient university of Cairo, ensured that his views were widely disseminated both in Egypt and more widely in the Middle East as a whole.[51]

There are thus significant differences of emphasis between Ahmad Khan and 'Abduh, which are in part due to the different contexts within which they worked. Ahmad Khan lived in an India which was explicitly and firmly part of the British Empire and 'Abduh lived in an Egypt where even if real power lay in the hands of the British Consul-General, Lord Cromer and his successors, the country still retained a nominal independence under its khedives. One point which was of considerable concern to both figures, however, was the activities of Christian missionaries, and to this we now turn.

Sayyid Ahmad Khan worked for the British East India Company. In such a position he both moved among the Muslim aristocracy in the cities in which he worked, and also knew many of the European residents of those cities, including Christian missionaries, and it was particularly in Agra, the city best known for one of its Islamic monuments, the Taj Mahal, that this became significant. Troll comments:

> Intense missionary activity, in Agra and elsewhere in the North-Western provinces, which ranged from written and oral debate (on a fairly high intellectual level), to preaching in bazaars and the distribution of thousands of copies of the Bible in vernacular languages, was perhaps a public novelty during those years in the province [the 1840's/c. 1255–1265].[52]

One feature of the situation in Agra which was not necessarily the case elsewhere was the fact that some of the senior officials of the British administration, particularly the Lieutenant-Governor James Thomason and an assistant of his, William Muir, were not afraid to make known their sympathy for the activities of the missionaries.

Muir became secretary to the government of the North-Western provinces in 1847/1263. He had already established something of a reputation as a commentator on the religious developments of the day in India, and he also became well-known as a scholar of Islam, on the basis of his *Life of Mahomet* and the *Annals of the Early Caliphate*, and went on to be the Principal of Edinburgh University. His view of Islam, however, was very negative. In one of his earliest works, 'The Mohammedan Controversy', published in *The Calcutta Review* in 1845/1261, the very first sentences read:

> Mohammedanism is perhaps the only undisguised and formidable antagonist of Christianity. From all the varieties of heathen religions Christianity has nothing to fear, for they are but the passive exhibitions of gross darkness which must vanish before the light of the Gospel. But in Islam we have an active and powerful enemy . . .[53]

Christian mission in Agra therefore seemed to operate on two levels. First of all there were those Christians who were explicitly functioning as missionaries, and of them one of the most famous was a German missionary, Karl Pfander (1803/1218–1865/1282), a skilful linguist who had gained a reputation as an effective debater in the context of the public discussions which sometimes took place in the bazaar.[54] Pfander's rather polemical approach, however, as illustrated in his book *Mīzān al-ḥaqq* (The Balance of Truth), produced a rather polemical response, not least from his opponent in a particularly important public debate which took place in Agra in 1854/1271, Raḥmat Allāh al-Kairanāwī (1834/1250–1891/1308). Having by most accounts bested Pfander in debate, Raḥmat Allāh in turn published a written reply to Pfander's book, entitled *Iẓhār al-ḥaqq* (The Demonstration of Truth), and like Pfander's work this has subsequently been reprinted many times so is still influential in some circles.[55]

The second level of missionary activity then was that which was not explicitly missionary in intent, but was carried out by sympathisers in the political and scholarly communities, such as Muir. He suggested in 1845/1261:

God be praised that Christianity is beginning gradually to assume her rightful position; and no sooner shall she have fully done so, than a light must break forth establishing before the world her truth and the unspeakable difference between it and every false religion.[56]

If Raḥmat Allāh's role was to rebut the efforts of Pfander, Sayyid Ahmad Khan's role was to refute the arguments of Muir; this he did particularly with reference to Muir's biographical studies of Muḥammad, which he attacked as manifesting prejudice and lack of objectivity.[57]

'Abduh's situation in Egypt was, as noted above, different from that of Sayyid Ahmad Khan in that Egypt had maintained its political independence, and there was not quite the same degree of sympathy between British administrators and Christian missionaries as was the case in Agra. Much of 'Abduh's work was an attempt to defend Islam against a remark by Lord Cromer, the Consul-General, that 'Islam reformed is Islam no longer', but Cromer's policies in Egypt were essentially inspired by pragmatism rather than any wish to diffuse the Gospel, and the perception of Christian missionaries as a threat did not develop to the same extent in Egypt as it did in India.

Muir, as we have seen, had a rather negative view of Islam, and a rather high view of the benefits which would be brought by the spread of Christianity in India. His thinking also seems to demonstrate a rather close identification between Christian mission and British rule. He had rather a high view, in other words, of the commonality of interests between the missionaries and the government of India. In reviewing the history of contacts between Christians and Muslims, he commented:

The fourth grand era of the connection of Christianity with Islam arose with the dominion of Europeans in India. And here every circumstance was in our favour. The presence of Europeans was generally the effect of conquest which, after the first feelings of irritation subside, invests the conqueror's faith and opinions with the prestige of power and authority . . . Now, at least, we might have expected that Christian Europe would early have improved her advantages for evangelizing the East; – that Britain, the bulwark of religion in the West, would have stepped forth as its champion in the East, and displayed her faith and her zeal where they were most urgently required. How different were the conclusions which the eighteenth century forces us to draw! England was then sadly neglectful of her responsibility; her

> religion was shown only at home, and she was careless of the spiritual darkness of her benighted subjects abroad; while her sons, who adopted India as their country, so far from endeavouring to impart to its inhabitants the benefits of their religion, too often banished it from their own minds, and exhibited to heathens and Mohammedans the sad spectacle of men without a faith . . .
>
> But the nineteenth century dawned with brighter prospects; and, as it advanced, the dark incubus of idolatry, superstition and bigotry began gradually to receive the light and teaching of the Gospel. Buchanan and Martyn, Brown and Thomason, are among the harbingers of this better era, in which Britain started from her lethargy; and, as if she had been treasuring up strength during her long inaction, came forth as a giant to the encounter. Her missionaries, with the venerable Carey at their head, led the van in strong array; many of her exiled sons began to perceive their responsibility for India's regeneration, and their number has since steadily increased. England now pours forth her gold in the merciful and blessed work of enlightening the people; while a material portion of her people in India has assumed a new aspect, and acknowledges by its deeds that its highest object is the enlightenment of India.[58]

Even apart from the fact that this passage was written by a Scotsman, this seems a remarkable statement, identifying as it does European dominion and the coming of the light and teaching of the Gospel, but if it appears at first sight to be an example of outstanding hubris, this impression surely has to be modified when it is put alongside the statement of Sayyid Ahmad Khan quoted earlier, which says something not so different from Muir when it refers to the Almighty bestowing all good things on England. Among the British, Muir was not necessarily typical or representative in this opinion; however, it is interesting that the Lieutenant-Governor under whom he served, James Thomason, was the son of Thomas Truebody Thomason, whom Muir refers to along with Buchanan, Martyn and Brown, the first Protestant missionaries to Muslims in India, as the bringers of light to the region. Equally, the situation in Agra was not necessarily typical of the whole of British India, but Muir's statement does at the very least make credible the suggestion which has been made by many modern commentators and historians, not only but perhaps particularly Muslims, that there was a close and intimate relationship between Christian mission and European imperialism.[59]

One widely influential statement of this case was made with reference to the Arab world by two Lebanese writers, Muṣṭafā Khālidī and 'Umar Farrūkh, in their book *Al-tabshīr wa'l-isti'mār fī'l-bilād al-'arabī* (Mission and Imperialism in the Arab World), published in Beirut in 1953/1372. On the basis of detailed examination of reports from missionary conferences, and books published by missionaries such as Samuel Zwemer, the authors were able to make a fairly strong case that Western politicians and Christian missionaries had frequently co-operated and helped each other in different parts of the Arab world, so it was not unreasonable to suggest that there was a close link between mission and imperialism. Many other works in the Arab world took up and developed this theme.[60]

It is a theme that was taken up more recently by Ayatollah Khomeini. His so-called *Little Green Book*, quoted by a Christian missionary in his account of the Iranian Revolution, said:

> Western missionaries, carrying out secret plans drawn up centuries ago, have created religious schools of their own within Muslim countries . . . These missionaries infiltrated our villages and our countryside to turn our children into Christians or atheists . . . The missionaries, as agents of imperialism, are also busy throughout the Muslim world perverting our youth – not by converting them to their own religion but by corrupting them . . . Propaganda centres . . . have been set up for the sole purpose of luring the faithful away from the commandments of Islam. Is it not our duty to destroy all these sources of danger to Islam?[61]

Among writers who wrote originally in English, the Palestinian Muslim A. L. Tibawi published particularly telling research. In his two books *British Interests in Palestine, 1800–1901*, and *American Interests in Syria, 1800–1901* he produced a compelling picture of the complicated interweaving of missionary, ecclesiastical, diplomatic, educational, literary, archaeological, and other interests in two neighbouring but rather different parts of the Arab world. And more recently the Islamic Foundation in Leicester has produced a series of briefer reports on the activities of Christian missions in different regions of the Muslim world which hint, at various points, at the political dimension of much missionary activity.[62]

Several attempts have also been made by Westerners to assess the accusation of close links between missionaries and colonial powers. Having suggested in his *History of Christian Missions* that 'missionaries in the nineteenth century had to some extent yielded to the colonial complex', Stephen Neill, who had himself been a Christian missionary, devoted a book-length study to the question, concluding that there was a huge spectrum of missionary opinion, and even if a large proportion of it was perhaps inclined to what would today be called 'cultural imperialism', any suggestion that all missionaries were imperialists is certainly not proven; while the situation is particularly difficult to assess with respect to Africa, in the world as a whole many areas were reached by missionaries before they were reached by diplomats or traders, and the activities of the latter were not infrequently opposed by missionaries. And Norman Daniel performed a valuable service in making clear that different attitudes predominated in different periods of the nineteenth/thirteenth century and that the different European powers were influenced by widely differing opinions.[63]

One last aspect of this long period of mission and imperialism, with all its complexity, must be investigated, and that is the phenomenon of conversion from Islam to Christianity. This was rarely a mass movement, so there is hardly anything comparable to the process whereby most of the Middle East was transformed by a gradual process of conversion from a situation where the majority of the population was Christian to one in which Islam became the faith of the majority, as we have investigated above. But there were instances of individuals converting to Christianity from Islam, often at considerable risk to themselves and their families because of the traditional Muslim laws concerning apostasy, and something must be said concerning their motivation and their influence.[64]

Just to take two examples, two notable nineteenth/thirteenth-century converts to Christianity were Sheikh Ṣāliḥ (1765/1179–1827/1242), a Muslim scholar in Lucknow, who, having become disillusioned with Islam as a result of an assassination plot which involved swearing on the Qur'ān, was drawn to Christianity through contact with Henry Martyn. He heard Martyn preach on the Ten Commandments and was attracted by his suggestion that the law needed to be interpreted in the light of the Sermon on the Mount. He therefore sought out contact with Martyn, through whom he was able to obtain Persian and Urdu translations of the New Testament, and after a period of reflection sought baptism. He was baptised in 1813/1228, taking the name Abdul Masih (Servant of Christ), and was later ordained as a minister, though the Anglican bishop initially refused to ordain him so he had to become a Lutheran, but became an Anglican once more in 1825/1240.[65]

A more recent convert, in Egypt, was Muḥammad Manṣūr, who, as a graduate of al-Azhar, was determined to refute the Christians of his village in Upper Egypt by logical argument but in his enthusiasm to prove that the Christian scriptures had been corrupted was won over by them. He was baptised as a Roman Catholic, but later joined the Evangelical Church through which he had first been exposed to the Christian scriptures, and for many years he continued to visit al-Azhar in order to discuss religious questions with both teachers and students. At his baptism he took as his Christian name Mikhail, after the preacher who had been so influential on him, and among those whom he persuaded to adopt the Christian faith as he had done was his brother Kāmil.[66]

Several other examples of individual conversion from Islam to Christianity could be referred to. As with the process of conversion to Islam which we looked at earlier, many factors and many different motives were no doubt involved. A number of recent studies have investigated both the process and the reasons for conversion of this kind, and it is clear that, even if not on the same scale as the earlier process of conversion to Islam, conversion from Islam has sometimes taken place and it represents one option in the range of Muslim responses to mission and imperialism.[67]

NOTES

1. See H. Trevor-Roper, *The Rise of Christian Europe*, London: Thames and Hudson, 1965, Chapter 4, and J. R. S. Phillips, *The Medieval Expansion of Europe*, Oxford University Press, 1988, Chapter 3.
2. N. Malcolm, *Kosovo: a Short History*, London: Macmillan, 1998, p. 61.
3. M. Vickers, *Between Serb and Albanian: a History of Kosovo*, London: Hurst, 1998, pp. 13–14.
4. Ibid., p. 14.
5. See Malcolm, *Kosovo*, pp. 77–80.
6. M. Ayoub, *Redemptive Suffering in Islam: a Study of the Devotional Aspects of 'Ashura in Twelver Shi'ism*, The Hague: Mouton, 1978, and W. Husted, 'Karbala made immediate: the Martyr as Model in Imami Shi'ism', in *Muslim World*, 83 (1993), pp. 263–78.
7. S. Runciman, *The Fall of Constantinople*, Cambridge University Press, 1965, and H. Inalcik, 'The Policy of Mehmed II toward the Greek Population of Istanbul and the Byzantine Buildings of the City', in *Dumbarton Oaks Papers*, 23/4 (1969–70), pp. 231–49.
8. See H. Inalcik, *The Ottoman Empire: the Classical Age, 1300–1600*, London: Weidenfeld and Nicolson, 1973, and M. A. Cook (ed.), *A History of the Ottoman Empire to 1730*, Cambridge University Press, 1976.
9. R. W. Southern, *Western Views of Islam in the Middle Ages*, Harvard University Press, 1962, pp. 105–6.
10. Ibid., pp. 106–7. On Wycliffe, see ibid., pp. 77–83, and on Joachim, see ibid., pp. 40–1. For other material on Luther, see C. U. Wolf, 'Luther and Mohammedanism', in *Muslim World*, 31 (1941), pp. 161–77; E. Grislis, 'Luther and the Turks', in *Muslim World*, 64 (1974), pp. 180–93 and 275–91; and S. Henrich and J. L. Boyce, 'Martin Luther – Translations of Two Prefaces on Islam', in *Word and World* (Luther Seminary, St. Paul, Minnesota), 16 (1996), pp. 250–74.

11. J. Slomp, 'Calvin and the Turks', in Y. Y. Haddad and W. Z. Haddad (eds), *Christian–Muslim Encounters*, University Press of Florida, 1995, p. 137.
12. Sermon 88 on Deuteronomy 38, quoted by Slomp, ibid., p. 135.
13. K. Vehlow, 'The Swiss Reformers Zwingli, Bullinger and Bibliander and their Attitude towards Islam (1520–1560)', in *Islam and Christian–Muslim Relations*, 6 (1995), pp. 229–54.
14. N. Matar, *Islam in Britain, 1558–1685*, Cambridge University Press, 1998, p. 11.
15. J. H. Parry, *The Age of Reconnaissance, 1450–1650*, London: Weidenfeld and Nicolson, 1963, esp. chapters 8 and 12.
16. A. S. Atiya, *A History of Eastern Christianity*, London: Methuen, 1968, p. 262.
17. See note 9 to Chapter 5 above.
18. D. M. Dunlop, 'A Christian Mission to Muslim Spain in the 11th Century', in al-Andalus, 17 (1952), pp. 259–310. See also T. Burman, *Religious Polemic and the Intellectual History of the Mozarabs, c. 1050–1200*, Leiden: Brill, 1994, esp. pp. 91–2, and P. Sj. van Koningsveld, 'Christian Arabic Literature from Medieval Spain: an Attempt at Periodization', in S. K. Samir and J. S. Nielsen (eds), *Christian Arabic Apologetics during the Abbasid Period (750–1258)*, Leiden: Brill, 1994, pp.203–24.
19. B. Z. Kedar, *Crusade and Mission: European Approaches toward the Muslims*, Princeton University Press, 1984.
20. J. R. H. Moorman, *Saint Francis of Assisi*, London: SCM, 1950, pp. 97–101; S. M. Zwemer, 'Francis of Assisi and Islam', in *Muslim World*, 39 (1949), pp. 247–51; G. Basetti-Sani, 'Muḥammad and St. Francis', in *Muslim World*, 46 (1956), pp. 345–53; and M. Mujeeb, 'St. Francis of Assisi', in *Islam and the Modern Age*, 8 (1982), pp. 67–75. There is a reproduction of a picture of Francis before the Sultan on the frontispiece of K. M. Setton (ed), *A History of the Crusades*, vol. V, University of Wisconsin Press, 1985.
21. E. A. Peers, *Fool of Love: the Life of Ramon Lull*, London: SCM, 1946; J. W. Sweetman, *Islam and Christian Theology*, Part II vol. I, London: Lutterworth, 1955, pp. 96–111; A. Bonner (ed.), *Doctor Illuminatus: a Roman Llull* [sic] *Reader*, Princeton University Press, 1993; and D. Urvoy, 'Ramon Lull et l'Islam', in *Islamochristiana*, 7 (1981), pp. 127–46. See also S.M. Zwemer, *Raymond Lull, first Missionary to Muslims*, New York: Funk and Wagnall, 1902.
22. Sweetman, *Islam and Christian Theology*, pp. 86–94 and 116–59, and L. M. Spath, 'Ricoldo da Monte Croce: Medieval Pilgrim and Traveller to the Heart of Islam', in *Bulletin of the Royal Institute for Inter-Faith Studies* (Amman), 1 (1999), pp. 65–102.
23. J. Glazik, 'Missionary Work of the Mendicants outside Europe', in H. Jedin and J. Dolan (eds), *Handbook of Church History*, vol. IV, London: Burns and Oates, 1970, pp. 391–400; K. S. Latourette, *A History of the Expansion of Christianity*, vol. II, London: Eyre and Spottiswoode, 1955, pp. 319–27; and M. W. Baldwin, 'Missions to the East in the Thirteenth and Fourteenth Centuries', in K. W. Setton (ed.), *A History of the Crusades*, vol. V, University of Wisconsin Press, 1985, pp. 452–518.
24. N. Horner, *Rediscovering Christianity where it Began*, Beirut: Near East Council of Churches, 1974, pp. 13–14; G. C. Anawati, 'The Roman Catholic Church and Churches in Communion with Rome', in A. J.

Arberry (ed.), *Religion in the Middle East*, vol. I, Cambridge University Press, 1969, Chapter 7; and C. A. Frazee, *Catholics and Sultans*, Cambridge University Press, 1983.

25. See W. H. McNeill and M. R. Waldman (eds), *The Islamic World*, Oxford University Press, 1973, pp. 386–7.
26. Ibid., p. 391.
27. See ibid., pp. 373–91, for extracts from the account of the whole of the two missions.
28. See S. C. Neill, *A History of Christian Missions*, London: Penguin, 1964, pp. 148–66 on the first three, and pp. 183–7 on the fourth.
29. See C. H. Payne, *Akbar and the Jesuits*, London: Routledge, 1926; E. R. Hambye, 'The First Jesuit Mission to Emperor Akbar', in C. W. Troll (ed.), *Islam in India: Studies and Commentaries*, vol. I, Delhi: Vikas, 1982, pp. 3–13; J. T. Addison, *The Christian Approach to the Moslems; a Historical Study*, Columbia University Press, 1942, Chapter 7; S. C. Neill, *A History of Christianity in India*, vol. I, Cambridge University Press, 1984, pp. 166–90 and 343–9; and A. Camps, *Jerome Xavier S. J. and the Muslims of the Moghul Empire: Controversial Works and Missionary Activity*, Switzerland: Schöneck-Beckenried, 1957.
30. L. L Vander Werff, *Christian Mission to Muslims: the Record*, Pasadena: William Carey Library, 1977, p. 19.
31. Ibid., p. 25.
32. Ibid., pp. 30–6; S. C. Neill, *A History of Christianity in India*, vol. II, Cambridge University Press, 1985, pp. 257–60; and C. E. Padwick, *Henry Martyn: Confessor of the Faith*, London: Inter-Varsity Fellowship, 1953. For the texts of the debates which Martyn held in Shiraz, see S. Lee, *Controversial Tracts on Christianity and Mohammedanism*, Cambridge: Smith, 1824.
33. See R. T. France, 'Henry Martyn', in S. M. Houghton (ed.), *Five Pioneer Missionaries*, London: Banner of Truth Trust, 1965, pp. 233–302, and D. Bentley-Taylor, *My Love Must Wait*, London: Inter-Varsity Press, 1975.
34. W. H. T. Gairdner, *The Reproach of Islam*, London: Church Missionary Society, 1909, 5th ed., entitled *The Rebuke of Islam*, London: Church Missionary Society, 1920.
35. S. M. Zwemer, *The Disintegration of Islam*, New York: Revell, 1915, and *The Cross above the Crescent*, Grand Rapids: Eerdmans, 1941; W. A. Rice, *Crusaders of the Twentieth Century*, London: Church Missionary Society, 1910.
36. On Gairdner, see C. E. Padwick, *Temple Gairdner of Cairo*, 2nd edn., London: SPCK, 1930, Vander Werff, *Christian Mission to Muslims*, pp. 187–224 and 277–84, and M. T. Shelley, *The Life and Thought of W. H. T. Gairdner, 1872–1928: a Critical Evaluation of a Scholar-Missionary to Islam*, unpublished PhD thesis, University of Birmingham, 1989; and on Zwemer, see Vander Werff, *Christian Mission to Muslims*, pp. 224–68 and 291–5, and P. Ipema, *The Islam Interpretations of Duncan B. Macdonald, Samuel M. Zwemer, A. Kenneth Cragg and Wilfred C. Smith: an Analytical Comparison and Evaluation*, unpublished PhD thesis, Hartford Seminary, 1971.
37. See T. Michel, 'Jesuit Writings on Islam in the Seventeenth Century', in *Islamochristiana*, 15 (1989), pp. 57–85.
38. Neill, *History of Chsitian Missions*, pp. 424–5 and 431–3.
39. See E. Hulmes, 'Walter Miller and the *Isawa*: an Experiment in Chris-

tian–Muslim Relationships', in *Scottish Journal of Theology*, 41 (1988), pp. 233–46.

40. See respectively P. Spear, *A History of India*, vol. II, London: Penguin, 4th edn., 1979, p. 133; M. S. Anderson, *The Eastern Question*, London: Macmillan, 1966, p. 342; and P. Mansfield, *The Arabs*, 3rd edn., London: Penguin, 1985, p. 206.
41. See G. H. Jansen, *Militant Islam*, London: Pan, 1979, p. 54; M. A. Noll, *A History of Christianity in the United States and Canada*, Grand Rapids: Eerdmans, 1992, pp. 292–3; and Neill, *History of Christian Missions*, p. 431.
42. See B. Stanley, 'Christian Responses to the Indian Mutiny of 1857', in W. J. Shiels (ed.), *The Church and War*, (Studies in Church History 20), Oxford: Blackwell, 1983, pp. 277–89; and S. Malik, 'God, England, and the Indian Mutiny: Victorian Religious Perceptions', in *Muslim World*, 73 (1983), pp. 106–32.
43. Inalcik, *The Ottoman Empire*, Plate I and p. 181.
44. P. J. Vatikiotis, *The Modern History of Egypt*, 4th edn., Weidenfeld and Nicolson, 1991, Chapter 5.
45. Quoted in K. Cragg, *Counsels in Contemporary Islam*, Edinburgh University Press, 1965, p. 49.
46. See B. Lewis, *The Emergence of Modern Turkey*, Oxford University Press, 1961, chapters 2 and 3; N. Berkes, *The Development of Secularism in Turkey*, 2nd edn., London: Hurst, 1998, chapters 4 to 8; and S. J. Shaw, *History of the Ottoman Empire and Modern Turkey*, vol. II, Cambridge University Press, 1977, chapters 1 to 3.
47. See J. O. Voll, *Islam: Continuity and Change in the Modern World*, 2nd edn., Syracuse University Press, 1994, Chapter 3; N. R. Keddie, *Religion and Rebellion in Iran: the Iranian Tobacco Protest*, London: Cass, 1966; and R. Peters, *Islam and Colonialism*, Mouton: The Hague, 1979.
48. See N. R. Keddie, *Sayyid Jamal al-Din 'al-Afghani': a Political Biography*, University of California Press, 1972, and *An Islamic Response to Imperialism: Political and Religious Writings of Sayyid Jamal al-Din 'al-Afghani'*, 2nd edn., University of California Press, 1983.
49. See C. W. Troll, *Sayyid Ahmad Khan: a Reinterpretation of Muslim Theology*, Delhi: Vikas, 1978, and J. M. S. Baljon, *The Reforms and Religious Ideas of Sir Sayyid Ahmad Khan*, 3rd edn., Lahore: Ashraf, 1964. For his views of the Bible, see C. W. Troll, 'Sayyed Ahmad Khan's Commentary on the Holy Bible', in *Islam and the Modern Age*, 7 (1976), pp. 35–45, M. D. Rahbar, 'Sir Sayyid Ahmad Khan's Principles of Exegesis Translated from his *Taḥrīr fī 'Usūl al-Tafsīr*', in *Muslim World*, 46 (1956), pp. 104–12 and 324–55, and H. P. Goddard, *Muslim Perceptions of Christianity*, London: Grey Seal, 1996, pp. 51–5.
50. M. Ayyub, 'Islam and Christianity: a Study of Muḥammad Abduh's View of the Two Religions', in *Humaniora Islamica*, 2 (1974), pp. 121–37, and Goddard, *Muslim Perceptions of Christianity*, pp. 43–7.
51. A. H. Hourani, *Arabic Thought in the Liberal Age*, Oxford University Press, 1962, chapters 6 and 7, and M. Abduh, *The Theology of Unity*, London: Allen and Unwin, 1966.
52. Troll, *Reinterpretation*, p. 65.
53. W. Muir, *The Mohammedan Controversy*, Edinburgh: T. and T. Clark, 1897, p. 2.
54. See Vander Werff, *Christian Mission to Muslims*, pp. 41–4, and S. M.

Zwemer, 'Karl Gottlieb Pfander, 1841–1941', in *Muslim World*, 31 (1941), pp. 217–26.

55. See A. A. Powell, *Muslims and Missionaries in pre-Mutiny India*, London: Curzon, 1993, especially chapters 5 and 8, and Goddard, *Muslim Perceptions of Christianity*, pp. 47–51 and 67–76.
56. Muir, *Mohammedan Controversy*, p. 50.
57. For his response to Muir's 'Biographies of Mohammed for India; and the Mohammedan Controversy', in his *The Mohammedan Controversy*, pp. 65–101, 'Value of Early Mahometan Historical Sources', in ibid., pp. 103–52, and *Life of Mahomet*, 4 vols, London: Smith Elder, 1858–61, see Troll, *Reinterpretation*, Chapter 4, esp. p. 132.
58. Muir, *Mohammedan Controversy*, pp. 5–6.
59. On Muir, see C. Bennett, *Victorian Images of Islam*, London: Grey Seal, 1992, Chapter 5.
60. See Goddard, *Muslim Perceptions of Christianity*, pp. 84–93.
61. P. Hunt, *Inside Iran*, London: Lion, 1981, pp. 106–7.
62. A. L. Tibawi, *British Interests in Palestine, 1800–1901*, Oxford University Press, 1961, and *American Interests in Syria, 1800–1901*, Oxford University Press, 1966; A. K. Khan, *Christian Missions in Pakistan: a Survey*, Leicester: Islamic Foundation, 1981, and *Christian Mission in Bangladesh: a Survey*, Leicester: Islamic Foundation, 1981; and A. von Denffer, *Indonesia: How Muslims are Made Christians*, Leicester: Islamic Foundation, 1981.
63. Neill, *History of Christian Missions*, p. 259, and *Colonialism and Christian Missions*, London: Lutterworth, 1966; and N. Daniel, *Islam, Europe and Empire*, Edinburgh University Press, 1966. A rather different view is adopted by B. Stanley, *The Bible and the Flag*, Leicester: Apollos, 1990, esp. pp. 183–4.
64. The traditional law of apostasy and its effects on conversion were investigated by Samuel Zwemer in his *The Law of Apostasy in Islam*, London: Marshalls, 1924. The law is a focus of considerable discussion among Muslims today, particularly in the context of discussion of human rights in general; see A. A. an-Na'īm, 'The Islamic Law of Apostasy and its Modern Applicability: a Case from the Sudan', in *Religion*, 16 (1986), pp. 197–224, and M. Ayoub, 'Religious Freedom and the Law of Apostasy in Islam', in *Islamochristiana*, 20 (1994), pp. 75–91.
65. Vander Werff, *Christian Mission to Muslims*, p. 39, and pp. 35–6 (on Martyn's role); and Powell, *Muslims and Missionaries*, pp. 110–17.
66. See J. G. Hunt 'Makhail (sic) Mansur: an Apostle of Christ', in *Muslim World*, 9 (1919), pp. 19–24, and C. E. Padwick's review of a biography of Mikhail Mansur by his brother, in *Muslim World*, 20 (1930), pp. 94–5.
67. For a personal account of conversion, see 'The Testimony of Pastor Marcus Abd-el-Mesih', in *Muslim World*, 35 (1945), pp. 211–15. Two studies of conversion which are based on the biographies of converts are S. Syrjänen, *In Search of Meaning and Identity: Conversion to Christianity in Pakistani Muslim Culture*, Helsinki: Finnish Society for Mission and Ecumenics, 1984, and J-M. Gaudeul, *Appelés par le Christ: ils Viennent de l'Islam*, Paris: Cerf, 1991. On the process of conversion see M. Jarrett-Kerr, *Patterns of Christian Acceptance*, Oxford University Press, 1972, pp. 196–201 and 318–20, and R. W. Hefner, 'Of Faith and

Commitment: Christian Conversion in Muslim Java', in Hefner (ed.), *Conversion to Christianity: Historical and Anthropological Perspectives on a Great Transformation*, University of California Press, 1993, pp. 99–125.

7

New Thinking in the 19th/13th and 20th/14th Centuries

THE GROWTH OF WESTERN ACADEMIC STUDY OF ISLAM

At the same time as the various activities associated with mission and imperialism were going on, a third important aspect of Western thinking about Islam was also developing, namely the growth of academic study of Islam. This is not to deny the existence of earlier Western scholarly writing about Islam, particularly the efforts of such people as Peter the Venerable to study Islam seriously on the basis of its own sources such as the Qur'ān; rather, it is to suggest that modern times, particularly since the Enlightenment and the Age of Reason, have witnessed the emergence of a new approach to the study of religion in general, as well as of Islam in particular, which is less explicitly theological in intention than the work of such figures as Peter, and strives to be objective and neutral in its description and assessment.[1]

This is not to say that Western scholarship of this kind has always succeeded in its aim of being impartial and fair in its judgements. The recent works of the Palestinian Christian scholar Edward Said have made this only too clear, demonstrating something of the extent to which Western scholars have sometimes reproduced uncritically or even reinforced older stereotypes and caricatures concerning Islam.[2] It is somewhat disconcerting for Western academics at the end of the twentieth/start of the fifteenth century to be reminded that such a distinguished anthropologist as E. E. Evans-Pritchard, Professor of Social Anthropology at Oxford and still regarded as one of the pioneers of serious anthropological study in the United Kingdom, undertook two of the three main studies for which he is best known for the following reasons: as regards the Nuer '[a]n urgent request from the government of the Sudan called him to report on an unruly Nilotic tribe whose insurrection would be put down by force unless someone could interpret their intentions';[3] and as regards the Sanusi, in Evans-Pritchard's own words:

> This account of the Sanusi of Cyrenaica would not have been written if a number of accidents had not led me to their country during the late war . . . I had been acquainted with some of the Sanusi exiles in Egypt as far back as 1932 and had visited Darna

> and Banghazi by sea; and it had long been my hope that I might some day, when the Italians had ceased to rule the country, have a chance to visit the interior. This wish came true when in November 1942 I was posted as Political Officer to the (third) British Military Administration of Cyrenaica.[4]

Western academics have clearly not always been able to pursue a disinterested search for the truth for its own sake. But the aspiration towards independence of thought and action has been there, with Evans-Pritchard only accepting the invitation to investigate the Nuer 'because there was the risk that unless some trusted means of communication could be established, the Nuer would fight until they were destroyed'.[5] Even if the ideal of independent analysis has not always been attained, the attempt to realise it does represent something of a new approach which we need to take some account of.

It is not an approach which Westerners should claim to have absolutely pioneered, however. E. J. Sharpe suggests that in the Middle Ages

> [a]lthough Christians were not seriously interested in other religions, except as opponents to be overcome, there were a number of Muslim writers of the period . . . who attempted to describe or otherwise confront those religions to which Islam was opposed. Tabarī (838–923) wrote about Persian religion; Mas'udī (d. 956) about Judaism, Christianity and the religions of India; and Alberūnī (973–c. 1050) about India and Persia. The honour of writing the first history of religion in world literature seems in fact to belong to the Muslim Shahrastanī (d. 1153), whose *Religious Parties and Schools of Philosophy* describes and systematises all the religions of the then known world, as far as the boundaries of China. This outstanding work far outstrips anything which Christian writers were capable of producing at the same period.[6]

The development of comparable studies of Islam in the West after the Middle Ages went through several stages. In 1539/946 the first Chair of Arabic was established at the Collège de France. By 1586/994 it had become possible to print works in Arabic for the first time. In 1613/1022 a Chair of Arabic was established in the University of Leiden. During the 1630s/1040s chairs of Arabic were established in both Oxford and Cambridge. The first complete English translation of the Qur'ān was made by Alexander Ross in 1649/1059, though almost a century had to pass before a more accurate one became available through the work of George Sale in 1734/1147. In 1705/1117 a Dutch scholar, Adriaan Reland, wrote an account of the religion of Islam which was based exclusively on Muslim sources, and between 1708/1120 and 1718/1130 Simon Ockley wrote his *History of the Saracens*, which attempted to make knowledge of Islamic history more accessible. A text of a very different sort became available when Antoine Galland translated *The Arabian Nights* into French between 1704/1116 and 1717/1129, with translations into English and German following early in the nineteenth/thirteenth century, and according to some estimations this work was second in popularity only to the Bible in eighteenth-twelfth-century Europe.[7]

These studies made texts available, and much of the interest in anything to do with Islam was actually inspired primarily by philological and linguistic concerns. But one major change which all this work brought about in Western perceptions of Islam was that new myths of Islam began to develop, with Muḥammad being presented as a tolerant ruler and Islam as a rational faith, in contrast to what Enlightenment thinkers saw as the characteristics of the Christian church of their day:

> Islam was seen as a rational religion, quite remote from those Christian tenets that most opposed reason. Moreover, Islam seemed to espouse few mythical concepts and mystical traditions, only what was deemed necessary to assure the following of the people. Beyond that, Islam appeared to balance the demand for a moral life with an understandable respect for the needs of the flesh, the senses and social interaction. It was, all told, a religion that approximated the Deism of most Enlightenment philosophers.[8]

Thus Edward Gibbon, in his *Decline and Fall of the Roman Empire*, published between 1776/1190 and 1788/1202, included a chapter (Chapter 50) on Muḥammad and the rise of Islam, which concluded with the following judgement on the prophet:

> The most bitter or most bigoted of his Christian or Jewish foes will surely allow that he assumed a false commission to inculcate a salutary doctrine, less perfect only than their own . . . The idols of Arabia were broken before the throne of God; the blood of human victims was expiated by prayer, and fasting, and alms, the laudable or innocent arts of devotion; and his rewards and punishments of a future life were painted by the images most congenial to an ignorant and carnal generation. Mahomet was, perhaps, incapable of dictating a moral and political system for

> the use of his countrymen: but he breathed among the faithful a spirit of charity and friendship; recommended the practice of the social virtues; and checked, by his laws and precepts, the thirst of revenge, and the oppression of widows and orphans.

Such a judgement is not always complimentary, but it does attempt to locate Muḥammad in the context of his own time and place, and to give praise where Gibbon saw it as being due.[9]

The eighteenth/twelfth and nineteenth/thirteenth centuries also saw new sources of information about, and knowledge of, Islam become available to Westerners, as a result of the activities of travellers and missionaries. The Englishwoman Lady Mary Wortley Montagu spent over a year in Istanbul with her husband, the British ambassador to the Ottoman sultan, between 1717/1129 and 1718/1130, and wrote an account of life in the city and at court, including those parts which were only accessible to women; her account was even translated later into Turkish.[10] The Frenchman Constantin François Chasseboeuf made available a meticulous account of his travels in the Middle East in his *Voyage en Égypte et en Syria*, published in 1787/1201 under his *nom de plume* of the Comte de Volney.[11] Some time later the Englishman E. W. Lane lived in Cairo for many years, and as well as translating *The Arabian Nights* into English he compiled a lexicon of the Arabic language which is still an indispensable reference work, and wrote *An Account of the Manners and Customs of the Modern Egyptians*, a work which, first published in 1836/1252, was both thorough and entertaining, and quickly became a bestseller.[12]

Travellers also visited parts of the Muslim world which were previously unknown to Europeans. One of the most celebrated was the Englishman Charles Doughty, who between 1876/1293 and 1878/1295 explored central Arabia, including previously unvisited towns such as Medā'in Ṣāliḥ, Ḥāyil, Khaybar, and Buraida, before travelling round Mecca to reach Jedda. His *Travels in Arabia Deserta*, first published in 1888, was another bestseller.[13] Doughty never dissimulated concerning his identity, never seeking to disguise that he was a Christian, and therefore travelled respectfully round the sacred area around the Holy City of Mecca; but other Europeans did not share his scruples.

The earliest European travellers to visit Mecca were probably the Italian Ludovico di Varthema (or Barthema), who was in Mecca and Medina in 1503/908, the Englishman Joseph Pitts, who having been taken prisoner by the Barbary pirates was forced to convert to Islam and went on the pilgrimage to Mecca in 1680/1091, and the Catalan Domingo Badia y Leblich, who travelled to Mecca disguised as an 'Abbasid prince, no less, 'Ali Bey al-'Abbasi, in 1897/1222. The most famous nineteenth/thirteenth-century visitors, however, were probably the Swiss John Louis Burckhardt, who had converted to Islam, and visited Mecca in 1814/1229, and the Englishman Sir Richard Burton, who travelled in the disguise of a Pathan Muslim and reached Mecca in 1853/1269. Burckhardt was probably the better observer of life in Mecca, but because of his other feats of exploration in Africa, Burton's account is the better known.[14]

Later, a number of Europeans managed not only to visit Mecca at the time of the pilgrimage but also to live there for some months. Perhaps the most famous were the Dutchman Snouck Hurgronje, who had completed a doctorate on the *ḥajj* and who spent more than six months in the city in 1885/1302, disguised as a Muslim, and the Englishman Eldon Rutter, who spent the best part of a year in Mecca and Medina in 1925/1343, though it is not clear whether or not he had converted to Islam. Each produced a vivid account of the city, with Hurgronje being able to describe the domestic life of the city in particular detail on the basis of having taken a local wife.[15]

All this additional information about and experience of Islam and the Muslim world had some interesting consequences, for example in the realms of Western art and architecture. In England, as early as the sixteenth/tenth century, rugs from the Islamic world were increasingly in demand; some of the portraits which exist of King Henry VIII show him standing on one, with arabesque designs on the curtains behind him. Stately homes such as Hardwick Hall in Derbyshire also have Turkish rugs from the 1590s/1000s. It is from 1750/1163 onwards, however, that the real passion for things Islamic develops in the artistic field, as seen in buildings such as Sezincote House in Gloucestershire, designed by Samuel Pepys Cockerell and built between 1804/1218 and 1805/1219, and, most famously, the Royal Pavilion in Brighton, built to the design of John Nash between 1815/1230 and 1822/1237. But perhaps the greatest extravaganza of Islamic-style architecture in Britain is to be found at Leighton House in London, designed by George Aitchison and built between 1877/1294 and 1879/1296. North America too was affected by this style, as seen in such constructions as the circus impressario P. T. Barnum's Iranistan, in Bridgport, Connecticut, built between 1846/1262 and 1848/1264, the mansion called Longwood in Mississippi, designed by Samuel Sloan in the following decade, and perhaps most remarkably the dome of the Armory building of the Colt pistol factory in Hartford, Connecticut, also from the 1850s/1270s.[16] The influence of Islam on the growth of Western civilisation generally was not forgotten either: the dome of the Reading Room of the Library of Congress in Washington DC, designed by Edwin Howland Blashfield and opened in 1897/1304, has a mural round the top of it which represents the twelve epochs or countries which made major contributions to the growth of American civilisation: between Egypt, Judaea, Greece, and Rome on the one hand, and the Middle Ages, Italy, Germany, Spain, England and France on the other, comes Islam, especially because of its contribution to science. (The twelfth element is America itself.)

Perhaps the most important legacy, however, was the continued growth and development of Islamic studies as one aspect of the Western study of the Orient, or Orientalism. In 1754/1167 William Jones founded the first society for the study of the Orient, the Asiatic Society of Bengal.[17] In Paris the Société Asiatique was founded in 1821/1236, and in London the Royal Asiatic Society followed in 1823/1238. In 1873/1290 the first international congress of Orientalists was held. In the wider society too considerable interest in Islamic themes was evident: Goethe's *Mahomets Gesang* (Song of Muḥammad) of 1774/1188 glorified Muḥammad, and his *West-Östlicher Divan* (Diwan/Collection of Poems of West and East) of 1819/1234 was heavily influenced by Persian Sufi poetry. In 1841/1257 Thomas Carlyle published his lectures on heroes, in which he accepted Muḥammad as a prophet.[18]

Hourani calls Silvestre de Sacy (1758/1171–1838/1254) 'in some ways the founder of modern Islamic and Arabic studies', and suggests that Paris and Leiden were the two great centres of Islamic studies in the nineteenth/thirteenth century.[19] Sacy was the first teacher of Arabic at the École des Langues Orientales Vivantes in Paris, which was set up in 1795/1210, and was the first president of the Société Asiatique. He also worked, unpaid, for the French Foreign Ministry, and at the end of the same century, Snouck Hurgronje, the Dutchman whom we have already referred to as one of the European visitors to Mecca, and in whom Hourani says 'the tradition of Leiden may be said to have reached its peak', worked as an adviser to the colonial government in the Dutch East Indies.[20]

A pioneering study of five significant European students of Islam looks at the Dutchman Hurgronje (1857/1273–1936/1355), the Hungarian Jew Ignaz Goldziher (1850/1266–1921/1339), the Prussian C. H. Becker (1876/1293–1933/1352), the Scot who worked for most of his life in North America, Duncan Black Macdonald (1863/1280–1943/1362), and the Frenchman Louis Massignon (1883/1300–1962/1382). All made considerable contributions to the development of Islamic Studies, in different ways: Hurgronje and Becker were active as advisers to governments, Becker serving as Prussian Secretary of State for a time; Massignon was active politically but often in opposition to his government; and the remaining two, Goldziher and Macdonald, confined themselves more strictly to the study of Islam as a religious system, in their *Vorlesungen über den Islam* (Lectures on Islam) and *Development of Muslim Theology, Jurisprudence and Constitutional Theory* respectively. For neither of them, however, was Islam simply an ancient system of thought and practice; both had a lively interest in contemporary Islam as well.[21]

The fact that these figures had no explicit political role has not rendered them immune, however, from accusations of 'Orientalism' in a pejorative sense – in other words, that they either formulated or perpetuated caricatures and stereotypes of Islam which are not accurate. Scholars of the next generation have also had the same accusation made against them. As well as the work of Edward Said which has already been referred to, a work entitled *Orientalism, Islam and Islamists* investigates scholars such as H. A. R. Gibb (1895/1312–1971/1391) and G. E. von Grunebaum (1909/1327–1972/1392), as well as Macdonald and the still living scholars Bernard Lewis and Kenneth Cragg, and suggests that all are, to one degree or another, guilty of errors of either description or interpretation.[22]

There are connections, it is true, between most of these modern Western scholars of Islam and either the Foreign Offices of the countries in which they lived and worked or Christian missions of one kind or another. Macdonald, Goldziher, and Hurgronje, for example, all met the Anglican missionary Temple Gairdner during his *Wanderjahr*, his year of absence from Cairo between 1910/1328 and 1911/1329; Macdonald, on the strength of a brief earlier meeting in Cairo, invited Gairdner to spend a term with him in Hartford, and afterwards, back in Europe, Gairdner had a three-hour talk, nearly all in Arabic, with Hurgronje, who suggested that he spend some time with Goldziher, which he did in the summer of 1911/1329. Both Macdonald and Goldziher tried to persuade Gairdner to devote himself to scholarship, but the demands of the mission in Egypt precluded this.[23] Gibb, having been orphaned at the age of two when his father, who was the manager of a land reclamation company in Egypt, died, was sent at the age of five to a school for the children of missionaries in Edinburgh while his mother continued to teach at the Church of Scotland school in Alexandria; and it is true, as Said remarks, that 'in his mature years Gibb was often to be met with speaking and writing for policy-determining organizations'.[24] But it is a rare human being who manages not be a member of a religious community (or a non-religious one), just as it is hard for someone who wishes to travel not to be a citizen of a particular state, or someone who wishes to communicate not to speak a particular language; and in the English-speaking world at least professors of English Literature are assured of a ready audience, but professors of Arabic or Islamic Studies are not. Involvement in policy-making may therefore be necessary rather than a matter of choice, and equally Edward Said's membership of the Palestinian National Council from 1977/1397 to 1991/1412 does not necessarily mean that he has nothing useful to say about the Middle East. Western scholars of Islam can therefore sometimes be judged too harshly; but the search for an impartial and self-critical understanding must continue.

CHANGING CHRISTIAN THINKING ABOUT ISLAM

All of this extra information and experience of the world of Islam is one factor which has contributed towards the emergence of new Christian thinking about Islam over the course of the past two centuries or so. But this new thinking was not simply the result of greater understanding and contact – it was also the result of the fresh thinking within the Christian community in the context of the emergence of modern theology. Thus in the context of English Deism, Lord Herbert of Cherbury (1583/991–1648/1058), suggested that there are five notions which are common to all religions, and these have been inscribed by God in all human hearts: religious communities have subsequently elaborated ceremonies, organisations, sacred books and other institutions, but these are simply different constructions on the original common foundation. Herbert was not always accurate in his description of other religious traditions, believing, for example, that Ramaḍān was observed twice each year, but he was at least aware of common patterns in different communities.[25] In Germany the last play of G. E. Lessing (1729/1141–1781/1195), entitled *Nathan the Wise,* includes a scene where a parable is told by Nathan, a rich Jew in Jerusalem, to the sultan Saladin. A man who is the possessor of a ring which has magic powers has three sons; he cannot pass the ring on to all of them so he has two identical rings made and gives one to each son; after his death, when they find out that there are three rings and not one, the sons begin to squabble about which is the original ring, but this cannot be proven. No more, suggests Lessing, can it be proven which of Judaism, Christianity and Islam is the genuine faith.[26]

The person who is usually described as the founder of modern Christian theology, Friedrich Schleiermacher (1768/1182–1834/1250), was influenced to some extent by Goethe and the Romantic movement and on this basis suggested that at the heart of all religion was not so much a system of belief or morality as a feeling of absolute dependence. This universal feeling has been developed, according to Schleiermacher, in different ways in different religious communities, each having a distinctive emphasis on some particular aspect of the relationship between God and human beings. Christianity and Islam, he says, are contending for the mastery of the world, but the relationship between them is not one of truth and falsehood, but rather one of truer and less true.[27] And as the nineteenth/thirteenth century moved into the twentieth/fourteenth century Ernst Troeltsch (1865/1282–1923/1341), whose detailed empirical investigation of Christian history led him to formulate the vital distinction between 'church' and 'sect' type organisations, also wrestled with the question of the relationship between Christianity and other religions: he sought to combine a retention of a view of the 'absoluteness' of Christianity and the development of a certain relativism as regards the historical development of different religious traditions. The tension between these two aspirations was something which Troeltsch never quite succeeded in resolving.[28]

On the basis of these foundations, twentieth/fourteenth-century Christian theology of religions has tended to crystallise around three main points of view. These are commonly called 'exclusivism', which holds that salvation (or being accepted by God) is realised only through belief in Christ and membership of the Christian community, a view represented by the Swiss Protestant theologian Karl Barth (1886/1303–1968/1388); 'inclusivism', which holds that salvation is made available through Christ, but that this should be understood inclusively, so that members of other religious communities may be saved, but through Christ, so that they are, in a difficult and controversial phrase of Karl Rahner (1904/1322–1984/1404), the German Roman Catholic theologian who is representative of this point of view, 'anonymous Christians'; and 'pluralism', which suggests that there is a plurality of ways to salvation, so that members of other religious communities may be saved through their own religious traditions, a view commonly associated with the British philosopher of religion, John Hick (b. 1922/1340).[29]

These three views are, of course, no more than convenient shorthand terms. Generally speaking 'exclusivism' is the dominant view among evangelical Protestant Christians, 'inclusivism' among Roman Catholic Christians, and 'pluralism' among liberal Protestant Christians, but these boundaries are by no means watertight, with some evangelical Christians, for example, moving towards 'inclusivism' and some Roman Catholic Christians coming closer to 'pluralism'. Equally some Eastern Orthodox theologians are more 'exclusivist' and some more 'inclusivist'. Additionally it is not uncommon for individual theologians to change their perspectives on this question, with John Hick being a well-known example of someone who moved from 'exclusivism' to 'pluralism'.[30] Each perspective, in other words, itself contains a broad spectrum of opinion, and the terms are no more than a shorthand guide to the discussion; nevertheless, they serve as convenient markers for the main options in the discussion.[31]

In this debate it might have been thought that Christian missionaries were uniformly solid supporters of 'exclusivism', given that part of the reason for the growth of missions, particularly Protestant ones, was a desire to bring the news of salvation through Christ to regions where it had not previously been heard, but this was not in fact the case. As E. J. Sharpe has made clear in his study of Christian attitudes towards Hinduism, missionary opinion was by no means unanimous or static, with the Scottish missionary J. N. Farquhar (1861/1277–1929/1347) becoming an early representative of a kind of 'inclusivism'.[32] Clinton Bennett has highlighted something similar with reference to missionary opinion about Islam, and Kenneth Cracknell, through a detailed study of some of the responses to a questionnaire which was sent out as part of the preparation for the Protestant World Missionary Conference of 1910/1328 in Edinburgh, has concluded that in some ways nineteenth/thirteenth-century Christian thinking, including that of some missionaries, was readier than subsequent Christian thought to contemplate continuity rather than discontinuity between Christianity and other religions; in that sense, he suggests, under the influence of Barth and Kraemer, the twentieth/fourteenth century has gone backwards rather than forwards.[33]

It has been suggested that the question of the relationship between Christianity and other religions is the most important question facing Christian theology today, as migration, travel and technology make contact and exchange between members of different religious communities easier and more common.[34] This has not prevented some important recent studies from failing to look at the question altogether.[35] But we must turn now from investigating Christian thinking about other religions in general to looking at Christian thinking about Islam in particular.

Here too we will find considerable diversity. As a representative, firstly, of a broadly 'exclusivist' stance, in the tradition of Karl Barth, we will look at Hendrik Kraemer (1888/1305–1965/1385). Kraemer was born in Amsterdam, and studied Oriental Studies at Leiden before going to Indonesia as a missionary, to work for the Dutch Bible Society. He was there between 1922/1340 and 1928/1346, and again between 1930/1349 and 1936/1355, and during the 1930s/1350s he also became increasingly influential in missionary circles worldwide.

Much controversy in those circles had been stimulated by the publication, in 1933/1352, of a report entitled *Rethinking Missions: a Laymen's Enquiry*, edited by an American Congregationalist, W. E. Hocking (1873/1290–1966/1386), who taught Philosophy of Religion at

Harvard.[36] This report suggested a radical re-appraisal of the traditional Christian understanding of mission, proposing instead co-operation between different religious traditions, which would lead to mutual discovery and interchange and eventually to the emergence of a world community. 'In such a scheme, conceptions of Christian uniqueness, absoluteness or finality were likely to disappear as barriers of interchange.'[37] Kraemer was the architect of a vigorous reaction against this view, which involved a reassertion of the uniqueness of the Christian message, its universal relevance, and the need, therefore, for a clear-cut sense of Christian mission. In 1937/1356 he returned to Europe, taking up the position of Professor of the History and Phenomenology of Religions at Leiden, and in the next year he published *The Christian Message in a Non-Christian World*, which is the clearest statement of his views, and was a kind of preparation for a large missionary conference held at Tambaram in South India.[38]

The influence of Barth on Kraemer, in terms of his stress on the discontinuity between the Gospel on the one hand, and religion on the other, was clear, but whereas Barth famously dismissed other religious traditions on the basis of his *a priori* assumptions, Kraemer at least wrote on the basis of considerable missionary experience, especially of Islam in Indonesia.[39] His conclusions concerning Islam, however, were pretty negative:

> Islam in its constituent elements and apprehensions must be called a superficial religion. The grand simplicity of its conception of God cannot efface this fact and retrieve its patent superficiality in regard to the most essential problems of religious life. Islam might be called a religion that has almost no questions and no answers. In a certain respect its greatness lies there, because this question-less and answer-less condition is a consistent exemplification of its deepest spirit, expressed in its name: Islam, that is, absolute surrender to God, the Almighty Lord.[40]
>
> This religion, so lacking in depth, is also, when one considers its origin and material, an unoriginal religion, and yet notwithstanding that it excels all other religions in creating in its adherents a feeling of absolute religious superiority. From this superiority-feeling and from this fantastic self-consciousness of Islam is born that stubborn refusal to open the mind towards another spiritual world, as a result of which Islam is such an enigmatic missionary object.[41]

> It is a very curious thing to note that in the really religious conceptions of Islam one can point to what might be called a process of super-heating. The conception of revelation in its ruthless consequence is super-heated. The same can be said about the conception of God. Islam is theocentric, but in a super-heated state. Allah in Islam becomes white-hot Majesty, white-hot Omnipotence, white-hot Uniqueness. His personality evaporates and vanishes in the burning-heat of His aspects. These de-personalized aspects, although of course not devoid of the personal connotation connected with Allah, are the real objects of religious devotion. The surrender to Allah, the fundamental religious attitude in Islam, has that same quality of absolute ruthlessness.[42]

Islam is thus unoriginal, superficial, simple, ruthless, stubborn, and has a superiority-complex, and even if, as has also been suggested with respect to Barth, Kraemer moderated his views somewhat towards the end of his life, his initial judgement was clearly quite harsh.[43]

Let us turn now to 'inclusivism'. We have already noted the dominance of this perspective in contemporary Roman Catholic thinking, and this can be illustrated with reference to Islam quite simply by quoting the ground-breaking statement concerning Islam which was formulated by the Second Vatican Council in 1965/1385:

> The Church also regards with esteem the Muslims who worship the one, subsistent, merciful and almighty God, the Creator of heaven and earth, who has spoken to man. Islam willingly traces its descent back to Abraham, and just as he submitted himself to God, the Muslims endeavour to submit themselves to his mysterious decrees. They venerate Jesus as a prophet, without, however, recognising him as God, and they pay honour to his virgin mother Mary and sometimes also invoke her with devotion. Further, they expect a day of judgement when God will raise all men from the dead and reward them. For this reason they attach importance to the moral life and worship God, mainly by prayer, alms-giving and fasting.
>
> If in the course of the centuries there has arisen not infrequent discussion and hostility between Christian and Muslim, this sacred Council now urges everyone to forget the past, to make sincere efforts at mutual understanding and to work together in protecting and promoting for the good and benefit of all men, social justice, good morals as well as peace and freedom.[44]

For a religious institution which at least since 1302/702 had held to the view that outside itself there was no salvation (*extra ecclesiam nulla salus*), the whole statement about other religions, within which this section about Islam appeared, represented a considerable shift of emphasis.[45] Part of the reason for the change was a shift towards the conciliar view of authority within the church as represented by a figure such as Nicholas of Cusa (1401/803–1464/868), whose views concerning Islam we referred to in Chapter 5, but a more important reason was the influence of the French Islamicist Louis Massignon (1883/1300–1962/1382).

Massignon's early life provides a fascinating key to the later evolution of his thought concerning Islam. Having lost the Christian faith into which he had been baptised during his teens, he recovered it as a result of the care with which he was looked after by a Muslim family while suffering from malaria in Iraq in 1908/1326. He went on to a distinguished academic career in France, during the course of which he published many books, particularly on Sufism and the figure who held a considerable fascination for him throughout his life, al-Ḥallāj (857/243–922/309), and he was intimately involved in many of the debates, political and otherwise, which took place during his lifetime. In 1950/1369 he was ordained a priest of the Greek Catholic church (which permits its priests to be married, as Massignon was). In the words of one recent commentator: 'By the force of his personality and the originality of his ideas Louis Massignon was perhaps the only Islamic scholar who was a central figure in the intellectual life of his time.'[46]

Massignon was convinced that the Holy Spirit was active in Islam, perhaps most dramatically in the life and death of al-Ḥallāj, which Massignon interpreted as being a kind of re-enactment of the life and death of Christ, since al-Ḥallāj was crucified in Baghdad after he had exclaimed 'Anā al-ḥaqq' ('I am the truth'). He went so far as to publish, privately, a book in which he expressed the hope that al-Ḥallāj might be recognised one day by the church as a martyr. But he did not present al-Ḥallāj as a pseudo-Christian, or an 'anonymous Christian', to use Rahner's phrase; rather, he suggested that al-Ḥallāj was an authentically Islamic figure, and his existence within the Islamic community was clear evidence that the grace of Christ was as real outside the Christian community as inside it. Breiner summarises:

> Massignon never sought to blur the distinctions between Christianity and Islam. He did not believe that Islam was a kind of 'close approximation' of Christianity and that its spiritual value rested in its approach to the teaching of Christianity. Nor did he have any doubts that Islam lacked something in comparison with

Christianity. But he did see believing Muslims as men and women of the Spirit, and he did see the grace of God, which is the grace of Christ, at work in Islam. He, therefore, had no doubts that Islam bound men and women to God.[47]

Great stress was therefore laid by Massignon on Islam as an Abrahamic religion, which in a sense provided a genealogy for the activity of the Spirit amongst Muslims, and the influence of his ideas on this can be seen in the careful wording of the statement of the Second Vatican Council. Among the many influential people with whom Massignon corresponded was Cardinal Montini, the Archbishop of Milan who in 1963/1383 became Pope Paul VI, and although Massignon himself died before Montini became Pope, it was partly through this contact that his ideas exerted so much influence at the Council.[48] Subsequently Massignon has enjoyed huge influence both among many of the leading Roman Catholic thinkers about Islam and beyond the Catholic church too; this includes considerable influence among Muslim thinkers from many different parts of the world, so it cannot be denied that he has been one of the major architects of new Christian thinking about Islam in the twentieth/fourteenth century.[49]

It would not be true, however, to suggest that 'inclusivism' has been influential only in Roman Catholic thinking about Islam. To take two other examples, the British Anglican scholar Bishop Kenneth Cragg (b. 1913/1331), has also sought to interpret Islam positively to Christians, as well as seeking to make traditional Christianity more comprehensible to Muslims, particularly in his *The Call of the Minaret*, and has perhaps gone further than any other Christian writer in seeking to weigh the spiritual meaning and significance of the Qur'ān for Christians.[50] Building in a sense on the work of Temple Gairdner, Cragg has worked hard to interpret the two faiths to each other, and this has sometimes resulted in harsh judgements being made on his work by members of both communities. Something of the hurt which this has caused to him, as well as a good insight into what might be described as the ambivalence of his position, can be seen in an article whose title is itself very revealing, 'Being Christian and Being Muslim: a Personal Debate'. Here Cragg makes clear both his admiration for some aspects of Islam, especially the Qur'ān's stress on 'letting God be God' and locating humanity in its proper place as the 'tenant' or 'trustee' (*khalīfa*) of creation, and also his negative reaction towards other aspects of Islamic teaching, especially the Qur'ān's view of divine omnipotence, which he suggests is so overwhelming as to depersonalise God altogether, and the Muslim view of Muḥammad as the passive recipient of divine revelation. These two features, Cragg suggests, together tend to result in the emergence of repressive societies. 'Islam both attracts and repels me', he therefore asserts.[51]

An Orthodox Christian who might also be called an 'inclusivist' is Georges Khodr, the Greek Orthodox Metropolitan of Mount Lebanon, who in a paper originally read to the Central Committee Meeting of the World Council of Churches in Addis Ababa in 1971/1390, suggested that Christians need to develop a fresh and wider appreciation of the activities of the Holy Spirit. An important part of the background to this idea, of course, is the dispute between Eastern and Western Christians about the 'procession' of the Holy Spirit, which has been referred to in Chapter 1 above: does the Holy Spirit proceed from the Father only (as the Eastern churches hold) or does the Spirit proceed from the Father and the Son (as opinion developed in the West)? If the first view is correct, then it is easier for Christians to perceive the activity of the Holy Spirit even where the Son is not specifically named, and Khodr suggests that:

> [C]ontemporary theology must go beyond the notion of 'salvation history' in order to rediscover the meaning of the *oikonomia*. The economy of Christ cannot be reduced to its historical manifestation . . . The very notion of economy is a notion of mystery . . . Within the religions, its task is to reveal to the world of the religions the God who is hidden within it, in anticipation of the final concrete unfolding and manifestation of the Mystery.[52]

Probably the best example of a Christian who adopts a broadly 'pluralist' approach towards Islam is the Canadian Wilfred Cantwell Smith (b. 1916/1334–2000/1420). Like Kraemer, Smith worked as a missionary for a number of years, in India, between 1941/1360 and 1945/1364, so he was there during the period which led to Indian independence from Britain in 1947/1366. This period witnessed considerable communal tension between Muslims and Hindus and eventually, when independence came, saw the migration of some five million Hindus from what became Pakistan to India, with the migration of a similar number of Muslims in the other direction, and the death of perhaps half a million people in communal massacres. It was in this context that Smith wrote his first book, *Modern Islam in India*, first published in 1943/1362, which is in effect a Marxist analysis of the different streams of thought which were then influential within the Muslim community. The experience of living in India at that period, together with the observations he was able to make concerning the practice of Islam in different regions of the Muslim world on the basis of a Rockefeller

Travelling Scholarship in 1948/1367, which were expressed in his second book, *Islam in Modern History*, seems to have made Smith particularly sensitive to the communal dimension of religious life and the distinction which needs to be drawn between the outward and the inward aspects of religion. This was articulated in his book *The Meaning and End of Religion*, where Smith distinguished between what he called 'the cumulative tradition', the outward manifestations of religion in terms of rituals, beliefs, communities and institutions, and 'faith', the attitude of trust which is at the core of all religious experience.[53]

With respect to Islam, Smith is therefore keenly aware that, like all religious traditions, Islam has outward manifestations and an inner spiritual core, and he insists that Islam can be a vehicle for the true knowledge of God:

> I should not think that any Muslim would be imperceptive who carefully read Aquinas, or Calvin, or Kierkegaard, and failed to see how valuably these men wrote about God, and about the human condition in relation to Him. Similarly, I should think that any Christian would be imperceptive who carefully read al-Ghazzali or al-Razi, and similarly failed. As a matter of fact, however, I myself have never actually met either a Muslim or a Christian who has done such reading and has not been deeply appreciative. If, of course, you feel, without having read them, that on principle these theologians could not possibly know anything about God worth reporting, because of the finite situation out of which they wrote concerning the infinite that had entered their lives, then this is a comment on your theology, not theirs . . .
>
> It has been argued, by some Christians, that outside the Christian tradition human beings may know God in part, but cannot know Him fully. This is undoubtedly correct, but the implications are precarious. One may well ask such theorists: Is it possible for a Christian to know God fully? I personally do not see what it might mean to say that anyone, Christian or Muslim or whatever, has a complete knowledge of God. The finite cannot encompass the infinite. Touching the hem of his garment, we apprehend transcendence – but we do not comprehend it . . .
>
> However one may take such observations, I would certainly say that I myself have never met a Christian who knew God fully. I have, however, met some Muslims who manifestly know Him more fully than certain of my fellow Christians seem to do. And I

> feel sure that here are Muslims who have met some Christians who, they have sensed, have known God less partially than certain of their nominally fellow Muslims appear to have. Such impressions are, of course, quite tentative; both they and I, in any case, would be quite content to leave the judgement to God. On one point I am not inclined to be tentative; that God, rather than you or I, is the one to pass that judgement.[54]

It is on the basis of thinking like this that Smith then formulates his ambitious and audacious project for moving towards the formulation of a World Theology.[55]

As has been suggested, other Christian thinkers also lean in the direction of 'pluralism'. It will be interesting, in particular, to see Hans Küng's forthcoming volume on Islam, which will complete his trilogy on the Abrahamic religions.[56] Many other Christian writers on Islam could, of course, have been examined.[57] Moreover, the limitations of the scheme of 'exclusivism', 'inclusivism', and 'pluralism' apply just as much to Christian thinking about Islam as they do to Christian thinking about other religions generally, but the writers we have looked at at least indicate something of the range of contemporary Christian thinking about Islam, and also the extent to which new approaches have emerged in recent years.[58]

CHANGING MUSLIM THINKING ABOUT CHRISTIANITY

As we turn now to contemporary Muslim thinking about Christianity, here too we will find considerable diversity of thought, and also some creative new thinking. We will also find that, to some extent, the categories of 'exclusivist', 'inclusivist', and 'pluralist' can also be applied to different Muslim writers, but these terms need to be used equally as cautiously in this context as they do with reference to contemporary Christian theology of religions.

An example of a Muslim writer who might be called an 'exclusivist', a kind of mirror-image to Hendrik Kraemer, is the Palestinian writer Ismā'īl al-Farūqī (1921/1339–1986/1406). Born in Jaffa in Palestine, Farūqī studied at the American University in Beirut, and after graduation he returned to Palestine to work in the Civil Service, rising to become District Governor of Galilee. The events of 1948/1367, however, involving the creation of the state of Israel and the effective partition of Palestine, made him and his family refugees, and he left Palestine for the United States. There he took two Masters degrees, and obtained his PhD in Philosophy from Indiana University in 1952/1371. Between 1954/1373 and 1958/1377 he studied at al-Azhar in Cairo, and then in 1959/1378 he returned to North America, at the invitation of

Wilfred Cantwell Smith, to join the Divinity Faculty of McGill University in Montreal, Canada.

At McGill Farūqī studied Judaism and Christianity, and this period was the genesis of his very important study *Christian Ethics*, which will be examined in more detail below. He later returned to the United States to set up an Islamic Studies programme at Syracuse University in New York, then went on to do the same at Temple University in Philadelphia. Throughout his life Farūqī travelled widely, lecturing in Pakistan and Malaysia among other places, and he also participated in a number of conferences on themes related to Judaism, Christianity and Islam, as well as being one of the founders of the International Institute of Islamic Thought and an adviser to the Muslim Students' Association of North America. The circumstances of his death, however, in 1986/1406, were extremely mysterious: both he and his wife were attacked and brutally stabbed to death in their home in the early hours of the morning, and no satisfactory explanation of the motives for the attack has ever been produced.[59]

Farūqī's first major publication focused on the concept of Arabism and the relationship between Arabism and Islam. Here he reflected on, and contributed to, a widespread debate which was going on in the Arab world concerning identity: did linguistic and ethnic identity have precedence, so that both Arab Christians and Arab Muslims shared an identity which transcended their religious differences, or was religious identity primary, with the result that there was a rather deep separation between Christian and Muslim Arabs?[60] Farūqī's contribution to this discussion was a paean of praise to Arabism, which he conceived as having a kind of world-redeeming mission since the Arabs were the bearers of a divine message. Arabism, in other words, was integrally related to Islam, while Judaism and Christianity, Farūqī suggested in Part I of the book, were respectively the first and second 'moments' of Arab consciousness. This view resulted in some rather puzzling statements such as: 'Arab consciousness . . . regards all Judaism, Christianity and Islam as moments of its long and arduous course of growth beginning, in childhood with Adam, and reaching the age of reason in Mohammed, the "seal of the prophets"', and 'Monotheism is exclusively an Arab thought'.[61]

His more detailed discussion of Judaism and Christianity, however, revealed that he had investigated their history and development carefully, and with respect to Christianity this was made even clearer in his next major work, *Christian Ethics: a Historical and Systematic Study of its Dominant Ideas*.[62] This work was the fruit of his period of studying Christianity in McGill, and the Foreword, by Stanley Brice Frost, the Dean of Graduate Studies and Research at McGill, makes it clear that Farūqī had made a considerable impact there:

Isma'il Faruqi for two years attended lectures, participated in seminars, read widely, and engaged in many a Senior Common Room debate. Looking back on those two years, it seems to me that they were one long, continuous, provocative discussion, in which my colleagues and I learned to appreciate Dr. Faruqi as a tenacious disputant, a stimulating colleague, and a warm-hearted friend.[63]

The Preface to the book was then written, shortly before his death, by Hendrik Kraemer, who called it 'the first serious attempt by a scholarly, well-trained Muslim to study Christian dogma and ethics according to his understanding of them and is based on a wide and penetrating study of their historical development'. Kraemer went on to say that 'Dr Faruqi deserves appreciation and recognition for writing a documented book on Christian ethics according to modern scientific methods of analysis and critical appraisal of source material.'[64] He does not attempt to disguise the fact, however, that the book is 'in fact (though not in intention) a vigorous refutation and rejection of Christianity, especially Western Christianity', or that it is 'polemical and condemnatory' in tone.[65]

Farūqī's main thesis is not in fact particularly original, suggesting as it does that the original message of Jesus is perfectly acceptable but that it has been corrupted subsequently by his so-called followers, beginning with Paul.[66] What is new about Farūqī's approach, however, is firstly the degree of detail which he is able to bring to his argument, based on his knowledge of original, as opposed to second-hand, sources: he has clearly read Biblical sources, describing Ezra and Nehemiah as 'racial fanatics', he is clearly at home with the Western Christian tradition, including Augustine and the Reformers, and he does not hesitate to discuss the works of contemporary figures such as Stephen Neill and Hendrik Kraemer, or Karl Barth, William Temple and Reinhold Niebuhr. Secondly, there is the language which he uses to present his case: he is perfectly at home with the language of *epoché* and metareligion, and Western Christianity, indeed, he sums up as having degenerated into 'peccatism' (or obsession with sin), and 'saviourism' (passive reliance on a third party for redemption), both of which, when combined with millennialism, Farūqī suggests, have led to Christians failing to work out their faith properly in the affairs of society. Moreover his basic thesis is developed in a rather original way, since he suggests that Jesus formulated an ethical breakthrough, in terms of challenging racialism and legalism and moving on to universalism and the interiorization of ethics, which later Western Christian thought then lost, whereas earlier Muslim exponents of the argument about Jesus's message being corrupted by his followers tended to state the opposite, namely that Jesus did adhere to Jewish law but his followers then decreed that to do so was no longer necessary.

A crucial element of Farūqī's biography, which explains some of his comments about Judaism and the Jewish background to Jesus, was his experience of Zionism in 1948/1367. He addressed the question of the relationship between Islam, Judaism and Zionism in his 1980/1400 publication *Islam and the Problem of Israel*.[67] But his antagonism towards Zionism did not prevent him from wrestling seriously with Judaism, and in 1982/1402 he edited a volume devoted to discussions between Judaism, Christianity, and Islam.[68] Equally the rather critical judgement on Christianity which we have seen above did not preclude his participation with Christians in many conferences devoted to Christian–Muslim relations, and many of the articles which he wrote at different stages of his career have been helpfully collected together in one volume recently by Dr Ataullah Siddiqui of the Islamic Foundation in Leicester.[69]

Eleven articles are collected together in this volume, with the first part focusing on the inter-relationship between Near Eastern Religions, including Judaism and Christianity but also including Ancient Mesapotamia and Egypt; the second on the relationship between Islam and Christianity in particular; and the third part containing two papers on the emotive subject of *da'wa* (mission), one of which was originally delivered to the 1976/1396 World Council of Churches Consultation of the topic, and the other to a Muslim audience in Kuala Lumpur five years later. The papers in Part I reflect something of the perspective of Farūqī's *On Arabism*, but the most relevant to our theme are those in Part II, and three in particular are significant: in one (Chapter 9), Farūqī outlines his views concerning the position of non-Muslims in Islamic societies, a topic which has been the focus of much subsequent discussion too.[70] Chapter 5, simply entitled 'Islam and Other Faiths', is a helpful overview of Farūqī's thinking, but perhaps the most interesting is Chapter 8, entitled 'Islam and Christianity: Diatribe or Dialogue?'[71]

Farūqī begins by stating clearly that neither of the two faiths can live in isolation, and they must be interested in each other's claims, which they should investigate through dialogue. Dialogue, he suggests, must lead to conversion, not to Christianity or Islam but to the truth, and this has some interesting consequences:

> In our day and age, exclusivism has a bad smell. Having worked with probabilities for three hundred years . . . and with sceptical

> notions of the truth for over half a century, we contract our noses whenever an exclusive claim to truth is made. As men of religion, I hope we all have the strength of our convictions, and feel neither offended or shamed by what our faiths claim. On the other hand, there is something shameful about exclusivism, just as there is about mission . . . We regard the exclusivist in science as stupid, even insane, for running in the face of evidence . . . But where the evidence is significant or conclusive, to flout it is a deficiency. . . . exclusivism is epistemological and hence not subject to moral considerations.
>
> Islam and Christianity cannot therefore be impervious to each other's claims; for just as it is irrefutably true that each lays claim to *the* truth and does so candidly, it is irrefutably true that the truth is one, and unless the standpoint is one of scepticism, of two diverse claims to *the* truth, one of both must be false![72]

For all his commitment to dialogue, therefore, and for all his contact and engagement with Christians and members of other religious communities, it seems that ultimately, Farūqī was, rather like Kraemer, an 'exclusivist', not perhaps in the traditional sense, but in a peculiarly personal sense. There is an element of paradox in much of Farūqī's thinking, and perhaps the key to this can be provided by the comments of two Western scholars. The first comes from Stanley Brice Frost in his Foreword to *Christian Ethics*, written relatively early in Farūqī's career: 'He became a man of two worlds, intelligently at ease in both and at peace with neither.'[73] And the second comes from a book written after his death about Islamic *da'wa* in the West:

> It perhaps appears contradictory that al-Faruqi has been cited in so many contexts. In actuality this is only indicative of the complexity of this individual. He was an ecumenicist with regard to the *devout* adherents of other faiths, but an activist dā'ī par excellence to those whom he considered secularized, be they nominally Muslim or blatantly non-Muslim.[74]

For all his undoubted knowledge about Christianity, therefore, rather like Kraemer with all his knowledge of Islam, Farūqī somehow lacked that inner sympathy which would have enabled him to gain a deeper appreciation of Christianity. Perhaps, on the other hand, like Kraemer, he moved on during the course of his life to a more open set of opinions, but fundamentally he seems to have remained an 'exclusivist'.[75]

As an example of a Muslim writer who would most naturally be described as an 'inclusivist', we will look at some of the writings of the

Tunisian scholar, Muḥammad al-Ṭālbī, who was born in the same year as Ismā'īl al-Farūqī, 1921/1339.

Until his retirement Ṭālbī was Professor of History in the University of Tunis. He had previously studied in Paris, where he obtained his doctorate in 1966/1386 on the history of the political history of the Aghlabid emirate, which dominated north Africa west of Morocco from 800/184 to 909/296, and was responsible for the Muslim conquest of Sicily. He later edited a medieval Spanish Muslim text on the important subject of *bid'a* (innovation), the *Kitāb al-ḥawādith wa'l-bid'a* (The Book of Cases and Innovation) of al-Ṭurṭūshī (d. 1126/520), and this detailed examination of the medieval arguments against innovation seems to have stimulated his own later thinking about the idea of development in Islamic thought.[76] In a conference paper he addressed the difficult question, which has been examined above in Chapter 4, of why the Christian church disappeared in north Africa.[77]

As a result of a number of experiences and contacts in Paris and elsewhere, Ṭālbī also developed an interest in Christian–Muslim relations, and he made an important contribution to their development with the publication in 1972/1392 of a short work entitled *Islam et Dialogue*.[78] Originally delivered as a public lecture in Rome, this paper stressed the importance for Islam of developing dialogue in order to re-establish contact with the world at large. Christianity, he suggested, had never lost this contact, as could be seen in the number of specialists in Islamic Studies:

> In every domain and in every scientific discipline the Church can produce people qualified to enter into dialogue . . . And what is Islam doing in face of such an unprecedented effort by the Church? It offers us a theology whose evolution practically came to an end in the 12th century.[79]

For the future the task is to avoid polemic and renounce the goal of the conversion of the other. Building on the precedent of Muslim writers such as al-Ghazālī (1058/450–1111/505) or Muḥammad 'Abduh (1849/1265–1905/1323), Ṭālbī suggests that there are certain circumstances in which non-Muslims can be saved, particularly on the basis of sincerity and an honest life.[80]

> It is not impossible, therefore, neither for Islam nor for Christianity, nor indeed for the other main religions, on the basis of their texts and with the support even of a certain ancient theological tradition, to elaborate a theology which would allow

> for a certain degree of plurality in the ways of salvation, were it only because one cannot forbid Divine Goodness from overflowing, in a gesture of justice, of mercy and of love, beyond the strict limits of any given Church in order to embrace all men of good will who live exemplary lives. In the end God remains entirely and freely the one who judges, and we must abandon ourselves confidently to His Wisdom. In any case we must abstain from passing judgement in His place.[81]

Ṭālbī does not go on to espouse 'pluralism' in the fullest sense, however: his reference to 'a certain degree of plurality' is therefore important, and he goes on to insist that he is aware of the danger of relativism. 'I trust that my readers will have understood that in my way of seeing things such a danger exists only for one who is not a true believer. For the true believer the epicentre of the faith he professes and to which he gives witness continues to be the Absolute.'[82]

In a more personal later article Ṭālbī provides an outline of how his thinking evolved towards these views.[83] His earliest schooling was in a French milieu. As he went to and fro from school he would pass a shop window which displayed parallel passages from the Bible and the Qur'ān; inside sat the (presumably Protestant) missionary at his desk. As he entered the new 'European' town, he would also pass a statue of Cardinal Lavigerie (1825/1240–1892/1309), the Archbishop of Algiers and the founder of the White Fathers. His time in Paris was very important: he attended Mass with his landlady, and he sat at the feet of Louis Massignon and Régis Blachère, who was an agnostic but whose critical approach to texts, including the Qur'ān, impressed him. Later he refers to two figures who influenced his thinking about religious diversity:

> The late German Jesuit Karl Rahner . . . was of the view that God is willing the salvation of everyone, and that this salvation has been made possible by the life, death and resurrection of Jesus Christ. He developed the idea that those who he calls 'the anonymous Christians' may be, within some parameters, saved by God's grace outside the confines of the 'visible church'. As far as I am personally concerned, and *mutatis mutandis* of course, I do not feel myself very far from Rahner's general frame of thought . . .
>
> More recently, and on a much larger scale, John Hick, who is more philosopher than theologian, questioned the uniqueness, decisiveness, and even the centrality of Jesus Christ as the single way of salvation. But Hick is a rather controversial figure, and his

> Copernican Revolution, putting *God*, and not Christianity, at the heart of our universe, has little chance of prevailing. If all religions, equally and without preliminary conditions, save, we cannot avoid relativism, and relativism is the ruin of the very notion of Truth.[84]

Most recently, in two works published in Tunis, Professor Ṭālbī has brought together in Arabic his reflections on many of the themes which have preoccupied him during his life. The first is entitled *'Iyāl allāh: afkār jadīda fī 'alāqāt al-muslim bi-ghayrihi* (The Children of God: New Thoughts on the Muslim's Relationships with Others), and the second *Ummat al-wasaṭ: al-islām wa taḥaddiyāt al-mu'āṣarāt* (The Middle Community: Islam and the Challenges of Modernity).[85] The first of these is based on conversations between Ṭālbī and two fellow professors in the University of Tunis; its three parts focus mainly on Professor Ṭālbī's autobiography, the text and meaning of the Qur'ān, particularly with respect to political questions, and questions relating to law, including such difficult issues as homosexuality and polygamy. The second volume then addresses modernity in general, Qur'ānic exegesis and Islamic history, including the significance of the early Muslim community's change of *qibla* (direction of prayer) from Jerusalem to Mecca, religious freedom, discussed both in the context of the modern debate about human rights and in the context of the ideals and the realities of medieval Andalucia, the significance of Darwin's theory of evolution, and the position of women, which is again discussed both with reference to particular Qur'ānic verses and the historical realities of medieval Spain. Throughout, in a clear testimony to the influence of Henri Bergson on Ṭālbī's thought, there is a stress on the great importance of a reading of the Qur'ān which is dynamic and forward-looking, rather than static and backward-looking; this, Ṭālbī insists, is not betrayal but fidelity to the original message of the Qur'ān.

Many of the ideas in these volumes are not new, building on and in some cases based on articles previously published elsewhere in either English or French, but their being made available in Arabic is extremely significant, and they have caused considerable controversy in some parts of the Arab world, including Morocco. In his discussion of the first of the two books, Ron Nettler highlights Ṭālbī's view that the best way to deal with religious pluralism (*al-ta'addudiyya*) is through a recognition of the simple fact of difference (*al-ikhtilāf*), a concept which is well-established within Islam with respect to the four schools of law, whose differences are regarded as permissible and are therefore tolerated, and which Ṭālbī suggests should be extended to incorporate different religious traditions.[86] The way in which Ṭālbī sees the relationship between Islam on the one hand and Judaism and Christianity on the other is therefore that the message of Islam succeeds but does not supersede the earlier messages: Islam completes or fulfils the earlier revelations, but this does not mean replacing them, for the Qur'ān itself speaks of its message both confirming and guarding what had come before (5: 48). Quoting the words of the New Testament, Matthew 5: 17, where Jesus says that he has come not to refute or abolish the law, but to complete or fulfil it, Ṭālbī thus suggests that Islam is to Judaism and Christianity as Christianity is to Judaism, and once again this makes clear the way in which his views are essentially 'inclusivist'.[87]

It is more difficult to point to any Muslim writer about Christianity or other religions in general who could easily be called a 'pluralist', in the sense in which the word has been used earlier with reference to John Hick or Wilfred Cantwell Smith. There is, however, what could be called a kind of 'proto-pluralism' which can be seen emerging in the writings of a number of young Turkish Muslim writers who have undertaken research either on different approaches to the philosophical question of religious pluralism or on different Christian approaches to Islam.

Thus Adnan Aslan, a Research Fellow at the Center for Islamic Studies in Istanbul, in his PhD thesis submitted to the University of Lancaster, investigated the attitudes to religious pluralism of John Hick and the Iranian thinker Seyyed Hossein Nasr (b. 1933/1352). The biographies and ideas of both thinkers are thoroughly surveyed and analysed, and Aslan shows how Hick was influenced by Wilfred Cantwell Smith, while Nasr was perhaps more influenced by a thinker such as the Swiss metaphysician who converted to Islam, Frithjof Schuon, and the ideas of the 'Perennial Philosophy'.[88] One consequence of these influences is that Hick is perhaps readier to acknowledge and support evolution, given Smith's concept of 'the cumulative tradition', whereas Nasr hankers after an understanding of tradition which has behind it the concept of the unchanging essence of sacred truth. Aslan makes quite explicit his preference for Nasr's view: Hick is too much of an empiricist for him, and he has a higher opinion of Nasr's emphasis on the transforming power of sacred knowledge, so that Nasr's 'traditional point-of-view', 'Islamic orthodoxy', and 'religious' hypothesis of religious pluralism is definitely preferred to Hick's 'modern outlook', 'liberalism', and 'secular' hypothesis of religious pluralism. But both writers' life-stories and systems of thought are thoroughly investigated and sympathetically discussed, and given the extent to which Hick's 'pluralist' views have been controversial within his own Christian community, this is no mean feat for a Muslim writer.[89]

Mahmud Aydin, who has more recently completed a PhD in the University of Birmingham, perhaps goes further. His thesis focused on modern Western Christian thinking, both Catholic and Protestant, about Islam, with particular reference to the person of Muḥammad and the Qur'ān, and the conclusion of the thesis makes some interesting suggestions concerning what Muslims might learn from the Western Christian re-thinking which has been examined earlier in the thesis. Four specific recommendations are made, involving the establishment of a Muslim organisation specifically devoted to Inter-faith Dialogue, the undertaking of more Muslim research on Christianity, the need to publish some guidelines concerning dialogue, and the importance of formulating a new theology of religions, which might include a re-reading of the Qur'ān. Elsewhere in the thesis Hick is specifically commended as an example for Muslims, because of his readiness to re-examine not only his tradition's view of other religious communities, but also his tradition itself, and this seems to be moving further towards a commendation of Hick's kind of 'pluralism'.[90]

There are, of course, many other Muslim writers whose opinions could have been referred to as illustrations of the diversity of contemporary Muslim thinking about Christianity, for example the great Indian-born scholar of Islamic thought, Fazlur Rahman (1919/1332–1988/1408), who wrote several articles on Judaism and Christianity. But Rahman's views on this topic are in many respects very traditional, and he does not seem to have had very much real engagement with contemporary Jews and Christians.[91] The book *Christian–Muslim Relations: Yesterday, Today, Tomorrow*, contains three papers in which there is some interesting analysis of the history of Christian–Muslim relations: the first includes the ready acknowledgement that there is a serious lack of systematic studies of Christianity by Muslims, and the second concedes that Christians should be given the credit for many positive initiatives to promote better understanding between the two communities; but the third is slightly more strident and alarmist in tone, and this rather undoes the more optimistic mood created by the first two papers.[92] One piece of work which is currently in progress, and whose publication is eagerly awaited not least because of its assured originality, is Shabbir Akhtar's biography of Paul. Some of Paul's teaching has been discussed by Muslim writers before, both in the medieval period by a writer such as 'Abd al-Jabbār and more recently by Ismā'īl al-Farūqī, but their development has never been located in the context of Paul's biography, so Akhtar's study should shed real light on an important stage of Christian development which may also have significant implications within the Muslim community, not least as regards the relationship between Arab and non-Arab Muslims.[93] Just as it has been possible to give only a sample of modern Christian thinking about Islam, however, so it has been possible to survey only some Muslim writers about Christianity. But even this gives some insight into the wide range of current Muslim thinking on this topic.[94]

NOTES

1. See J. Waardenburg (ed.), *Classical Approaches to the Study of Religion*, 2 vols, The Hague: Mouton, 1973 and 1974, and F. Whaling (ed.), *Contemporary Approaches to the Study of Religion*, 2 vols, Berlin: Mouton, 1983 and 1985.
2. E. Said, *Orientalism: Western Conceptions of the Orient*, 2nd edn, London: Penguin, 1995, *Covering Islam: how the Media and the Experts Determine how we see the Rest of the World*, 2nd edn, London: Vintage, 1997, and *Culture and Imperialism*, London: Chatto and Windus, 1993. See also the articles of the Palestinian Muslim A. L. Tibawi, 'English-speaking Orientalists: a Critique of their Approach to Islam and Arab Nationalism', in *Muslim World*, 53 (1963), pp. 185–204 and 298–313, and 'Second Critique of English-speaking Orientalists and their Approach to Islam and the Arabs', in *Islamic Quarterly*, 13 (1979), pp. 3–54.
3. M. Douglas, *Evans-Pritchard*, London: Fontana, 1980, p. 43.
4. E. E. Evans-Pritchard, *The Sanusi of Cyrenaica*, Oxford University Press, 1949, p. iii.
5. Douglas, *Evans-Pritchard*, p. 43.
6. E. J. Sharpe, *Comparative Religion: a History*, 2nd edn, London: Duckworth, 1986, p. 11. For the first three Muslim writers see H. P. Goddard, *Muslim Perceptions of Christianity*, London: Grey Seal, 1996, Chapter 2. On al-Shahrastānī, see A. K. Kazi and J. G. Flynn, *Muslim Sects and Divisions*, London: Kegan Paul International, 1984; W. M. Watt, 'A Muslim Account of Christian Doctrine', in *Hamdard Islamicus*, 6 (1983), pp. 57–68; and B. B. Lawrence, *Shahrastani on the Indian Religions*, The Hague: Mouton, 1976.
7. See M. Rodinson, 'Western Views of the Muslim World', in Rodinson, *Europe and the Mystique of Islam*, London: I.B. Tauris, 1988, pp. 3–82, esp. pp. 40–8; A.H. Hourani, *Islam in European Thought*, Cambridge University Press, 1991, pp. 7–60, esp. pp. 12–14; G. Endress, *An Introduction to Islam*, Edinburgh University Press, 1988, Chapter 2; N. Matar, *Islam in Britain, 1558–1685*, Cambridge University Press, 1998, Chapter 3; and C. E. Butterworth and B. A. Kessel (eds), *The Introduction of Arabic Philosophy into Europe*, Leiden: Brill, 1994.
8. Rodinson, 'Western Views . . .', pp. 46–7.
9. For some readings which illustrate the full range of attitudes towards Islam in this period, see D. A. Pailin, *Attitudes to Other Religions: Comparative Religion in Seventeenth and Eighteenth Century Britain*, Manchester University Press, 1984, pp. 81–104, 198–222, and 269–73.
10. R. Halsband, C. Pick, and D. Murphy (eds), *Embassy to Constantinople: the Travels of Lady Mary Wortley Montagu*, London: Century, 1988. See also B. Lewis, *Islam in History*, London: Alcove, 1973, pp. 37–40, and E.

W. Fernea, 'An Early Ethnographer of Middle Eastern Women: Lady Mary Wortley Montagu (1689–1762)', in *Journal of Near Eastern Studies*, 40 (1981), pp. 329–38.

11. See A. H. Hourani, 'Volney and the Ruin of Empires', in Hourani, *Europe and the Middle East*, London: Macmillan, 1980, pp. 81–6.
12. E. W. Lane, *An Account of the Manners and Customs of the Modern Egyptians*, 5th edn, reprinted New York: Dover, 1973. For Said's view, see *Orientalism*, pp. 158–66.
13. C. Doughty, *Travels in Arabia Deserta*, 2 vols, 3rd edn, reprinted New York: Dover, 1979.
14. R. Burton, *Personal Narrative of a Pilgrimage to al-Madinah and Meccah*, 2 vols, Memorial edn, reprinted New York: Dover, 1964. See also A. Ralli, *Christians at Mecca*, London: Heinemann, 1909; A. Jeffery, 'Christians at Mecca', in *Muslim World*, 19 (1929), pp. 221–35, and R. Bidwell, *Travellers in Arabia*, London: Hamlyn, 1976. For Said's view of Burton, see *Orientalism*, pp. 194–7.
15. S. Hurgronje, *Mekka*, 2 vols, The Hague: Nijhoff, 1888 and 1889, vol. II translated into English by J. H. Monahan, *Mecca in the Latter Part of the Nineteenth Century*, Leiden: Brill, 1931, and E.C. Rutter, *The Holy Cities of Arabia*, 2 vols, New York: Putnams, 1928.
16. See J. Sweetman, *The Oriental Obsession: Islamic Inspiration in British and American Art and Architecture 1500–1920*, Cambridge University Press, 1987, esp. pp. 12, 13, 104–11, 189–92, and 219–21.
17. See A. Murray, (ed.), *Sir William Jones 1746–94: a Commemoration*, Oxford University Press, 1998; Pailin, *Attitudes*, pp. 247–52; and Said, *Orientalism*, pp. 77–9.
18. See Rodinson, 'Western Views . . .', pp. 53–4 and 56–7; Hourani, *Islam in European Thought*, pp. 19 and 34; Endress, *Introduction to Islam*, pp. 12–13; and Said, *Orientalism*, pp. 167–8 and 152.
19. Hourani, *Islam in European Thought*, pp. 32–3, and Said, *Orientalism*, pp. 123–30.
20. Hourani, *Islam in European*, p. 41, and Said, *Orientalism*, pp. 255–7.
21. J. Waardenburg, *L'Islam dans le Miroir de l'Occident*, Paris: Mouton, 1962. See also Hourani, *Islam in European Thought*, pp. 36–41 on Goldziher, and p. 50 on Macdonald, and Said, *Orientalism*, pp. 209–10 on Goldziher and Macdonald, and pp. 276–8 on Macdonald. For more detail on the two figures see R. Simon, *Ignaz Goldziher: his Life and Scholarship as Reflected in his Works and Correspondence*, Leiden: Brill, 1986; Macdonald's own autobiographical notes in *Hartford Seminary Foundation Bulletin*, 1 (June 1946); and P. Ipema, *The Islam Interpretations of Duncan B. Macdonald, Samuel M. Zwemer, A. Kenneth Cragg and Wilfred C. Smith: an Analytical Comparison and Evaluation*, unpublished PhD thesis, Hartford Seminary, 1971. Goldziher's lectures were originally published in 1910 (Heidelberg: Winter), and translated into English as *Introduction to Islamic Theology and Law*, Princeton University Press, 1981; Macdonald's work was first published in 1903 by Russell and Russell, New York.
22. A. Hussain, R. Olson, and J. Qureshi (eds), *Orientalism, Islam and Islamists*, Brattleboro VT: Amana, 1984. See Chapter 5 (G. E. Pruett) on Macdonald, Chapter 6 (Z. H. Faruqi) on Gibb, Chapter 7 (B. S Turner) on von Grunebaum, Chapter 8 (J. Qureshi) on Cragg, and Chapter 9 (S. S. Nyang and S. Abed-Rabbo) on Lewis; there is also considerable discus-

sion of Gibb and von Grunebaum in Chapter 3 (G. E. Pruett). For a different view of Gibb, see A. H. Hourani, 'H. A. R. Gibb: the Vocation of an Orientalist', in Hourani, *Europe and the Middle East*, London: Macmillan, 1980, pp. 104–34. Said discusses Gibb and Massignon in *Orientalism*, pp. 255–84.

23. C.E. Padwick, *Temple Gairdner of Cairo*, 2nd edn, London: SPCK, 1930, pp. 204–20.
24. See Hourani, 'H.A.R. Gibb. . .', p. 104; the unpublished diary of a trip to Egypt in 1902/1319 by Mrs. J. M. Campbell, pp. 16–17; and Said, *Orientalism*, p. 275.
25. See his 'Common Notions concerning Religion' from his *De Veritate*, in O. C. Thomas (ed.), *Attitudes toward Other Religions*, London: SCM, 1969, pp. 32–48, and also in R. Plantinga (ed.), *Christianity and Pluralism*, Oxford: Blackwell, 1999, pp. 169–81. See also Pailin, *Attitudes*, pp. 162–70 and 266–91, and R. A. Johnson, 'Natural Religion, Common Notions and the Study of Religions: Lord Herbert of Cherbury (1583–1648)', in *Religion*, 24 (1994), pp. 213–24.
26. See Plantinga, *Christianity and Pluralism*, pp. 182–7, and K-J. Kuschel, *Abraham: a Symbol of Hope for Jews, Christians and Muslims*, London: SCM, 1995, p. 193.
27. See the extract from his *On Religion*, in Thomas, *Attitudes toward other Religions*, pp. 51–69, and the extract from *The Christian Faith* in Plantinga, *Christianity and Pluralism*, pp. 190–208, and also Hourani, *Islam in European Thought*, pp. 23–4.
28. See on the one hand his *The Absoluteness of Christianity and the History of Religions*, first published in 1902, English translation by David Reid, Richmond VA: John Knox Press, 1971, and on the other his lecture 'The Place of Christianity among the World Religions', a lecture originally delivered in Oxford in 1923/1342, shortly before his death, in Thomas, *Attitudes towards Other Religions*, pp. 73–91, and also in Plantinga, *Christianity and Pluralism*, pp. 211–22 and J. Hick and B. Hebblethwaite (eds), *Christianity and Other Religions*, London: Fontana, 1980, pp. 11–31. See also R. Bernhardt, *Christianity without Absolutes*, London: SCM, 1994, pp. 96–9.
29. There is now an abundance of material on these three points of view, but see especially A. Race, *Christians and Religious Pluralism*, London: SCM, 2nd edn, 1993; P. K. Knitter, *No Other Name! A Critical Survey of Christian Attitudes toward the World Religions*, London: SCM, 1985; M. Barnes, *Christian Identity and Religious Pluralism: Religions in Conversation*, London: SPCK, 1989, Part I; and G. D'Costa, *Theology and Religious Pluralism*, Oxford: Blackwell, 1986, which investigates the question through a focus on three representative thinkers, Hendrik Kraemer (who will be investigated further below), Karl Rahner, and John Hick. See also the anthologies of Thomas, *Attitudes towards Other Religions*, Hick and Hebblethwaite, *Christianity and Other Religions*, and Plantinga, *Christianity and Pluralism*, and for a robust debate between 'inclusivists' and 'pluralists', J. Hick and P. Knitter (eds), *The Myth of Christian Uniqueness*, London: SCM, 1987, and G. D'Costa (ed.), *Christian Uniqueness Reconsidered: the Myth of a Pluralistic Theology of Religions*, Maryknoll NY: Orbis, 1990.
30. For an evangelical who leans towards 'inclusivism' see J. Sanders, *No Other Name*, London: SPCK, 1994; for a suggestion that the Roman

Catholic theologian Hans Küng has become a 'pluralist' see S. Cowdell, 'Hans Küng and World Religions: the Emergence of a Pluralist', in *Theology*, March 1989, pp. 85–92. For an account of Hick's change of opinion by Hick himself, see his 'Introduction: a Spiritual Pilgrimage', in his *God Has Many Names*, London: Macmillan, 1980, pp. 1–9.

31. See I. Markham, 'Creating Options: Shattering the "Exclusivist, Inclusivist, and Pluralist" Paradigm', in *New Blackfriars*, January 1993, pp. 33–41 (with a reply by G. D'Costa).
32. E. J. Sharpe, *Faith Meets Faith: Some Christian Attitudes to Hinduism in the Nineteenth and Twentieth Centuries*, London: SCM, 1977, and *Not to Destroy but to Fulfil: the Contribution of J.N. Farquhar to Protestant Missionary Thought in India before 1914*, Uppsala: Swedish Institute of Missionary Research 1965.
33. C. Bennett, *Victorian Images of Islam*, London: Grey Seal, 1992, and K. Cracknell, *Justice, Courtesy and Love: Theologians and Missionaries Encountering World Religions, 1846–1910*, London: Epworth, 1995.
34. See the statement to this effect in the report of the Doctrine Commission of the Church of England, *Believing in the Church*, London: SPCK, 1981, esp. pp. 258 and 300–1, and the Commission's later attempts to address the question in *We Believe in God*, London: Church House Publishing, 1987, esp. pp. 13–14 and 133–5, and *The Mystery of Salvation*, London: Church House Publishing, 1995, Chapter 7.
35. See for example C. Gunton (ed.), *The Cambridge Companion to Christian Doctrine*, Cambridge University Press, 1997; P. Esler (ed.), *Christianity in the Twenty-First Century*, Edinburgh: T. and T. Clark, 1998; and D. G. Mullan (ed.), *Religious Pluralism in the West: an Anthology*, Oxford: Blackwell, 1998, which looks only at intra-Christian (i.e. denominational) pluralism, rather than inter-religious pluralism.
36. W. E. Hocking (ed.), *Rethinking Missions: a Laymen's Enquiry*, New York: Harper, 1933.
37. T. Yates, *Christian Mission in the Twentieth Century*, Cambridge University Press, 1994, p. 72.
38. See D'Costa, *Christian Uniqueness Reconsidered*, Chapter 3; Yates, *Christian Mission*, pp. 105–17; and C. F. Hallencreutz, *Kraemer towards Tambaram: a Study in Hendrik Kraemer's Missionary Approach*, Uppsala: Swedish Institute of Missionary Research, 1966.
39. See Race, *Christians and Religions Pluralism*, p. 16, for Barth's remark.
40. H. Kraemer, *The Christian Message in a Non-Christian World*, London: Edinburgh House Press, 1938, pp. 216–17.
41. Ibid., p. 220.
42. Ibid., p. 221.
43. See Race, *Christianity and Religious Pluralism*, pp. 14–16 and 23–4. For a later statement by Kraemer himself, see Plantinga, *Christianity and Pluralism*, pp. 245–66.
44. From Hick and Hebblethwaite, *Christianity and Other Religions*, pp. 82–3; also in Plantinga, *Christianity and Pluralism*, pp. 305–8.
45. See Plantinga, *Christianity and Pluralism*, pp. 124–5 for the 1302/702 statement and pp. 305–8 for the whole 1965/1385 statement.
46. A. O'Mahony, 'Mysticism and Politics: Louis Massignon, Shi'a Islam, Iran and 'Ali Shari'ati – a Muslim-Christian Encounter', in A. Jones (ed.),

University Lectures in Islamic Studies, vol. II, London: Altajir World of Islam Trust, 1998, pp. 115–16.

47. B. Breiner, 'Louis Massignon: an Interpretive Essay', in *Newsletter of the Centre for the Study of Islam and Christian–Muslim Relations*, (Birmingham), No. 14 (May 1985), p. 25.

48. See R. Caspar, 'Islam according to Vatican II', in M. L. Fitzgerald and R. Caspar, *Signs of Dialogue: Christian Encounter with Muslims*, Philippines: Silsilah Publications, 1992, Chapter 11, and D. Macpherson, 'The Second Vatican Council and the Future of Christian–Muslim Dialogue', in Jones, *University Lectures*, pp. 31–47.

49. An early study of Massignon was in J. Waardenburg, *L'Islam dans le Miroir de l'Occident*, The Hague: Mouton 1962. For Catholic appreciations see C. W. Troll, 'Islam and Christianity Interacting in the Life of an Outstanding Christian Scholar of Islam: the Case of Louis Massignon (1883–1962)', in *Islam and the Modern Age*, 15 (1984), pp. 157–66; S. H. Griffith, 'Sharing the Faith of Abraham: the "credo" of Louis Massignon', in *Islam and Christian–Muslim Relations*, 8 (1997), pp. 193–210; and D. B. Burrell, 'Mind and Heart at the Service of Muslim-Christian Understanding: Louis Massignon as Trail-Blazer', in *Muslim World*, 88 (1998), pp. 268–78. For other views see J. Baldick, 'Massignon: Man of Opposites', in *Religious Studies*, 23 (1987), pp. 29–39; N. Robinson, 'Massignon, Vatican II and Islam as an Abrahamic Religion', in *Islam and Christian–Muslim Relations*, 2 (1991), pp. 182–205; and Breiner, 'Louis Massignon. . .', pp. 19–26. For his influence on Muslims, see S. H. Nasr, 'In Commemoration of Louis Massignon: Catholic Scholar, Islamicist and Mystic', in *Traditional Islam in the Modern World*, London: Kegan Paul International, 1987, pp. 253–72; O'Mahony, 'Mysticism and Politics. . .', pp. 113–34; and H. P. Goddard, 'Christianity from the Muslim Perspective: Varieties and Changes', in J. Waardenburg (ed.), *Islam and Christianity: Mutual Perceptions since the mid-Twentieth Century*, Louvain: Peters, 1998, pp. 213–55, esp. pp. 221, 248, and 250. See also D. Massignon (ed.), [Massignon's son], *Presence de Louis Massignon: Hommages et Témoignages*, Paris: Maisonneuve et Larose, 1987; M. L. Gude, *Louis Massignon: the Crucible of Compassion*, University of Notre Dame Press, 1996; and H. Fattah, 'Report on the Conference "Louis Massignon: the Vocation of a Scholar": Notre Dame University, Indiana, 2–5.10.1997', in *Bulletin of the Royal Institute for Inter-Faith Studies*, 1 (1999), pp. 212–17.

50. See A. K. Cragg, *The Call of the Minaret*, 2nd edn, London: Collins, 1985, and his three books on the Qur'ān, *The Event of the Qur'ān: Islam in its Scripture*, London: Allen and Unwin, 1971, *The Mind of the Qur'ān: Chapters in Reflection*, London: Allen and Unwin, 1973, and *Readings in the Qur'ān*, London: Collins, 1988.

51. A. K. Cragg, 'Being Christian and Being Muslim: a Personal Debate', in *Religion*, 10 (1980), pp. 196–207. The quotation is from p. 197. On Cragg, see Ipema, *Islam Interpretations*; Yates, *Christian Mission*, pp. 150–5; C. Lamb, *The Call to Retrieval: Kenneth Cragg's Christian Vocation of Islam*, London: Grey Seal, 1997; and J. Qureshi, ' "Alongsidedness – in Good Faith?": an Essay on Kenneth Cragg', in Hussain, Olson and Qureshi, *Orientalism, Islam and Islamists*, pp. 203–58. The editors' Introduction to this book contains a particularly snide comment on Cragg's work, which could serve very well as an example of what might

be called 'secular fundamentalism': 'Cragg's writings, as perhaps could be expected from a Christian clergyman, suffer from the intrinsic limitations of his own world views.' (Ibid., p. 4).

52. G. Khodr, 'Christianity in a Pluralistic World: the Economy of the Holy Spirit', in *Sobornost*, 6 (1971), p. 170.
53. W. C. Smith, *Modern Islam in India*, 2nd edn, Lahore: Ashraf, 1946, *Islam in Modern History*, Princeton University Press, 1957, and *The Meaning and End of Religion*, New York: Macmillan, 1962.
54. W. C. Smith, 'Christian–Muslim Relations: the Theological Dimension', in *Studies in Inter-Religious Dialogue*, 1 (1991), pp. 22–3. See also W. C. Smith, *On Understanding Islam*, The Hague: Mouton, 1981, esp. Part IV, 'Muslim-Christian Relations.'
55. W. C. Smith, *Towards a World Theology*, London: Macmillan, 1981. On Smith see E. J. Hughes, *Wilfred Cantwell Smith: a Theology for the World*, London: SCM, 1986; L. Gilkey and H. Smith, 'Wilfred Cantwell Smith: Early Opus and Recent Trilogy', in *Religious Studies Review*, 7 (1981), pp. 298–310; and Ipema, *Islam Interpretations*; and for a comparison of Cragg and Smith, see R. J. Jones, 'Wilfred Cantwell Smith and Kenneth Cragg on Islam as a Way of Salvation', in *International Bulletin of Missionary Research*, 16 (1992), pp. 105–10.
56. H. Küng, *Judaism*, London: SCM, 1992, and *Christianity*, London: SCM, 1995.
57. See J. I. Smith, 'Some Contemporary Protestant Theological Reflections on Pluralism: Implications for Christian–Muslim Understanding', in *Islam and Christian–Muslim Relations*, 8 (1997), pp. 67–83, which as well as Zwemer, Cragg, Smith and Hick, looks at Phil Parshall and John B. Cobb Jr.
58. On the limitations of the scheme, see H. P. Goddard, 'The Salvific Value of Other Faiths with Special Reference to Islam', *Christian–Muslim Reflections*, Centre for the Study of Islam and Christian–Muslim Relations, (Birmingham), 2 (1994), pp. 1–15. For an overview of Christian thinking about Islam during the last fifty years, see the first three chapters of J. Waardenburg (ed.), *Islam and Christianity: Mutual Perceptions since the mid-Twentieth Century*, Louvain: Peters, 1998, which look respectively at Catholic (C.W. Troll), Protestant (J.-C. Basset), and Orthodox (A. Argyriou) opinion; and for a survey of both popular and scholarly contemporary Christian literature about Islam, see K. Zebiri, *Muslims and Christians Face to Face*, Oxford, Oneworld, 1997, esp. Chapters 3 and 5.
59. See *Arabia*, No. 59 (July 1986), pp. 14–17.
60. See A. H. Hourani, *Arabic Thought in the Liberal Age, 1798–1939*, 2nd edn, Oxford University Press, 1970, Chapter 11; G. Antonius, *The Arab Awakening*, London: Hamish Hamilton, 1939; and I. J. Boullata, *Trends and Issues in Contemporary Arab Thought*, State University of New York Press, 1990.
61. I. R. al-Faruqi, *On Arabism: 'Urubah and Religion*, Amsterdam: Djambatan, 1962, pp. 11 and 12.
62. I. R. al-Faruqi, *Christian Ethics: a Historical and Systematic Analysis of its Dominant Ideas*, McGill University Press, 1967.
63. Ibid., p. vi.
64. Ibid., p. vii.
65. Ibid.

66. This line of argument can be traced back at least as far as 'Abd al-Jabbār (d. 1025/416). See S. M. Stern. ''Abd al-Jabbar's Account of how Christ's Religion was Falsified by the Adoption of Roman Customs', in *Journal of Theological Studies*, 19 (1968), pp. 128–85.
67. I. R. al-Faruqi, *Islam and the Problem of Israel*, London: Islamic Council of Europe, 1980. There is an extract from Chapter 10 of this book in J. L. Esposito (ed.), *Voices of Resurgent Islam*, Oxford University Press, 1983, pp. 261–7.
68. I. R. al-Faruqi (ed.), *Trialogue of the Abrahamic Faiths*, Washington DC: International Institute of Islamic Thought, 1982.
69. I. R. al-Faruqi, *Islam and Other Faiths*, ed. A. Siddiqui, Leicester: Islamic Foundation, 1998.
70. I. R. al-Faruqi, 'Rights of non-Muslims under Islam: Social and Cultural Aspects', originally published in *Journal of the Institute of Muslim Minority Affairs*, 1 (1979), pp. 90–102. See also the discussion in the same journal, vols. 6 and 7.
71. I. R. al-Faruqi, 'Islam and Christianity: Diatribe or Dialogue?', originally published in *Journal of Ecumenical Studies*, 5 (1968), pp. 45–77.
72. Faruqi, *Islam and Other Faiths*, p. 247.
73. Faruqi, *Christian Ethics*, p. v.
74. L. Poston, *Islamic Da'wah in the West: Muslim Missionary Activity and the Dynamics of Conversion to Islam*, Oxford University Press, 1992, p. 191, note 7.
75. See also J. L. Esposito, 'Ismail R. Al-Faruqi: Muslim Scholar-Activist', in Y. Y. Haddad (ed.), *The Muslims of America*, Oxford University Press, 1991, pp. 65–79, and K. Zebiri, 'Relations between Muslims and non-Muslims in the Thought of Western-Educated Muslim Intellectuals', in *Islam and Christian–Muslim Relations*, 6 (1995), pp. 258–62, and A. Siddiqui's 'Introduction' in Faruqi, *Islam and Other Faiths*, pp. xi-xxix.
76. Abū Bakr Muḥammad ibn al-Walīd al-Ṭurṭūshī, *Kitāb al-ḥawādith wa'l-bid'a*, ed. M. Ṭālbī, Tunis: al-maṭba'a al-rasmiyya li'l-jumhūriyya al-tūnisiyya, 1959, reviewed by M. S. Kister in *Journal of Semitic Studies*, 6 (1961), pp. 137–42.
77. M. Talbi, 'Le Christianism Maghrébin: de la Conquête Musulmane à sa Disparition', in M. Gervers and R. J. Bikhazi (eds), *Conversion and Continuity: Indigenous Christian Communities in Islamic Lands, Eighth to Eighteenth Centuries*, Toronto: Pontifical Institute of Medieval Studies, 1990, pp. 313–51.
78. M. Talbi, *Islam et Dialogue: Reflexion sur un Thème d'Actualité*, Tunis: Maison Tunisienne de l'Edition, 1972. An English translation can be found in R. W. Rousseau (ed.), *Christianity and Islam: the Struggling Dialogue*, Scranton PA: Ridge Row Press, 1985, pp. 53–73, reproduced in P. J. Griffiths (ed.), *Christianity through non-Christian Eyes*, Maryknoll NY; Orbis, 1990, pp. 82–101.
79. Rousseau, *Christianity and Islam*, pp. 56–7.
80. The relevant texts, together with two others, by the medieval Ihkwān al-Ṣafā (The Brethren of Purity) and Muḥammad Kāmil Ḥusain of Egypt (1901/1318–1977/1397), have been assembled by a pupil of Professor Ṭālbī, Professor Abdelmajid Charfi, in 'L'Islam et les Religions Non Musulmanes: Quelques Textes Positifs', in *Islamochristiana*, 3 (1977), pp. 39–63.

81. Rousseau, *Christianity and Islam*, p. 63.
82. See ibid., p. 63, but this translation is mine since the version used by Rousseau suggests that the believer continues to be the epicentre!
83. M. Talbi, 'Unavoidable Dialogue in a Pluralist World: a Personal Account', in *Encounters*, 1 (1995), pp. 56–69.
84. Ibid., p. 64.
85. M. Ṭālbī, *'Iyāl allāh: afkār jadīda fī 'alāqāt al-muslim bi-ghayrihi*, ed. H. ibn 'Uthmān, Tunis: Dār Sirās, 1992, and *Ummat al-wasaṭ: al-islām wa taḥaddiyāt al-mu'āṣarāt*, Tunis: Cérès, 1996.
86. See also M. Talbi, 'Is Cultural and Religious Co-Existence Possible? Harmony and the Right to be Different', in *Encounters*, 1 (1995), pp. 74–84.
87. See R. L. Nettler, 'Mohamed Talbi: "For Dialogue between All Religions" ', in R. L. Nettler and S. Taji-Farouki, (eds), *Muslim-Jewish Relations: Intellectual Traditions and Modern Politics*, Amsterdam: Harwood Academic Publishers, 1998, pp. 171–99. See also R. L. Nettler, 'Mohamed Talbi's Ideas on Islam and Politics: a Conception of Islam for the Modern World', in J. Cooper, R. L. Nettler, and M. Mahmoud, (eds), *Islam and Modernity: Muslim Intellectuals Respond*, London: Tauris, 1998, pp. 129–55; Zebiri, 'Relations between Muslims . . .', pp. 267–70; and H. P. Goddard, 'Christianity from the Muslim Perspective: Varieties and Changes', in Waardenburg, *Islam and Christianity*, pp. 246–9.
88. See F. Schuon, *The Transcendent Unity of Religions*, London: Faber, 1953, *Islam and the Perennial Philosophy*, with a Preface by S. H. Nasr, London: World of Islam Festival Publishing, 1976, and *Christianity/Islam: Essays on Esoteric Ecumenicism*, Bloomington IN: World Wisdom Books, 1985.
89. A. Aslan, *Religious Pluralism in Christian and Islamic Philosophy: the Thought of John Hick and Seyyed Hossein Nasr*, London: Curzon, 1998.
90. M. Aydin, *Modern Western Christian Theological Understanding of Muslims since the Second Vatican Council*, unpublished PhD thesis, University of Birmingham, 1998. See also Aydin, 'Common Values and Common Aims', in *Islam and Christian–Muslim Relations*, 6 (1995), pp. 279–84, and the article of another Turkish writer, B. Senay, 'The "Religious Other" in Islam: Revelation, Diversity, and "Living Together" ', in *Discernment*, 5 (1998), pp. 10–35, which seems to hover on the frontier between 'inclusivism' and 'pluralism'.
91. See F. Rahman, 'The People of the Book and Diversity of "Religions" ', in Rahman, *Major Themes of the Qur'ān*, Minneapolis: Bibliotheca Islamica, 1980, pp. 162–70; Rahman, 'Islam's Attitude towards Judaism', in *Muslim World*, 72 (1982), pp. 1–13; and Rahman, 'Non-Muslim Minorities in an Islamic State', in *Journal of the Institute of Muslim Minority Affairs*, 7 (1986), pp. 13–24. See also Zebiri, 'Relations between Muslims . . .', pp. 262–4.
92. M. A. Anees, S. Z. Abedin, and Z. Sardar, *Christian–Muslim Relations: Yesterday, Today, Tomorrow*, London: Grey Seal, 1991.
93. On Akhtar see my paper in Waardenburg, *Islam and Christianity*, pp. 223–6.
94. See H. P. Goddard, *Muslim Perceptions of Christianity*, London: Grey Seal, 1996; Goddard, 'Modern Pakistani and Indian Muslim Perceptions of Christianity', in *Islam and Christian–Muslim Relations*, 5 (1994), pp.

165–88; and Goddard, 'Christianity from the Muslim Perspective: Varieties and Changes', in Waardenburg, *Islam and Christianity*, pp. 213–55. See also the papers by A. Charfi, A. S. Moussalli, and W. Hassab Alla (chapters 4 to 6) in the same volume, and Zebiri, *Muslims and Christians Face to Face*, esp. chapters 2 and 4.

8

Dialogue or Confrontation?

THE DIALOGUE MOVEMENT

One of the results of the fresh thinking which Christians and Muslims have been doing about each other in the twentieth/fourteenth century has been the emergence of a significant move towards dialogue between the two communities. This is not a completely new development, as in earlier centuries we have seen that there have been both disputations and debates between Christians and Muslims, but dialogue is rather different from both of those activities, involving as it does both a greater philosophical sophistication, which has become easier with the growth of modern critical study of religion, and a greater willingness to listen as well as to assert.

The Second Vatican Council was an important landmark in this development, since as well as significantly moving Christian thinking on from its traditional 'exclusivism' towards Islam and other religious traditions, it also called on Christians and Muslims to forget the past and strive sincerely for mutual understanding. This call had already been given an institutional form even before the Council's statement by the establishment in 1964/1384 of the Secretariat for non-Christians, which in 1989/1409 was renamed the Pontifical Council for Inter-Religious Dialogue. A parallel shift in opinion was beginning to take place among other Christians at roughly the same time, though it took slightly longer to develop any institutional form: only in 1971/1391 did the World Council of Churches set up a Sub-Unit for Dialogue with People of Living Faiths and Ideologies, but this was the focus of some discord between Protestant member churches, some of whom entertained some suspicions of the whole idea of dialogue, and some of the Orthodox churches which were generally much more positive. In 1991/1411, as part of a major shake-up of its structure, the WCC (World Council of Churches) disbanded the Sub-Unit, and its responsibilities were taken over by the Office on Inter-Religious Relations within the General Secretariat.

Each of these bodies produced a set of guidelines for dialogue. The Catholic ones, written by Louis Gardet and Joseph Cuoq, were published in 1969/1389, and a second edition, with revisions by Maurice Borrmans, was published in 1981/1401, with an English translation following in 1990/1410.[1] It is interesting to compare the two editions,

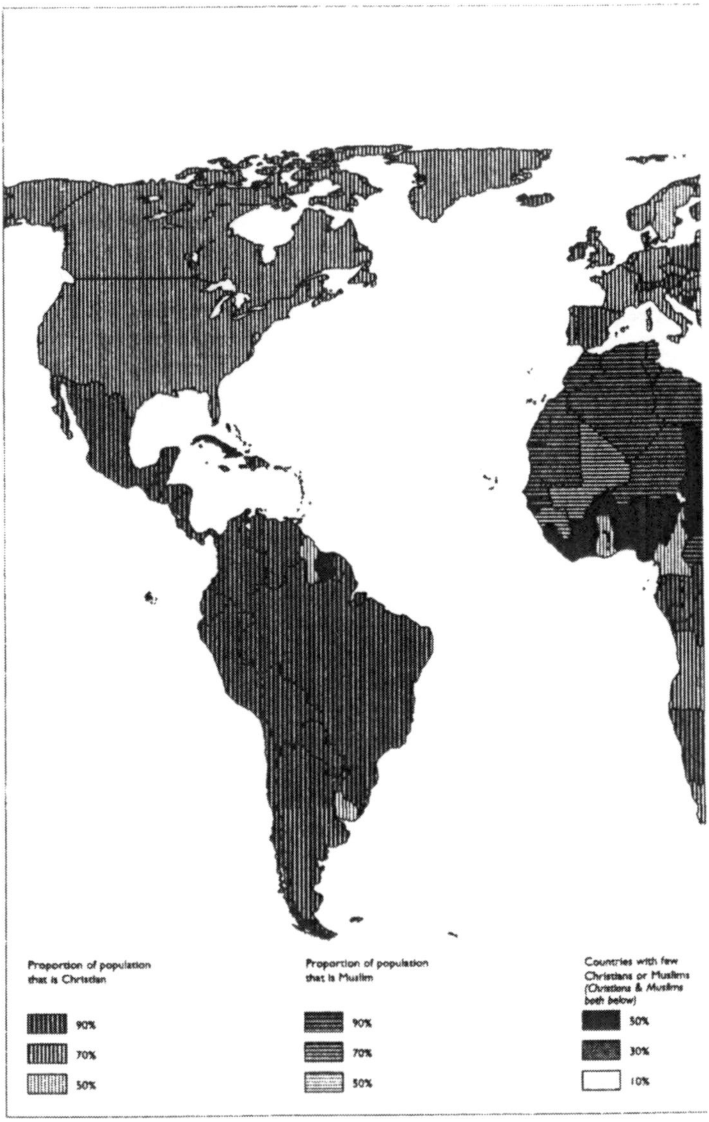

Map 2 The Christian and Muslim Worlds Today

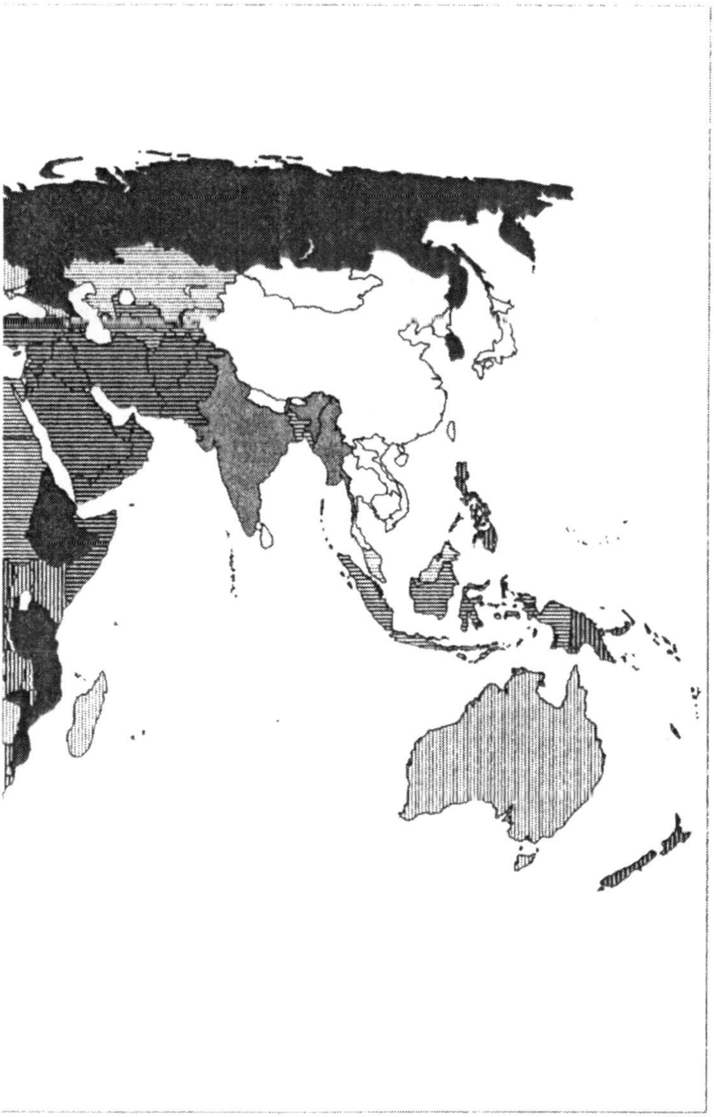

since the changes clearly show the lessons learnt from all the experience of Christian–Muslim dialogue accumulated during the 1970s/1390s: the first edition thus devotes much attention to how Christians should prepare themselves both practically and spiritually for dialogue, not least by informing themselves properly about Islam, whereas the second, while not neglecting these things, is rather more specific in terms of some of the obstacles to mutual understanding which exist in both communities, and in terms of areas where Christians and Muslims can co-operate or agree, both in the practical arena and on theological questions. The English translation of the second edition also includes an Appendix which lists the almost thirty international conferences on Christian–Muslim dialogue which took place between 1969/1389 and 1988/1419, with details of their sponsors and organisers.[2]

The World Council of Churches never produced any guidelines specifically for Christian–Muslim dialogue, but it did formulate, in 1979/1399, some guidelines on Dialogue with People of Living Faiths, and these were widely discussed and debated. Because of the nature of the World Council of Churches, which by definition is more decentralised than the Vatican, these never acquired the same status and authority as the Catholic guidelines, but they were disseminated and discussed in different national and local contexts and undoubtedly contributed to raising the awareness of inter-faith issues and helping those involved to reflect on what they were doing. Some time later, in 1992/1412, the WCC's Office on Inter-Religious Relations produced a document entitled *Issues in Christian–Muslim Relations: Ecumenical Considerations*, which was intended as a follow-up to the earlier guidelines, but it is a much slighter document than the Catholic guidelines.[3]

Both the Pontifical Council and the WCC Sub-Unit also arranged conferences and seminars, sometimes nationally or regionally and sometimes internationally, and one of the most positive features of these was the co-operation between the Vatican and the WCC which was more or less taken for granted, so that Roman Catholic representatives would attend and contribute to conferences organised by the WCC and vice versa as a matter of course. One of the most successful was the consultation arranged by the WCC in Broumana in Lebanon in 1972/1392, which brought together twenty-five Christians and twenty-two Muslims from all regions of the world to discuss four topics: Religions, Nations, and the Search for a World Community; Truth, Revelation and Obedience; Community Relationship between Christians and Muslims; and Prayer and Worship. The Memorandum which was published at the end of the consultation expressed something of the very positive atmosphere at the meeting, as well as summarising the main elements of the discussion and outlining participants' hopes for the future.[4]

One of the most interesting Christian–Muslim conferences more recently was one held at the Institute for Theology of Religions at the Theological Faculty of St Gabriel in Vienna in 1993/1413, at the instigation of Dr Alois Mock, the Foreign Minister of Austria, on the theme of peace for humanity. Twenty-three Christians and twenty-three Muslims from all over the world met for three days to discuss this theme, with papers presented by, among others, the Muslims Dr Esmat Abdel-Meguid (the Secretary General of the Arab League), Mohammed Khatami (who became President of Iran in 1997), Prince Hasan of Jordan, Gad al Haq (the Sheikh of al-Azhar), and Nurcholish Madjid (the Director of the Indonesian Institute of Sciences in Jakarta), and the Christians Georges Khodr (Orthodox Bishop of Mount Lebanon), Henri Teissier (Archbishop of Algiers), Cardinal Franz König of Vienna (who led one of the earliest Christian delegations to al-Azhar, in 1965/1385) and Cardinal Francis Arinze (the President of the Pontifical Council for Inter-religious Dialogue). An official 'Vienna Declaration' was issued at the end of the conference, and this addressed not only the world's Christians and Muslims but also the world's legal and political authorities.[5]

Many other conferences, far too many to refer to individually, have been held in different parts of the world.[6] Of those who have attended many of them, it is interesting to compare the reflections on them of two people intimately involved in the Vatican and WCC ventures, Michael Fitzgerald and Dirk Mulder.[7] In general terms the former is much more optimistic than the latter, who points to the opposition to the whole idea of dialogue in some quarters within the WCC. The Roman Catholic initiative therefore seems to have developed more momentum and stamina, not least in recent years because of the personal interest of Pope John Paul II, and the vision and initiative of the current head of the Pontifical Council, Cardinal Francis Arinze, who comes originally from Nigeria, a part of the world where relationships between Christians and Muslims are a matter of urgent practical concern.[8]

Many interesting and important topics have been addressed during these conferences, including such controversial subjects as mission, and the position of religious minorities. Two of the conferences at which discussion became most heated took place in 1976/1396: the first took place in Libya, at the initiative of the Arab Socialist Union of that country, in collaboration with the Secretariat for non-Christians, and caused considerable controversy when the final communiqué included a number of references to Zionism; and the second, arranged by the WCC in Switzerland, focused on mission and *da'wa*, with the summaries of the discussions that took place only hinting at the strength of feeling which this issue sometimes provoked in the participants, who included Ismā'īl al-Farūqī.[9] More recently, the issue of religious minorities was discussed at a workshop of a 1982/1402 conference in Sri Lanka, which was organised jointly by the WCC and the World Muslim Congress (*Mu'tamar al-'ālam al-islāmī*), and the opening paper of this workshop, by Tom Michel, provoked a lively debate in the pages of the *Journal of the Institute of Muslim Minority Affairs*.[10]

The discussion of this kind of issue illustrates the extent to which practical factors stimulated the growth of the dialogue movement; it was not simply a theological or intellectual venture, therefore. New social developments were also significant: in a Western context, with migration, especially of Muslims, from former colonies to the different countries of Western Europe, and continuing immigration from all continents to North America, led to the emergence of much more religiously diverse societies; this was matched by the demographic realities of religious pluralism in many of the newly independent nations of Africa and Asia. Situations such as the Civil War in the Lebanon between 1975/1395 and 1991/1411 also gave added importance to the task of promoting better understanding and relations between Christians and Muslims. Wider trends in the study of theology, religion and philosophy also helped to foster the dialogue movement, with Christians being compelled to undertake some radical rethinking about Christian-Jewish relations in the wake of the Holocaust, and the ideas of two Jewish thinkers, Martin Buber (1878/1295–1965/1385), with his stress on the importance of encounter for perceiving truth, and Emmanuel Levinas (1906/1324–1995/1416), with his insistence on the primacy of the ethical in relationships, being particularly important in philosophy. It was developments such as these which stimulated interest in dialogue among academic philosophers and historians of religions too, as can be seen in the convening of a conference in Birmingham in 1970/1390 on Truth and Dialogue, and the debates which took place in the International Association for the History of Religions concerning Inter-faith Dialogue.[11]

The review of the dialogue movement so far might appear to suggest that all of the initiatives for it tended to come from Christians. This is acknowledged to some extent by Muslim writers such as M. A. Anees, who recognises that 'in the Muslim world . . . there remains a definite lack of systematic study of Christianity', and the Moroccan jurist, Muḥammad Lyazghi, who at a conference for Christians working in

Muslim countries stated: 'Muslims are in a period of transition where they first have to dialogue with each other, but this will lead to a time when people will allow Muslims and Christians to be together.'[12] But this does not mean that Muslims have not been involved, both in attending and addressing conferences as individuals and through Muslim organisations such as the World Muslim Congress (*Mu'tamar al-'ālam al-islāmī*), based in Karachi, the Muslim World League (*Rābitat al-'ālam al-islāmī*), based in Mecca, or the World Islamic Call Society (*Jam'iyyat al-da'wa al-islāmiyya al-'ālamiyya*), based in Tripoli (Libya).[13] Other Muslim groups which have initiated or sponsored dialogue between Christians and Muslims include the High Council for Islamic Affairs in Cairo, a Saudi delegation led by the Minister of Justice, which sponsored a conference on Human Rights in the two traditions, the Center for Economic and Social Studies and Research of the University of Tunis, the Arab Socialist Union of Libya, al-Azhar University in Cairo, and most recently the Āl al-bayt Foundation of Jordan, which has organised a number of conferences in collaboration both with St George's House Windsor, an Anglican conference centre, and the Orthodox Centre of the Ecumenical Patriarchate in Switzerland.[14]

An individual Muslim scholar such as Muḥammad Ṭālbī is quite open about the impact which participation in dialogue between Christians and Muslims had on him personally:

> [I]n November 1971, I was invited to Rome by what is now known as the Pontificio Instituto di Studi Arabi e d'Islamistica (PISAI) to lecture the students there on the history of the medieval Islamic civilization. Spontaneously, I chose the theme 'Islam and Dialogue: Some Reflections on a Current Topic'. I spoke without a written text, almost without notes. In fact I was badly in need of clarifying my own ideas and almost unconsciously I grasped the opportunity that presented itself to me in Rome. In that very town that had earlier challenged and destroyed Carthage, that in its turn had been sacked (August-November 846) by my Aghlabid ancestors, and where some years earlier, the promising Council of Vatican II had been held.[15]

Another important Muslim initiative came in 1985/1405, when King Hassan II of Morocco (1962/1381–1999/1420) invited Pope John Paul II to address 80,000 young Moroccans in a sports stadium in Casablanca on the theme of the common fellowship and the shared responsibilities of Christians and Muslims. One of the advantages which the Vatican has over other Christian organisations such as the WCC in seeking to build relations with Muslims is the fact that as well as being a religious institution it is also a state. Anachronistic as this seems to many Western Catholics today, it has certain advantages in relationships with the Muslim world as it means that as well as representing the world's largest religious community and having religious representatives in most of the countries of the world, it also has a diplomatic presence through the Papal Nuncios, and this gives readier access to governments than would be possible through the heads of the local Catholic communities. In addition, four mainly Muslim states – Egypt, Turkey, Iran, and Indonesia – have separate diplomatic representatives to the Vatican, and this too is indicative of the special significance of the Vatican in Christian–Muslim Relations. (Most other countries combine the post of Ambassador to the Vatican with that of Ambassador to the Republic of Italy). One of the consequences of this is the regular stream of political as well as religious visitors to the Vatican, which gives it a unique relationship with the Muslim world as a whole.[16]

As a result of all this activity, a series of institutions have emerged across the world which are interested and involved in dialogue between Christians and Muslims, and their publications provide an invaluable source of information for developments, both positive and negative, around the world. Just to mention a few of these institutions we now have, in the Muslim world, the Royal Institute for Inter-Faith Studies in Amman, Jordan, set up by Prince Hasan in 1994/1415, for the study of religious issues in the Arab and Islamic worlds, with particular reference to Christianity in the Arab world, on which a book has been published.[17] Conferences have also been organised, in association with the Āl al-bayt Foundation, as mentioned above, and in 1999/1419 the first issue of a new journal, the *Bulletin of the Royal Institute for Inter-Faith Studies*, appeared, including articles on Ricoldo da Monte Croce and a conference held in Amman in 1998/1419 on Religion and Community, and a detailed report of the 1997/1418 conference held at Notre Dame University on Louis Massignon. In the West, the Islamic Foundation in Leicester has, since 1995/1415, been producing *Encounters: Journal of Inter-Cultural Perspectives*, which is devoted to the study of the issues associated both with inter-religious dialogue and with the relationship between Islam and the West.

Among Orthodox Christians it is perhaps the University of Belamend in the Lebanon which has done most to further the cause of Christian–Muslim understanding and dialogue, through conferences and a summer school. The current Executive Secretary of the WCC's Office on Inter-Religious Relations is also a Lebanese Orthodox Christian, Tarek Mitri.[18] And in the West *The Greek Orthodox Theological Review* has made more widely known some of the discussions which have taken place in North America between Orthodox Christians and Muslims on the relationships between their two communities.[19]

In Rome we have already referred to PISAI, the Pontifical Institute for Arab and Islamic Studies. Set up originally in Tunis by the White Fathers, PISAI moved to Rome in 1964/1384 and since then, as well as being one of the engine-houses of Christian–Muslim dialogue, in collaboration with the Pontifical Institute for Inter-Religious Dialogue, it has since 1975/1395 been the place of publication of the journal *Islamochristiana*, which as well as publishing articles on the history and theology of Christian–Muslim relations, performs an invaluable service by publishing reports of interesting developments in the field from all over the world, both in terms of meetings and conferences and reviews of publications. It is also not afraid to solicit Muslim comment on areas of controversy within the Roman Catholic church itself, and this self-critical approach has done much to further its reputation in both communities.[20]

Among Protestant Christians significant institutions are the Centre for the Study of Islam and Christian–Muslim Relations in Selly Oak in Birmingham, set up by Professor David Kerr in 1976/1396, now part of Birmingham University, and the publisher of *Islam and Christian–Muslim Relations*, together with the newer Center for Muslim-Christian Understanding, set up by Professor John Esposito in 1993/1414, within the School of Foreign Service of Georgetown University, which is a Jesuit Foundation, in Washington DC. Also in North America, Hartford Seminary in Connecticut has been one of the major centres for Islamic Studies in the region since 1894/1312, when Duncan Black Macdonald joined the Faculty of the Seminary. *The Muslim World* was first published there in 1910/1328, under the editorship of Samuel Zwemer, and although Zwemer's perspective was very much a traditional missionary one, the journal evolved a totally different approach while Kenneth Cragg was one of the editors between 1951/1371 and 1960/1380, and together with the new Duncan Black Macdonald Center for the Study of Islam and Christian–Muslim Relations, set up by Willem Bijlefeld, it is committed to a more dialogical approach.

Moreover, in different parts of the Christian and Muslim worlds groups of scholars and religious leaders have been meeting regularly for some years now to discuss issues of mutual interest, and it is important to refer to at least some of them. Perhaps the most effective has been the Groupe de Recherche Islamo-Chrétien (GRIC), a Francophone group involving mainly North African Muslim scholars, including Muhammad Ṭālbī, and Christians from the Lebanon as well as France and Belgium, which has met over a number of years in the form of both regular local meetings and an annual international gathering to discuss some of the most serious and difficult issues of Christian–Muslim dialogue, including the relationship between the Bible and the Qur'ān, and the relationship between Religion and the State.[21] The Anglophone world has not yet managed to produce a Christian–Muslim group of the same status, or work of the same quality, though in the United Kingdom the Inter-Faith Network has done useful work focusing on wider inter-faith relationships. Other parts of the world have groups which have managed to meet regularly, such as the Cénacle Libanais, the *Jamā'at al-akhā' al-dīnī* (The Association of Religious Brotherhood) in Cairo, and the Pakistan Association for Inter-Religious Dialogue (PAIRD).[22] PISAI and the Gregorian University in Rome have also set up an interesting exchange scheme with a number of universities in Turkey, and Indonesia has also provided some positive examples of Christian–Muslim collaboration.[23]

Sometimes, it cannot be denied that dialogue between Christians and Muslims has seemed to be a struggle. The title of one of the useful anthologies of documents concerning the dialogue actually includes the word 'struggle' in it.[24] Sometimes too, more recently, it has appeared that even the progress which has been made is somewhat vulnerable, as seen in the discussions which have been taking place in Rome concerning the relationship between Dialogue and Proclamation, and the position of Father Jacques Dupuis, who has been involved in dialogue with Asian religions rather than Islam, but whose views concerning the relationship between Christianity and other religions in general have been subjected to some interrogation.[25] But logically, in terms of verbal communication the only alternative to dialogue is either a monologue or a total silence, and it is hard to see how dialogue could be completely set aside.

THE POLITICAL CONTEXT

All of these developments in terms of inter-religious dialogue have taken place within a political context which has also been changing. Since 1945/1364, the era of colonialism has come to an end almost everywhere, and the majority of the Muslim world has therefore regained its political independence. Independence has been gained, however, within boundaries which in many cases were agreed by colonial powers, and serious problems sometimes ensued. This was the case, for example, in the Lebanon, which during the period of the French mandate between the two World Wars had its borders expanded from its historic heartland in order to make it more economically viable, but in the process the religious diversity of the population was considerably increased; and it was also the case in Africa, where political borders did not necessarily correspond to traditional ethnic or linguistic boundaries.

It was in this context, then, that alongside inter-religious dialogue, political dialogue also developed. This was particularly the case between the countries on opposite sides of the Mediterranean Sea, between whom there was in some cases a considerable amount of economic migration, for example from Morocco to the Netherlands and from Turkey to Germany, and for whom there was a considerable degree of economic interdependence, most obviously because of European dependence on oil for much of its energy needs. Thus as well as Christian–Muslim dialogue, we have also had a Euro-Arab dialogue or a Western-Arab dialogue.[26] Sometimes too the terminology becomes a little confused, so that there is dialogue between a religious unit, Islam, and a political or geographical unit, the West, and it becomes the relationship between Islam and the West which is discussed, by, for example, Professor Samuel Huntington, as referred to in the Introduction, or in the widely reported speech of Prince Charles to the Oxford Centre for Islamic Studies in 1993/1414.[27]

It is not always possible to compartmentalise or tidily separate the religious from the political, as memorably described by Charles Kimball, one of a delegation of seven American clergymen who went to Iran in 1980/1400 to meet with some of the Iranian leaders who were then holding fifty-three of his fellow citizens hostage in their embassy, on the basis of allegations that they were spies. During the course of a meeting with the Iranian students who had occupied the embassy, one of the students declared: 'The taking and holding of these spies is a great Islamic act!' Kimball explains how, to the mild surprise of his colleagues, he replied:

> That is nonsense . . . I think I understand your political motivations for seizing this embassy and holding these people hostage . . . Even so, you must know that your actions are not only illegal, they are immoral. And they are certainly not Islamic. Your responsibility as Muslims is to protect the foreigner in your midst . . .

And Kimball adds that, after a pause, the student said softly: 'What we are doing may not be Islamic, but it is revolutionary!'[28] Equally, when in 1996/1416 seven French Trappist monks, following the footsteps of Charles de Foucauld in seeking to live the spiritual life in the desert in the interior of Algeria, were kidnapped and murdered two months later by the GIA (Groupe Islamique Armée), it is not absolutely clear whether the motivation for this action was primarily religious or political; in other parts of the world the distinction may be even more difficult to make.[29]

Thus if in Nigeria there is tension and violence between two of the country's largest ethnic groups, the Yoruba and the Hausa, with some sixty Hausas being killed in the southern town of Sagamu and then some thirty Yorubas being killed in the northern town of Kano when news of the first massacre reached the town, as happened in July 1999/ Rabiʿ al-ākhir 1420, is this to be understood as a Christian–Muslim clash or a Yoruba-Hausa one?[30] The situation is complicated because the Hausa are almost all Muslim, while the Yoruba are evenly divided between Christians and Muslims, and in many other parts of the world too the religious and ethnic/linguistic balance is a very delicate one.[31] Instances of supposed conflict between Christians and Muslims in today's world, therefore, must always be located in their immediate political context.[32]

For the future perhaps one of the most difficult issues for Christians and Muslims to face is that of religious minorities. There are Christian minorities in the Muslim world which are in some cases the remnant of ancient once-dominant Christian majorities, as for example in Egypt or Palestine/Israel, and in others the legacy of more recent Christian missionary endeavour, as is the case in Pakistan or Indonesia; and newer Muslim minorities in the West, both in Europe and in North America. How will the dominant communities respond to and treat these minorities? In the world of Islam, will the suggestion of Muḥammad Ṭālbī – that the Muslim world should move away from the classical concept of the Christian as *dhimmī* back towards the situation of much fuller equality and participation envisaged by the Constitution of Medina – be taken up, or will the view of some medieval Muslim writers that Christians should be brought low and made to feel brought low be revived and come to predominate?[33] And in the West, will Muslim communities follow the example of Ismāʿīl al-Fārūqī and shift the primary marker of their identity from being an ethnic/ linguistic one towards a religious one, as Fārūqī shifted his emphasis from Arabism towards Islam, or will factors of language and culture predominate? These are questions which it is very hard to answer at this stage, but they are clearly both religious and political in their implications.[34]

FELLOW-PILGRIMS?

It is something of a truism to say that both the Christian and Muslim communities are 'debating communities'.[35] Within each community, therefore, it could be said that there are broadly two types of understanding of the faith: we have already seen the categorisation of the medieval poet al-Maʿarrī, with his reference to the world being divided into two sects, those with religion but no brains and those with brains but no religion, and this could be parallelled by statements such as those of W. B. Yeats, 'The best lack all conviction; the worst are full of passionate intensity', Bertrand Russell, 'People are zealous for a cause when they are not quite positive it is true', or John Henry Newman, 'Those who are certain of a fact are indolent disputants'. If this is true as regards the internal dynamics of both of the communities which we have been looking at, so it is also true with reference to their attitudes towards each other, where we can discern within each community a more positive and a more negative stream of thought.

Thus in medieval Spain, just to take one historical example, among Christians there is an obvious contrast between the attitudes of Ferdinand III of Castile (1230/627–1252/650) and his son Alfonso X 'the Wise' (1252/650–1284/683), with their tolerance towards Muslims and their openness towards Islamic culture, as seen in the inscription composed by Alfonso for the tomb of his father in Seville, which was written in Latin, Castilian, Hebrew and Arabic on each side of the tomb, and the attitudes of Ferdinand and Isabella two centuries later, whose tomb in Granada refers to them as the 'prostrators' of the sect of Muḥammad and the 'extinguishers' of the heretical stubbornness (i.e. Judaism). And among the Muslims there is an equally striking contrast between the tolerance of the Umayyad caliphate in Cordoba (756/138–1031/422) and the later much harsher rule of the Almoravids (*al-Murābiṭūn*) (1086/479–1145/540) and the Almohads (*al-Muwaḥiddūn*) (1145/540–1228/625), with the former seeing the deportation of the Mozarabs, Arabic-speaking Christians, to Morocco in 1127/521, and the latter ordering the Jews to convert to Islam in 1147/542, on pain of death. Many of the Jews fled to the (then) more tolerant Christian territory.[36]

In recent history too, a similar division can be seen. A Western traveller, admittedly from a Catholic background, while passing though Pakistan, recorded a remark of her Muslim host about the significant differences he had noticed between the attitudes of the Catholic and Protestant missionaries in the country: 'The Protestants seem to come here because they hate Islam and the Catholics because they love God.'[37] And it is true that among Western Christians today there does seem to be a significant contrast between some Protestant, particularly evangelical, Christian opinion on the one hand, and other, more ecumenically minded, Protestant and Roman Catholic opinion on the other. Some evangelical Christians, it appears, even if they do not hate Islam, are rather scared of Islam.

Why is this? On the one hand there are theological reasons for this view: one is the high view held by many evangelicals of the Bible as scripture, to the extent of it sometimes being referred to as infallible, a view to which the Qur'ān is a particular challenge given the Muslim claim that it was dictated by God; another is the high view of Christ (Christology) which is also held by many evangelicals, under the influence of Karl Barth whose Christology was so high that it was described by Paul Knitter as 'Christomonism', identifying Christ so much with God that Christology almost took the place of theology.[38] This view, with its stress on the finality of Christ, again finds Islam, as a post-Christian religion, particularly challenging.

On the other hand there are also wider cultural and religious reasons for the rather negative attitude towards Islam among some evangelicals: one is their tendency to identify faith and culture rather closely, as we have seen in the context of nineteenth/thirteenth-century mission, and thus to react rather strongly to the challenge of Islam to Western culture, which some evangelicals identify as 'Christian'; and another is the widespread influence, particularly in North America, of Christian Zionism, which gives rather uncritical support to the state of Israel, even its expansionist ambitions, which are seen as being in some way a fulfilment of Biblical prophecies. This view leads almost inevitably to some kind of demonisation of Islam, and it is significant that in 1999/1420, when the former Israeli Prime Minister Benjamin Netanyahu visited the United States, he was received far more warmly by evangelical leaders such as Rev. Jerry Falwell than he was by leaders of the Jewish community.[39] Muslims, on this view, almost become 'untouchables', and given the worldwide influence of this kind of evangelicalism, it has a significant negative impact on Christian–Muslim relations in many different parts of the world, not least in Africa, where the attitude towards Islam of an evangelist such as the South African Reinhard Bonnke, as demonstrated in some of his 'crusades' in Nigeria, is very different indeed from that of, say, Cardinal Francis Arinze.[40]

In the Christian community as a whole, however, as we have seen, there are many other opinions about Islam which are held, not least those associated with Rahner and Massignon, or Hick and Smith, and perhaps one of the ways in which the future relationships of Christians and Muslims could be ameliorated would be through the development of a rather greater generosity of spirit towards Islam among some evangelical Christians. Instead of the slightly haughty tone of some evangelical documents such as the Open Letter which was circulated within the Church of England in 1991/1412 concerning the necessity of the proclamation of the Christian message to those of other faiths during the Decade of Evangelism, and opposing the use of Anglican church buildings for any kind of inter-faith worship, we might therefore have a rather more inclusive attitude, such as that demonstrated by Professor John Macquarrie at the end of his book on modern views of Jesus, where he discusses the list of exemplars of faith which is found in the eleventh chapter of the Epistle to the Hebrews:

> [I]n Hebrews the procession of the men and women begins before Abraham, with some universal human figures. Should we not include some after Abraham as well? Suppose the progression has reached that point where Moses is passing, for obviously Christians too look back to him, as well as Jews.
>
> 'By faith Moses, when he came of age, refused to be called the son of Pharaoh's daughter, choosing rather to suffer affliction with the children of God than to enjoy the pleasures of sin for a season.
>
> 'By faith Mohammed, when he saw the people of Mecca degraded by idolatries, brought them the message of the one invisible God who is righteous and merciful.'[41]

Macquarrie goes on to insist, with the Epistle itself, that the history of faith reaches its fulfilment in Jesus Christ, but he adds that that does not imply the slightest disrespect for those who have found a relation to God in some other faith.[42]

Among Muslims too, a huge range of opinion about and attitudes towards Christianity is evident in the world today. Let us just take an example of contrasting Muslim attitudes in one region of the world, in South Africa: here on the one hand we have the polemical pamphlets and videos of Ahmad Deedat (b. 1918/1336), with their eye-catching titles such as *Crucifixion or Cruci-Fiction?* or *Resurrection or Resuscitation?*[43] These are extremely antagonistic towards Christianity, and Kate Zebiri comments 'the extensive popularity and influence of his works are unquestionable . . . even though they are undeniably inauspicious for Christian–Muslim relations', but Deedat's works have been translated into many languages, and he was even awarded the Feisal award for services to Islam in Saudi Arabia in 1986/1406.[44] On the other hand we have the writings of Farid Esack, which demonstrate how in the context of South Africa some Muslims were perfectly happy to co-operate with members of other religious communities in the struggle against apartheid. Esack observes rather tetchily that in Deedat's works the only reference to apartheid is in a polemical context, where it is simply asserted that Christianity is the cause of it and Islam is the solution to it. Esack thus seeks to work out an Islamic theology of liberation, which for many Muslims goes too far in the direction of hermeneutical revisionism, but does at least discuss in some detail the Qur'ānic attitude towards the 'other', not least in the context of how the term *mushriqūn* (literally 'associators', but usually translated as 'idolaters' or 'polytheists') should be understood and whether or not it should be applied to the *ahl al-kitāb* (People of the Book).[45]

There is therefore a huge range of Muslim opinion within the relatively small Muslim community in that one country, and this is echoed and amplified many times across the Muslim world as a whole. In Jordan a Royal Institute for Inter-Faith Studies is established and teaching on Christianity is a compulsory element of the religious education of all Jordanian school-children, while in neighbouring Saudi Arabia Christian worship is not permitted in public; this is just one example of differing attitudes towards the position of Christians in Muslim societies. Equally, on the one hand President Khatami of Iran was received at the Vatican by Pope John Paul II in March 1999/Dhū al-Qa'da/1419, and on the other continuing reports emerge from Iran of harassment of local Christians. Complete consistency is rarely achieved in any one context, let alone across the whole of a worldwide religious community.[46]

One change in the Muslim community which might do much to improve the climate of Christian–Muslim relations worldwide, would be the recognition by some of those Muslims who display a certain animus in their attitude towards Christians that Christians are not, after all, tritheists. The issue here is clearly the complex and hotly debated one, both among Christians and between Christians and Muslims, of the Trinity. Trinitarianism, it is true, is not Unitarianism, but equally it is not tritheism either, and Muslim recognition of this, as well as aiding better understanding of Christianity, would also help to remove some of the bitter antagonism which has clearly been felt towards Christianity by some Muslims. Difficult linguistic as well as theological issues are of course involved here, and the Arabic Christian term for Trinity, *tathlīth*, does certainly not help the process of understanding. Most Arabic words can be traced back to a three letter root or foundation, in this case the letters corresponding to the sounds 'th' 'l' and 'th' in the Latin alphabet, which together make up the word *thalātha*, meaning 'three'. *Tathlīth*, then, to use the technical grammatical terminology, is derived from the *maṣdar* (verbal noun) of the second form of the verb derived from this root, which usually involves the idea of 'making', so *tathlīth* could therefore appear literally to mean 'making three'. This is horribly asymmetrical to the Arabic word *tawhīd*, which has the same grammatical form but is derived from the root 'w' 'ḥ' 'd', which together make up the world *wāḥid*, meaning 'one'; *tawḥīd* therefore could be taken to mean 'making one'. This is very different from 'making three', so if some revision or refinement to the Christian Arabic terminology could be agreed, this might be constructive in helping Muslims to appreciate the distinction between Trinity and tritheism.

The issue is a complex one even within Christian theology, of course, with significant differences of emphasis existing between Eastern and Western Christians, so that, for example, the Cappadocian Fathers of the fourth century CE in the East seem readier to speak of plurality with reference to the Trinity than Augustine in the West. Perhaps unhelpfully for our purposes, the Cappadocians are also currently very influential in Western Christian thought about the Trinity, but further reflection both among Christians and between Christians and Muslims on this question would certainly be enlightening.[47]

Taking account of all the diversity which exists not only between the Christian and Muslim communities but also within the two communities, what is the best model for the future of the relationship between Christians and Muslims? In my view, it is the one described by Kenneth Cracknell that sees them as 'fellow-pilgrims to the truth that none of us has yet grasped in its immensity'.[48] The truth, in other words, is always beyond us as human beings, since it is always greater than us. Put another way, our appreciation of it is always provisional, but in seeking to further and develop that appreciation, both Christians and Muslims can bring valid and useful insights, not least since on many issues they share common understandings. Even on those topics concerning which they differ, however, mutual benefit can be derived from dialogue and constructive engagement, as can be seen in the reports of the Groupe de Recherche Islamo-Chrétien. Such vigorous and demanding dialogue may or may not result in agreement, but it certainly seems to advance the perception of the truth. Christians and Muslims are therefore, along with others, fellow-pilgrims on the route towards the perception of the truth, rather than either of them being, as some Christians and Muslims seem to like to think, already the proud possessors of the truth.

One of the leading centres of the Muslim community in the United Kingdom is Bradford.[49] The Anglican diocese of Bradford, as well as covering the city of Bradford also includes most of the nearby Yorkshire Dales, an area of outstanding natural beauty, and it is in the midst of the Dales, near the small villages of Appletreewick and Skyreholme, that the diocese has its centre for spiritual retreats and conferences, Parcevall Hall. It is an interesting building, a traditional Yorkshire farmhouse which was restored, extended, and modernised around 1927/1345 by Sir William Milner, who died in 1960/1380. His sister was married to Lord Linlithgow, the Viceroy of India between 1936/1355 and 1943/1362, and through that contact Sir William developed an interest in Indian culture and architecture, with the result that when he laid out the gardens of Parcevall Hall, he did so on Moghul lines, so that they reproduce, on a small scale and in a very different setting, the great Moghul gardens of Kashmir and Lahore. More recently, since 1993/1414, the diocese has laid out in the gardens the Stations of the Cross, a traditional kind of mini-pilgrimage whereby Christians can meditate on the last days of Jesus's life by following a laid-out route to the different stations, each of which represents a particular incident. The fourteenth, which represents the body of Jesus being laid in the tomb, is in the part of the garden which is perhaps the most typically Moghul in design, with water running down a series of steps into a small pool at the foot, in a manner highly reminiscent of the Shalimar Gardens in Lahore. Water is symbolic of the resurrection, and, incongruous as it may seem, given that Muslims believe in neither the crucifixion nor the resurrection of Jesus, that small piece of the Parcevall Hall gardens may perhaps serve as a small parable of what Christian–Muslim relations could become if the two communities are able to draw on the best of each of their traditions. Parcevall Hall provides a small example of Christian spirituality in the physical environment of a Moghul-inspired garden, which could no doubt be matched by an example of Muslim spirituality in a Christian-inspired physical environment, and it can perhaps serve to symbolise Christians and Muslims as fellow-pilgrims on the road towards the truth, which neither has yet grasped in its immensity.

NOTES

1. Secretariat for non-Christians, *Guidelines for a Dialogue between Christians and Muslims*, Rome: Ancora, 1969; 2nd edn, M. Borrmans, *Orientations pour un Dialogue entre Chrétiens et Musulmans*, Paris: Cerf, 1981, English translation, *Guidelines for Dialogue between Christians and Muslims*, translated by Marston Speight, Mahwah NJ: Paulist Press, 1990.
2. See Borrmans, *Orientations*, English edition, pp. 115–21.
3. World Council of Churches, *Guidelines on Dialogue with People of Living Faiths*, Geneva: WCC Publications, 1979, and Office on Inter-Religious Relations, *Issues in Christian–Muslim Relations: Ecumenical Relations*, Geneva: WCC Publications, 1992.
4. S. J. Samartha and J. Taylor (eds), *Christian–Muslim Dialogue: Papers Presented at the Broumana Consultation*, Geneva: World Council of Churches, 1973. The final Memorandum can be found on pp. 156–63.
5. A. Bsteh (ed.), *Peace for Humanity: Principles, Problems and Perspectives of the Future as Seen by Christians and Muslims*, Delhi: Vikas, 1996. The final Declaration can be found, in German, English, French and Arabic, on pp. 274–83.

6. For WCC sponsored conferences, see *Christians Meeting Muslims: WCC Papers on Ten Years of Christian–Muslim Dialogue*, Geneva: World Council of Churches, 1977, and S. E. Brown, (ed.), *Meeting in Faith: Twenty Years of Christian–Muslim Conversations Sponsored by the World Council of Churches*, Geneva: WCC Publications, 1989. For Catholic involvement, see M. Borrmans, 'The Muslim-Christian Dialogue of the Last Ten Years', in *Pro Mundi Vita*, Brussels, No. 74 (1978), and note 2 above.
7. M. L. Fitzgerald, '25 Years of Christian–Muslim Dialogue: a Personal Journey', in *Proche-Orient Chrétien*, 40 (1990), pp. 258–71, and D. Mulder, 'A History of the Sub-Unit on Dialogue of the World Council of Churches', in *Studies in Inter-religious Dialogue*, 2 (1992), pp. 136–51.
8. See T. Michel, 'Pope John Paul II's Teaching about Islam in his Addresses to Muslims', in *Islam and the Modern Age*, 18 (1987), pp. 67–76; I. M. Abu-Rabi', 'Pope John Paul II and Islam', in *Muslim World*, 88 (1998), pp. 279–96; and F. Arinze, 'Christian–Muslim Relations in the Twenty-first Century', in *Pro Dialogo*, Rome, No. 97 (1998), pp. 81–92, and Arinze, *Meeting Other Believers*, Leominster: Gracewing, 1997.
9. See M. Borrmans, 'Le Séminaire du Dialogue islamo-chrétien de Tripoli (Libye), (1–6 Février 1976)', in *Islamochristiana*, 2 (1976), pp. 135–70, and D. Kerr and K. Ahmad (eds), 'Christian Mission and Islamic Da'wah', in *International Review of Mission*, 65 (1976), pp. 365–460, reprinted Leicester: Islamic Foundation, 1982.
10. See T. Michel, 'The Rights of non-Muslims in Islam: an Opening Statement', in *Journal of the Institute of Muslim Minority Affairs*, 6 (1985), pp. 7–20, with replies and comments in the succeeding issues of the same journal by Muḥammad Hamidullah, Fazlur Rahman and Hasan Askari, with further Christian contributions from William Shepard and Andreas D'Souza.
11. See J. Hick (ed.), *Truth and Dialogue*, London: Sheldon Press, 1974, and E. J. Sharpe, *Comparative Religion: a History*, 2nd edn, London: Duckworth, 1986, Chapter 11.
12. See M. A. Anees, 'The Dialogue of History', in M. A. Anees, S. Z. Abedin, and Z. Sardar, *Christian–Muslim Relations: Yesterday, Today, Tomorrow*, London: Grey Seal, 1991, p. 13. Lyazghi is quoted by C. McVey, in the Preface to *The World of Islam*, special issue of *New Blackfriars*, February 1990, p. 56.
13. See A. Siddiqui, *Christian–Muslim Dialogue in the Twentieth Century*, London: Macmillan, 1997, Chapter 11, on these groups.
14. A full list can be found in Borrmans, *Orientations*.
15. M. Talbi, 'Unavoidable Dialogue in a Pluralist World: a Personal Account', in *Encounters*, 1 (1995), p. 62.
16. See the publication of the Pontifical Council for Inter-religious Dialogue, *Recognize the Spiritual Bonds which Unite Us*, Vatican City, 1994, pp. 137–42 of which provides a partial list of the religious and political leaders of the Muslim world who visited the Vatican between 1978/1398 and 1993/1414.
17. El Hassan bin Talal, *Christianity in the Arab World*, Amman: Royal Institute for Inter-Faith Studies, 1994, British edition, London: SCM, 1998.
18. See T. Mitri (ed.), *Religion, Law and Society: a Christian–Muslim Discussion*, Geneva: WCC, 1995.

19. See N. M. Vaporis (ed.), *Orthodox Christians and Muslims*, (papers from the *Greek Orthodox Theological Review*), Brookline MA: Holy Cross Orthodox Press, 1986.
20. See M. Talbi, 'Les Réactions non Catholiques à la Déclaration de Vatican II "Dignitatis Humanae" – Point de Vue Musulman', in *Islamochristiana*, 17 (1991), pp. 15–20, and M. Arkoun, 'Réflexions d'un Musulman sur le "Nouveau Catéchisme"', in *Islamochristiana*, 19 (1993), pp. 43–54.
21. See the English translation of their first report, Muslim-Christian Research Group, *The Challenge of the Scriptures*, Maryknoll NY: Orbis, 1989, the report of the group's second series of discussions, on Religion and the State, by R. Caspar, in *Islamochristiana*, 12 (1986), pp. 49–72, and J.-P. Gabus, 'L'expérience de Dialogue Islamo-Chrétien dans le Cadre du GRIC', in *Islamochristiana*, 19 (1993), pp. 117–24.
22. See J. Corbon, 'Le Cénacle Libanais et le Dialogue Islamo-Chrétien', in *Islamochristiana*, 7 (1981), pp. 227–40, C. Van Nispen, 'L'Association de la Fraternité Religieuse', in *Islamochristiana*, 5 (1979), pp. 253–8, and A. D'Souza, 'Dialogue in the Islamic Republic of Pakistan', in *Islamochristiana*, 14 (1988), pp. 211–18.
23. T. Michel, 'Teaching the Christian Faith in the Faculties of Theology of Turkey', in *Encounter*, Rome, No. 164 (1990); T. Taher (The Indonesian Minister for Religious Affairs), 'Pancasila Fifty Years On', in *Islamochristiana*, 21 (1995), pp. 87–94; and I. M. Abu-Rabi', 'Christian–Muslim Relations in the Twenty-First Century: Lessons from Indonesia', in *Islamochristiana*, 24 (1998), pp. 19–35.
24. See R. W. Rousseau (ed.), *Christianity and Islam: the Struggling Dialogue*, Scranton PA: Ridge Row Press, 1985. Another useful anthology of texts on dialogue, with a more positive title, is L. Swidler (ed.), *Muslims in Dialogue: the Evolution of a Dialogue*, Lewiston: Edwin Mellen Press, 1992.
25. See 'Dialogue and Proclamation: Reflections and Orientations on Inter-religious Dialogue and the Proclamation of the Gospel of Jesus Christ', jointly published by the Pontifical Council for Inter-religious Dialogue and the Congregation for the Evangelization of Peoples, and containing introductions and a joint statement by the heads of the two bodies, Cardinal Francis Arinze and Cardinal Jozef Tomko, Vatican City, 1991, with the comment by M. Fitzgerald in *Pro Dialogo*, (Bulletin of the Pontifical Council for Inter-Religious Dialogue), 28 (1993), pp. 23–33; and the reports of the investigation of Fr. Dupuis's *Towards a Christian Theology of Religious Pluralism*, Maryknoll NY: Orbis, 1997, in *The Tablet*, 21 November 1998, with a defence of Father Dupuis by Cardinal König on 16 January 1999 and a reply by Cardinal Ratzinger on 13 March 1999.
26. See S. Al-Mani' and S. Al-Shaikhly, *The Euro-Arab Dialogue*, London: Pinter, 1983; D. Hopwood (ed.), *Euro-Arab Dialogue: Relations between the Two Cultures*, London: Croom Helm, 1985; H. A. Jawad, *Euro-Arab Relations*, London: Macmillan, 1992; and J. S. Nielsen and S. A. Khasawnih, *Arabs and the West: Mutual Images*, Amman: University of Jordan Press, 1998.
27. See HRH Prince Charles, *Islam and the West*, Oxford Centre for Islamic Studies, 1993, also in *Islam and Christian–Muslim Relations*, 5 (1994), pp. 67–74.

28. C. Kimball, *Striving Together: a Way Forward in Christian–Muslim Relations*, Maryknoll NY: Orbis, 1991, p. 1–2.
29. See C. de Foucauld, *Letters from the Desert*, London: Burns and Oates, 1977.
30. Report in *The Economist*, 31 July 1999.
31. See J. O. Hunwick (ed.), *Religion and National Integration in Africa: Islam, Christianity, and Politics in the Sudan and Nigeria*, Evanston IL: Northwestern University Press, 1992; and H.P. Goddard, 'Christian–Muslim Relations in Nigeria and Malaysia', in L. Ridgeon (ed.), *Islamic Interpretations of Christianity*, London: Curzon, forthcoming in 2000.
32. See S. Joseph and B. L. K. Pillsbury (eds), *Muslim-Christian Conflicts*, Boulder CO: Westview Press, 1978.
33. See Ṭālbī's discussion of this topic in *'Iyāl allāh*, as discussed by R. L. Nettler in 'Mohamed Talbi: "For Dialogue between All Religions" ', in R. L. Nettler and S. Taji-Farouki (eds), *Muslim-Jewish Relations: Intellectual Traditions and Modern Politics*, Amsterdam: Harwood Academic Publishers, 1998, pp. 190–3.
34. J. S. Nielsen (ed.), *Religion and Citizenship in Europe and the Arab World*, London: Grey Seal, 1992, and Y. Y. Haddad and A. T. Lummis, *Islamic Values in the United States*, Oxford University Press, 1987.
35. Compare the title of M. M. J. Fischer and M. Abedi, *Debating Muslims: Cultural Dialogues in Postmodernity and Tradition*, Madison: University of Wisconsin Press, 1980.
36. F. de B. de Medina, 'Islam and Christian Spirituality in Spain: Contacts, Influences, Similarities', in *Islamochristiana*, 18 (1992), pp. 87–108. On the Jews, see M. R. Cohen, *Under Cross and Crescent: the Jews in the Middle Ages*, Princeton University Press, 1994.
37. D. Murphy, *Full Tilt*, London: Century, 1983, p. 138.
38. P. Knitter, 'Christomonism in Karl Barth's Evaluation of the non-Christian Religions', in *Neue Zeitschrift für Systematische Theologie*, 15 (1973), pp. 38–64.
39. See P. C. Merkley, *The Politics of Christian Zionism, 1891–1948*; London: Cass, 1998; R. Fuller, *Naming the Antichrist: the History of an American Obsession*, Oxford University Press, 1995; and P. Boyer, *When Time Shall Be No More: Prophecy Belief in Modern American Culture*, Harvard University Press, 1992.
40. See P. Gifford, ' "Africa Shall be Saved": an Appraisal of Reinhard Bonnke's Pan-African Crusade', in *Journal of Religion in Africa*, 17 (1987), pp. 63–92; Gifford, *The New Crusaders: Christianity and the New Right in Southern Africa*, 2nd edn, London: Pluto, 1991, esp. pp. 108–15; Gifford, *Christianity and Politics in Doe's Liberia*, Cambridge University Press, 1993, esp. pp. 257–71.
41. J. Macquarrie, *Jesus Christ in Modern Thought*, London: SCM, 1990, pp. 421–2. See also his *The Mediators*, London: SCM, 1995, esp. Chapter 9, on Muḥammad.
42. Macquarrie, *Jesus Christ*, p. 422. For the full text of the Open Letter, see J. Wolffe (ed.), *The Growth of Religious Diversity: Britain from 1945 – a Reader*, London: Open University, 1994, pp. 205–6.
43. Distributed free by the Islamic Propagation Centre International, Durban, and first published in 1984 and 1978 respectively.
44. K. Zebiri, *Muslims and Christians Face to Face*, Oxford: Oneworld, 1997, p. 46.

45. F. Esack, *Qur'ān, Liberation and Pluralism: an Islamic Perspective of Interreligious Solidarity against Oppression*, Oxford: Oneworld, 1997, esp. pp. 154–5 on the *mushriqūn* and pp. 218–19 on Deedat; and Esack, *On Being a Muslim: Finding a Religious Path in the World Today*, Oxford: Oneworld, 1999, esp. pp. 153–4 on Deedat.
46. See the reports of the discussions at the Lambeth Conference of the Anglican Communion in 1998/1419, concerning the considerable diversity which exists with regard to the position of Christians in different parts of the Muslim world, in *The Church Times*, 31 July 1998.
47. For a Christian attempt to make the Trinity accessible to Muslims, see D. Brown, *The Divine Trinity*, London: Sheldon Press, 1969. For a more technical historical discussion, see R. Haddad, *La Trinité Divine chez les Théologiens Arabes, 750–1050*, Paris: Beachesne, 1985.
48. K. Cracknell, *Considering Dialogue*, London: British Council of Churches, 1981, p. 1.
49. See P. J. Lewis, *Islamic Britain: Religion, Politics and Identity among British Muslims – Bradford in the 1990's*, London: Tauris, 1994.

Bibliography

Full details of material used for each topic addressed in this book can be found in the notes to each section. The following books are relevant to the overall theme of Christian–Muslim relations.

General books on Christian–Muslim relations

Anees, M. A., Abedin, S. Z., and Sardar, Z. (1991), *Christian–Muslim Relations: Yesterday, Today, Tomorrow*, London: Grey Seal.

Gaudeul, J.-M. (1984), *Encounters and Clashes: Islam and Christianity in History*, 2 vols, Rome: Pontifical Institute of Arabic and Islamic Studies.

Goddard, H. P. (1995), *Christians and Muslims: from Double Standards to Mutual Understanding*, London: Curzon.

Haddad, Y. Y., and Haddad, W. Z. (eds) (1995), *Christian–Muslim Encounters*, Gainesville FL: University Press of Florida.

Mohammed, O. N. (1999), *Muslim-Christian Relations: Past, Present, Future*, Maryknoll NY: Orbis.

Sweetman, J. W. (1945, 1947, 1955, and 1967), *Islam and Christian Theology*, 4 vols, London: Lutterworth. (Rather dated, but still valuable on the medieval intellectual exchanges between Christians and Muslims.)

Watt, W. M. (1991) *Muslim-Christian Encounters: Perceptions and Misperceptions*, London: Routledge.

Christian Perceptions of Islam over the centuries

Hourani, A. (1991), *Islam in European Thought*, Cambridge University Press.

Plantinga, R. J. (ed.) (1999), *Christianity and Plurality*, Oxford: Blackwell. (Does not address Islam in particular, but an invaluable survey of Biblical and Christian thinking about other religions.)

Southern, R. W. (1962), *Western Views of Islam in the Middle Ages*, Harvard University Press.

Waardenburg, J. (1962), *L'Islam dans le Miroir de l'Occident*, The Hague: Mouton.

Muslim Perceptions of Christianity over the centuries

Goddard, H. P. (1996), *Muslim Perceptions of Christianity*, London: Grey Seal.

Robinson, N. (1991), *Christ in Islam and Christianity: the Representation of Jesus in the Qur'ān and the Classical Muslim Commentaries*, London: Macmillan.

Waardenburg, J. (ed.) (1999), *Muslim Perceptions of Other Religions throughout History*, Oxford University Press.

Christian–Muslim Relations today, including dialogue

Borrmans, M. (1990), *Guidelines for Dialogue between Christians and Muslims*, Mahwah NJ: Paulist Press.

Griffiths, P. J. (ed.) (1990), *Christianity through non-Christian Eyes*, Maryknoll NY: Orbis. Part II (Islamic Perceptions of Christianity in the Twentieth Century).

Joseph, S., and Pillsbury, B. L. K. (eds) (1978), *Muslim-Christian Conflicts: Economic, Political, and Social Origins*, Boulder CO: Westview.

Muslim-Christian Research Group (1989), *The Challenge of the Scriptures: the Bible and the Qur'ān*, Maryknoll NY: Orbis.

Rousseau, R. W. (ed.) (1985), *Christianity and Islam: the Struggling Dialogue*, Scranton PA: Ridge Row Press.

Siddiqui, A. (1997), *Christian–Muslim Dialogue in the Twentieth Century*, London: Macmillan.

Waardenburg, J. (ed.) (1998), *Islam and Christianity: Mutual Perceptions since the Mid-20th Century*, Louvain: Peeters.

Watt, W. M. (1983), *Islam and Christianity Today*, London: Routledge and Kegan Paul.

Zebiri, K. (1997), *Muslims and Christians Face to Face*, Oxford: Oneworld.

Index

'Abbās I, 118–19
'Abbasid Revolution, 50
'Abd Allāh al-Hāshimī, 53–4, 115
'Abd al-Jabbār, 167
'Abd al-Malik, 47–8
'Abd al-Qādir, 129
'Abduh, Muḥammad, 130, 132, 163
Abraham, 24, 27, 35, 36, 37, 41, 48, 59, 104, 153, 155, 158, 191
Abū Ṭālib, 20
Abū 'Ubaida ibn al-Jarrāḥ, 44, 46
Abyssinia *see* Axum
Aceh, 129
Acre, 88, 89, 114, 116
Acts, Book of, 7, 8, 9
Adam, 93, 159
Addis Ababa, 156
Addison, J. T., 86
Aden, 126
Afghānī, Jamāl al-dīn, al-, 129
Afghanistan, 34, 126
Africa, 109, 124, 125, 135, 146, 182, 187
  see also North Africa; South Africa
Aghlabid emirate, 163, 183
Agra, 130–1, 132, 133
Ahmad Khan, Sayyid, 128, 129, 130, 132, 133
'Ain Jalūt, 89
Aitchison, George, 146
Ajmir, 1, 4n3, 112
Akbar, 120–1
Akhtar, Shabbir, 167–8
Āl al-bayt Foundation, 183, 184
Alberūnī (al-Bīrūnī), 143
Albigensians, 116
Aleppo, 87, 112
Alexandria, 6, 13, 14, 50, 54, 55, 148
Alexius I, 84
Alfonso VI, 98, 99
Alfonso X ('the Wise'), 189
Algeria, 187
Algiers, 116, 125, 126, 129, 164, 181
'Alī, 104
Aligarh, 128
Almohad dynasty, 101, 189
Almoravid dynasty, 189
American Board of Foreign Missions, 122
Amman, 184
Amos, 95
Amsterdam, 151
Andrae, Tor, 24, 39
Andrew of Longjumeau, 116, 117
Anees, M. A., 182
Anglican Christians, 118–19, 122, 124–5, 135, 155–6, 190–1, 193–4
Anonymous monk of France, 113
Anonymous Nestorian monk, 36
Antichrist, 10, 39, 40, 81–4, 85, 94, 96, 111
Antioch, 8, 13, 14, 85, 87
Apocalyptic, 81, 82, 84, 96, 111
  see also Millennialism
Apollyon, 92
Apostasy, 135, 140n64
Appletreewick, 193
Aqṣā, al- (mosque), 88
Aquinas, Thomas, 102–3, 116, 157
Arabia, 15–17, 19, 23, 24–6, 28, 29, 34, 39, 42–3, 46, 144, 145–6
Arabian Mission, 124
Arabian Nights, 144, 145
Arabism, 159, 161
Arab League, 181
Arab Socialist Union, 183
Arianism, 39
Arinze, Francis, 181, 190
Aristotle, 10, 14, 52, 97, 99, 101, 102, 103, 104
Arius, 94
Armenian church, 73, 117
Ash'arī, al-, 60–1, 66
Asherah, 5

Asia, 109, 111, 112, 124, 182
  see also Central Asia
Asia Minor, 56, 58, 85, 87, 88, 113
  see also Turkey
Aslan, Adnan, 166
Assassins, 87
Assisi, 114, 115
Association of Religious Brotherhood, 186
Athens, 9, 50
Augustine, 70, 71, 79, 81, 160, 193
Austria, 126, 181
Averroes *see* Ibn Rushd
  Averroists, 102, 116
Avicenna *see* Ibn Sīnā
Avignon, 96
Axum, 16, 20, 22, 23
Aydin, Mahmud, 167
Azhar, al-, 99, 130, 135, 136, 158, 181, 183
Aziz, Tariq, 73

Baal, 5
Bacon, Roger, 95–6
Baghdad, 52, 54, 80, 97, 116, 154
Baḥīrā, 20, 22–3, 39
Baḥrain, 16
Balkans, 110
Baltic, 89
Baptist Missionary Society, 122
Bāqillānī, al-, 61–2
Barelvi, Sayyid Amad, 129
Barnum, P. T., 147
Barth, Karl, 150, 151, 152, 153, 160, 190
Basques, 81
Basra, 53
Bat Ye'or, 68
BBC, 90
Becker, C. H., 147
Bede, the Venerable, 80
Beirut, 158
Belamend, 184
Belgium, 186
Bellini, 128
Benedict de Goes, 121
Bengal, 125, 147
Bennett, Clinton, 151
Bergson, Henri, 165
Bernard of Clairvaux, 87, 93, 97
Bethlehem, 88
Bible, 5–11, 35, 39, 60, 87, 95, 110, 123, 135, 144, 160, 164, 186, 190
  Translation into Arabic, 55, 117, 123
  Genesis 21: 12–13, 35
  Genesis 21: 18, 35
  Genesis 25, 35
  Genesis 25: 1, 36
  1 Kings 18, 5
  Isaiah 45: 1, 5
  Daniel 7, 82
  Jonah 4: 2, 6
  Malachi 1: 11, 5–6
  Matthew 2: 1–12, 9, 23
  Matthew 3: 7, 10
  Matthew 5: 17, 166
  Matthew 27: 25, 7–8
  Matthew 28: 19–20, 122
  Mark 13, 83
  John 14: 6, 10
  Acts 2: 23, 8
  Acts 4: 12, 10
  Acts 10, 9
  Acts 11: 26, 14
  Acts 17, 9
  Acts 19 and 20, 9
  Hebrews 11, 191
  1 Peter 3: 15, 95
  1 John 2: 22, 10
  1 John 4: 2–3, 10, 40
  Revelation 13: 8, 83
  see also Genesis; Revelation
Bijlefeld, Willem, 185
Birmingham, 167, 182, 185
Blachère, Regis, 164
Blashfield, Edwin Howland, 146
Boethius, 97
Bohemia, 89
Bologna, 96, 100
Bonnke, Reinhard, 190
Borrmans, Maurice, 177
Bosnia, 2
Bosphorus, 91
Bradford, 193
Breiner, Bert, 154–5
Bridgport, 146
Brighton, 146
British and Foreign Bible Society, 122
Broumana, 180
Buber, Martin, 182
Bugia, 116

Bukhara, 97
Bulliet, Richard, 69–70
Burckhardt, John Louis, 146
Burgundy, 87, 93
Burton, Sir Richard, 146
Bushire, 123
Byblos, 89
Byzantine empire, 14, 15, 16, 22, 34, 37, 38, 41, 42, 44, 47, 50, 52, 56–9, 62, 64, 73, 84, 88, 91, 98, 111, 113

Caesarea, 44
Cairo, 99, 128, 130, 148, 158, 183, 186
Calcutta, 123
Calvin, John, 111–12, 157, 160
Cambridge, 100, 123, 143
Canada, 159
  see also North America
Cape Horn, 112
Cape of Good Hope, 109
Cappadocian Fathers, 193
Carey, William, 122, 133
Carlyle, Thomas, 147
Carmelite order, 117–20
Carthage, 79, 183
  see also Hippo
Casablanca, 183
Castile, 99
Cathars, 89
Caucasus, 126, 129
Cénacle Libanais, 186
Center for Muslim–Christian Understanding, 185
Central Asia, 34, 61, 64, 73, 89, 121, 125, 126
Centre for the Study of Islam and Christian–Muslim Relations, 185
Cerinthus, 10
Chalcedon, Council of, 14, 15, 37, 38, 41
Chaldaean church, 73
Charfi, Abdelmajid, 60, 64
Charlemagne, 80
Charles V, 89, 117
Charles Martel, 80
Charles, Prince, 187
Chasseboeuf, Constantin François, 145
China, 113, 120, 143
Chosroes/Khusro, 22
Christian church, divisions of, 12–15
  see also Eastern (Orthodox) churches
Christian Zionism, 190
Christology, 13–14, 22, 26, 28, 29, 37, 41, 48, 53, 57, 62, 63, 93, 94, 121, 190, 191
  see also Jesus
Chrysostom, John, 8
Church Missionary Society, 122, 124, 125
Clement IV, 95
Clement VIII, 117
Clement of Alexandria, 9
Clermont, 84, 91
Cluny, 93
Cockerell, Samuel Pepys, 146
Collège de France, 143
Colt factory, 146
Columbus, Christopher, 109
Conrad III, 87
Constantine, 8, 11–12, 13, 113
Constantinople, 13, 14, 37, 47, 58, 85, 89, 96, 111, 128
  see also Istanbul
Constitution of Medina, 29–30, 31, 41, 66, 188
Conversion to Christianity, 46, 59, 73, 83, 128, 135–6, 161
Conversion to Islam, 31, 45, 46, 54, 68–74, 135, 136, 145, 146, 161, 189
Convivencia, 101
Cook, Michael, 36, 42, 44
Coptic Christians, 24, 37, 47, 56, 71–2, 117
Cordoba, 81–4, 98, 101, 189
Cornelius, 9
Covenant of 'Umar, 44–6, 66
Cracknell, Kenneth, 151, 193
Cragg, Kenneth, 148, 155–6, 185
Creation, 102
Crimea, 126
Cromer, Lord, 130, 132
Crone, Patricia, 36, 42, 44
Crusades, 1, 2, 3, 64, 84–92, 93, 96, 109, 110, 111, 114, 190
Cuoq, Joseph, 177
Cyprian, 70
Cyprus, 65, 88
Cyrenaica, 142–3
  see also Libya

Cyril, 113
Cyrus (Byzantine official), 37
Cyrus (Persian king), 5

Damascus, 38, 43, 47, 65, 87, 91
Damietta, 89, 114
Daniel, Norman, 93, 135
Dante, 104
Danube, 91, 110
Darwin, 165
David, 104
Da'wa (mission), 161–2, 182
 see also Mission
Debate, Christian–Muslim, 41, 53, 118–19, 121–2, 123, 131–2, 177
Deedat, Ahmad, 191
Dhimma (Covenant), 46–7
Dhimmī (Protected minorities), 46, 59, 66–7, 161, 188
 see also religious minorities
Dialogue, Christian–Muslim, 41, 54, 161–2, 163, 167, 177–86, 193–4
Diana/Artemis, 9
Diaspora, Jewish, 6
Diocletian, 48n11
Dome of the Rock, 88
Dominic, 116
Dominican order, 103, 116, 117
Dominic Gundisalvus, 101
Donatism, 13, 71
Doughty, Charles, 145
Dress regulations, 45–6, 66–7, 77n45
Druzes, 72
Dupuis, Jacques, 186

Eastern (Orthodox) churches, 150, 156, 177, 184–5, 193
 see also Christian church, divisions of; Melkites; Monophysite Christians; Nestorian Christians
Ebionism, 10
Edessa, 87
Edinburgh, 148, 151
 Edinburgh University, 131
Edirne (Adrianople), 109
Egypt, 14, 15, 34, 37, 47, 56, 69, 71–2, 88, 89, 114, 126, 128, 129, 130, 132, 135, 142, 145, 148, 161, 184, 188
El Cid, 99
Elijah, 5, 63
England, 88, 100, 121–2, 123, 128, 132–3, 146
 see also United Kingdom
Enlightenment, the, 142, 144
English in Iran, 118–19
English Levant Company, 112
Ephesus, 9
 Council of, 14
Eritrea, 16
Esack, Farid, 191–2
Esmat Abdel-Meguid, 181
Esposito, John, 185
Ethiopia, 16
Euclid, 97, 99, 104
Eulogius, 81–4
Euro–Arab dialogue, 187
Eutyches, 14
Evangelical Christians, 125, 136, 150, 189–91
Evans-Pritchard, E. E., 142–3
Ezekiel, 63
Ezra, 28, 160

Fakhry, Majid, 52
Falsafa (Islamic philosophy), 50
Falwell, Jerry, 190
Fārābī, al-, 55, 99, 101
Farquhar, J. N., 151
Farrūkh, 'Umar, 134
Farūqī, Ismā'īl al-, 158–62, 163, 167, 182, 188
Ferdinand III, 189
Ferdinand and Isabella, 109, 189
Filioque (and the Son), 13, 156
First World War, 123
Fitzgerald, Michael, 181
Foucauld, Charles de, 187
France, 80–1, 87, 88, 89, 97, 100, 102, 116, 154, 185
Francis I, 117
Francis of Assisi, 114–15, 117, 120
Franciscan order, 114, 115, 117
 Mission in the Holy Land, 117
Frederick II, 88, 98, 100
Frederick Barbarossa, 88
Free will and predestination, 41, 53, 118–19, 122
French Revolution, 123
Frost, Stanley Brice, 159, 162

Gabriel, 20
Gabriel II, 56

Gad al Haq, 181
Gairdner, Temple, 124–5, 148, 155
Galen, 99, 104
Galland, Antoine, 144
Gama, Vasco da, 109
Gardet, Louis, 177
Gaza, 42
Genesis, Book of, 80
see also Bible
Genoa, 112
Georgetown University, 185
Gerard of Cremona, 99, 101
Gerbert of Aurillac, 97
Germany, 87, 88, 93, 111, 113, 187
Ghassān, tribe of, 15, 16
Ghazālī, al-, 61, 99, 101, 124, 157, 163
Gibb, H. A. R., 148
Gibbon, Edward, 144–5
Gibelet, 89
Gnosticism, 10, 40
Goa, 121
Goethe, 147, 149
Goldziher, Ignaz, 147–8
Gospel, 20, 27, 55
see also Bible
Goths, 113
Granada, 109, 189
Great Schism, 12–13, 79
Greece, 74
Greek Catholic church, 154
Gregorian University, 186
Gregory VII, 70
Groupe Islamique Armée, 187
Groupe de Recherche Islamo-Chrétien (GRIC), 185–6, 193
Grunebaum, G. E. von, 148
Gulf, Persian, 16
Gundeshapur, 50, 52, 54
Guy de Lusignan, 88

Hagar, 35, 36
Hagarism, 36, 44
Ḥākim, al-, 71–2
Ḥallāj, al-, 154
Ḥanafī (school of Islamic law), 71
Hardwick Hall, 146
Ḥārith ibn Jabala, 15
Harran, 53, 54
Hartford, 146, 148
Hartford Seminary, 185
Hārūn al-Rashīd, 52, 80–1
Harvard, 152
Hasan, Prince, 181, 184
Hāshimī, al-, 53–4, 114
Hassan II, 183
Hattin (Ḥiṭṭīn), 88
Hausa, 188
Hellenism, Christian attitudes to, 8–10, 79
Hellenism, Muslim attitudes to, 50
Henry VIII, 146
Heraclius, 22, 23, 34, 37
Herbert of Cherbury, Lord, 149
Herman of Dalmatia, 98
Ḥibat Allāh ibn al-'Assāl, 55
Hick, John, 150, 164, 166, 167, 190
High Council for Islamic Affairs, 183
Hijaz, 17, 42
see also Mecca; Medina
Ḥimyar, 30, 31, 44
Hinduism, 120, 151, 156
Hippo (Carthage), 71
Hippocrates, 99, 104
Ḥīra, al-, 16, 52
Hocking, W. E., 151–2
Holocaust, 182
Holy Roman Empire, 98
Holy Sepulchre, 86, 88
Holy Spirit, 13, 90, 154, 156
Hospitallers, 88
Hourani, A. H., 147
Hūd, 24
Hulagu, 73
Ḥunayn ibn Isḥāq, 52
Hungary, 111, 125, 126
Hunt, Paul, 134
Huntington, Samuel, 4n4, 187
Hurgronje, Snouck, 24, 146, 147, 148
Hussites, 89

Ibn al-Nadīm, 55
Ibn 'Asākir, 45
Ibn Isḥāq, 19–22, 30–1, 44
Ibn Rushd, 99, 101–2, 103, 104
Ibn Sab'īn, 102
Ibn Sa'd, 31
Ibn Sīnā, 97, 99, 101, 103, 104
Ibn Taimiyya, 64–6, 68
Ibrāhīm *see* Abraham
Ibrāhīm (son of Muammad), 24
Icons, 59
Idrīsī, al-, 98
Ikhwān al-Ṣafā, 3

Imperialism, European, 3, 109–13, 125–7, 133–5, 147–9
India, 69, 103, 120–2, 123, 124, 125, 126, 128, 129, 130–3, 143, 156, 194
Indian Mutiny, 126, 127
Indian Ocean, 109
Indonesia, 127, 151, 152, 181, 184, 186, 188
Innocent IV, 117
Institute of Muslim Minority Affairs, 182
Inter-Faith Network, 186
International Institute of Islamic Thought, 159
Iran, 14, 34, 72–3, 79, 111, 117–20, 123, 125, 126, 128, 129, 134, 181, 184, 187, 192
Iraq, 14, 16, 34, 36, 43, 47, 50, 52, 60, 72–3, 126, 154
ʿĪsā *see* Jesus
Isaac, 35
Isawas, 125
Isfahan, 122
Ishmael, 35, 37, 41, 48, 80
Ishmaelites, 35–6, 39
Islamic Foundation, 134, 161, 184
Islamophobia, 1
Ismāʿīl (Khedive), 128
Israel, 72, 127, 158, 188, 190
  see also Zionism
Istanbul, 128, 145, 166
  see also Constantinople
Italy, 98, 99, 100, 103, 126, 184

Jaʿfar ibn Abū Ṭālib, 20–1
Jaffa, 158
Jahangir, 2, 120, 121
Jāḥiẓ, al-, 3, 60, 67
Jakarta, 181
James I, 2, 4n3
Japan, 120
Jedda, 145
Jeremiah, 37
Jerusalem, 2, 9, 13, 15, 35, 37, 44, 48, 59, 83, 84, 85, 86, 87, 88, 91, 120, 149, 164
  Council of, 7
  Jewish temple in, 7, 11, 44, 85
Jesuit order, 120–2, 123, 125, 164, 185
Jesus, 6, 8, 9, 10, 14, 21, 22, 23, 24, 26, 27, 29, 31, 39, 40, 57, 61, 65, 66, 84, 87, 93, 95, 118, 122, 125, 153, 154, 155, 160, 161, 164, 166, 191, 194
  see also Christology
Jewish–Christian relations, 6–8, 29, 60, 182
Jews, 6–8, 19, 24, 25, 26, 28, 29–30, 30–1, 41, 42, 43, 46, 47, 56, 57, 59–60, 66–7, 68, 85, 86, 92, 94, 101, 102, 115, 144, 146, 149, 167, 182, 189, 190, 191
  see also People of the Book
Jihād (struggle), 57, 128–9
Jizya (poll-tax/tribute), 26, 31, 44, 45, 47, 81
Joahim of Fiore, 111
John, 7, 11
John de Carpini, 116–17
John of Damascus, 38–41, 44, 53, 55, 56, 58, 94
John of Segovia, 96
John of Seville, 101
John Paul II, 114–15, 181, 183, 192
John the Baptist, 95
Jonah, 6, 7
Jones, William, 147
Jordan, 72, 181, 183, 184, 192
Jubail, 89
Judaism, 7, 8, 19, 29, 68, 143, 149, 159, 161, 166, 167, 189
Justin Martyr, 9
Justinian, 50
Justinian II, 47

Kabul, 126
Kairanāwī, Raḥmat Allāh al-, 131–2
Kairouan, 79
Kalām (Islamic Theology), 41, 60, 64, 66
Kano, 188
Karachi, 183
Karakorum, 117
Kashmir, 194
Kerr, David, 185
Keturah, 36
Khadīja, 20, 56
Khālid ibn al-Walīd, 31, 43
Khālidī, Muṣṭafā, 134
Khatami, Mohammed, 181, 192
Khaybar, 30, 31, 41, 42, 145
Khodr, Georges, 156, 181
Khomeini, Ayatollah, 134

Khoury, A-T[h.], 58
Kierkegaard, 157
Kiev, 113
Kimball, Charles, 187
Kinda, tribe of, 17, 53
Kindī, 'Abd al-Masīh al-, 53–4, 56, 93, 114
Kindī, Abū Yūsuf Ya'qūb ibn Isḥāq al-, 50
Knitter, Paul, 190
König, Franz, 181
Kosovo (battle of), 109–11
Kosovo (province of), 2, 109–11
Kraemer, Hendrik, 3, 151–3, 156, 158, 160, 162
Kritzeck, James, 93, 94, 95
Kuala Lumpur, 161
Kufr (unbelief), 27–8
Küng, Hans, 158, 171n30
Kuyper, Abraham, 127

Lahore, 194
Lakhm, tribe of, 16
Lancaster, 166
Lane, E. W., 145
Lapidus, I. M., 71
Lavigerie, Cardinal, 125, 127, 164
Lazar, Prince, 109–11
Lazarus-Yafeh, Hava, 59–60
League of Nations, 126
Lebanon, 69, 72, 89, 92, 117, 126, 156, 180, 181, 182, 184, 185, 186
Leblich, Domingo Badia y, 145
Leicester, 134, 161, 184
Leiden, 143, 147, 151, 152
Leighton House, 146
Leo III, 47, 58–9
Leon, 98
Lepanto, 112
Lessing, G. E., 149
Levinas, Emmanuel, 182
Levtzion, Nehemiah, 68
Lewis, Bernard, 148
Library of Congress, 146–7
Libya, 126, 129, 181, 183
see also Cyrenaica
Linlithgow, Lord, 194
Logos, 14
London, 68, 146, 147
London Missionary Society, 122
Longwood, Mississippi, 146
Los Angeles, 68
Louis VII, 87
Louis IX, 89, 117
Loyola, Ignatius, 120
Lucknow, 135
Lull, Raymond, 96, 115–16, 117, 120, 121
Luther, Martin, 111, 160
Lyazghi, Muḥammad, 182–3

Maalouf, Amin, 90
Ma'arrat al-Nu'mān, 90
Ma'arrī, Abū'l-'Alā' al-, 90, 104, 189
McAuliffe, Jane, 26
Maccabees, 6
Macdonald, Duncan Black, 147–8, 185
McGill University, 159
McKinley, William, 127
Macquarrie, John, 191
Madjid, Nurcholish, 181
Magellan, Ferdinand, 112
Mahdī, al-, 52
Mahound, 92
Maimonides, Moses, 101, 102
Majorca, 115
Makdisi, George, 100–1
Malaysia, 159
Malay states, 126
Malcolm, Noel, 109–10
Malik al-Kāmil, al-, 114
Mālikī (school of Islamic law), 70–1
Ma'mūn, al-, 52, 53, 54, 55, 56, 71, 114
Manichaeans, 52, 57
Mansūr, al-, 52
Manṣūr ibn Sargūn, 38
Manṣūr, Kāmil, 136
Manṣūr, Muḥammad/Mikhail, 135–6
Manuel I, 59, 64
Manzikert, 73, 84
Māriya, 24
Mark of Toledo, 101
Maronite church, 92, 117
Marshall, David, 28
Martyn, Henry, 123, 133, 135
Martyrdom, 111, 115, 116, 154
Mary, 21, 27, 28, 153
Massignon, Louis, 147–8, 154–5, 164, 184, 190
Mas'ūdī, al-, 143
Māturīdī, al-, 61, 62–4

Mauritania, 126
Mawardī, al-, 69
Mecca, 19, 20, 23, 24, 25, 28, 30, 39, 47, 59, 145, 147, 164, 183, 191
Meccans, 21
  see also Quraish
Medina, 19, 22, 23, 24, 25, 26, 29–30, 31, 36, 47, 70, 145, 146
  see also Constitution of Medina
Mehmed II, 111, 128
Melkites, 38, 48n13, 53, 55, 64, 117
Mendicant orders, 114
Mesapotamia, 161
Methodius, 113
Meyendorff, John, 59
Michael III, 57, 58
Michael the Syrian, 37
Michelangelo, 104
Michel, Tom, 65–6, 182
Midian, 36
Milan, 155
Millennialism, 160
  see also Apocalyptic
Milner, Sir William, 193–4
Mindanao, 112
Missions to Muslims, Christian, 114–25, 129, 130–5, 148, 151, 152, 181, 182, 189
  see also *Da'wa*
Mitri, Tarek, 185
Mock, Alois, 181
Moghul empire, 120–2, 125, 126
Moghul gardens, 194
Moluccan islands, 112
Monasticism, Christian, 16
Mongols, 73, 89, 116, 117
Monophysite Christians, 14, 15, 16, 17, 20, 22, 37, 41, 47, 52, 54, 62
Montagu, Lady Mary Wortley, 145
Montini, Cardinal, 155
Montpellier, 100
Moorhead, John, 35–6
Morocco, 101, 114, 125, 126, 163, 165, 182, 183, 187, 189
Moses, 24, 35, 63, 95, 104, 191
Mozarabs, 189
Mt Sinai, 42
Muḥammad, 15, 17, 19–32, 34, 35, 36, 39, 40, 41, 42, 43, 44, 46, 54, 56, 57, 59, 60, 61, 64–5, 83, 92, 93, 94, 95, 100, 104, 111, 112, 113, 116, 132, 144, 145, 147, 155, 159, 167, 189, 191
Muḥammad ibn 'Abd Allāh al-Hāshimī, 53
Muir, William, 53, 54, 131–3
Mulder, Dirk, 181
Muqtadir, al-, 113
Murad I, 109, 110
Murad (son of Akbar), 121
Murcia, 116
Murphy, Dervla, 189
Mūsā *see* Moses
Muslim Students' Association, 159
Muslim World League, 183
Mutawakkil, al-, 57, 66–7
Mu'tazila, 61, 62, 66

Nahum, 6
Na'īm, A. A. al-, 140n64
Najd, 16
Najrān, 16, 17, 22, 26, 31, 43, 44, 114
Naples, 100, 102
Narbonne, 80
Nash, John, 146
Nāṣir al-dīn, 129
Nasr, Seyyed Hossein, 166
Nayed, Aref, 76n28
Nazareth, 89
Nebuchadnezzar, 37
Negus, 20–1, 22
Nehemiah, 160
Neill, Stephen, 134–5, 160
Neoplatonism, 52
Nero, 11
Nestorian Christians, 14–15, 16, 37, 41, 47, 52, 53, 54, 62, 72, 73, 94, 113, 117
Nestorius, 14, 40
Netanyahu, Benjamin, 190
Netherlands, 127, 187
Nettler, Ron, 165–6
Newman, John Henry, 189
Nicetas (historian), 89
Nicetas of Byzantium, 57–8, 92
Nicholas of Cusa, 96, 154
Nicopolis, 110
Niebuhr, Reinhold, 160
Nigeria, 2, 125, 181, 188, 190
Nineveh, 6
Noah, 27, 104
Nobili, Robert de, 120

Normans, 98
North Africa, 13, 34, 36, 69, 70–1, 79, 89, 92, 125, 126, 163, 185
North America, 146, 147, 158, 159, 182, 185, 188, 190
 see also Canada; United States
Notre Dame University, 184
Nottingham, 122
Nuer, 142, 143
Nu'mān ibn Mundhir, 16
Numerals (Arabic), 103
Nūr al-dīn, 87

Ockley, Simon, 144
Open Letter, 190–1
Orientalism (Western study of the Orient), 147–9
Orthodox Centre of the Ecumenical Patriarchate, 183
Orthodox Christians *see* Eastern (Orthodox) churches
Ottoman Turks, 61, 74, 96, 109, 110, 111, 112, 117, 118, 119–20, 125, 126, 127–8, 145
Otto of Freising, 93
Oxford, 96, 100, 142, 143, 187
Özcan, Hanifi, 63

Pakistan, 34, 156, 159, 188, 189
 Pakistan Association for Inter-Religious Dialogue, 186
Palermo, 98
Palestine, 6, 38, 53, 55, 56, 72, 88, 89, 109, 116, 126, 158, 188
Palestinian National Council, 148
Parcevall Hall, 193–4
Paris, 80, 96, 100, 102, 116, 128, 147, 163, 164
Parliament, British, 1
Paul, 7, 9, 73, 160, 167
Paul III, 120
Paul VI, 155
Paul Alvarus, 81–4
Paul of Antioch, 64–6
People of the Book, 27, 42, 44, 46, 192
 see also Dhimmī; Jews
Pepin, 80
Peter, 8, 10–11
Peter the Hermit, 85, 97
Peter the Venerable, 93–5, 98, 101, 103, 115, 142
Petrus Alfonsi, 92–3
Pfander, Karl, 131–2
Philip II (Augustus), 88
Philip II (of Spain), 112
Philip the Arab, 15
Philippines, 2, 112, 127
Philo, 6, 14
Pietist movement, 122
Pilate, Pontius, 7
Pinheiro, Emmanuel, 121
Pitts, Joseph, 145
Pius II, 91
Plato, 10, 14, 104
Poland, 119
Poll-tax *see Jizya*
Polo, Marco, 117
Pontifical Council for Inter-Religious Dialogue, 177, 180, 181, 185
 see also Secretariat for non-Christians
Pontifical Institute for Arabic and Islamic Studies, 183, 185, 186
Porphyry, 94, 97
Portugal, 109, 119, 121
Pristina, 109
Protestant Christians, 118–20, 122–3, 124–5, 133, 150, 151, 164, 177, 185, 189
 see also Calvin; Luther
Provence, 80, 99
Ptolemy, 97, 99, 104
Pyrenees, 99
Pythagoras, 104

Qarāfī, al-, 65
Quraish, 20
 see also Meccans
Qur'ān, 24–9, 39, 45, 46, 53, 54, 57, 58, 61, 62, 63, 65, 83, 94, 95, 100, 125, 135, 142, 155, 164, 165, 166, 167, 186, 190, 192
 Translation into English, 143
 Translation into Latin, 93
 2:62, 26
 3:18–19, 95
 3:55, 26
 3:61, 95
 3:199, 27
 4:171, 21, 53
 5:14, 12
 5:48, 166
 5:66, 27

5:72–3, 28
5:82–3, 25, 26
5:116, 28
9:8, 46
9:10, 46
9:29, 26, 28, 42, 44, 45
9:30, 28
19, 21
28:52–5, 27
29:46, 95
57:27, 27
96:1–5, 20
112, 39

Radulph of Caen, 90
Rahman, Fazlur, 167
Rahner, Karl, 150, 154, 164, 190
Raimundo, Archbishop of Toledo, 98
Raphael, 104
Raymond of Aguilers, 85
Raymond of Châtillon, 88
Raymond of Penaforte, 116
Rāzī, al-, 157
Reconquista, 98
Reformed Christians, 124–5
see also Calvin
Reland, Adriaan, 144
Religious minorities, 181, 182, 188
see also Dhimmī
Revelation, Book of, 11, 29
see also Bible
Ricci, Matthew, 120
Rice, W. A., 125
Richard I, 1, 2, 88
Ricoldo of Montecroce, 116, 184
Robert of Ketton, 93, 98
Roccasecca, 103
Rodrigo Diaz de Viva (El Cid), 99
Roe, Sir Thomas, 1, 2, 4n3, 112, 122
Roger II, 98
Roman Catholic Christians, 48n13, 73, 150, 153, 155, 185, 189
see also Carmelite order; Dominican order; Franciscan order; Jesuit order; Vatican
Roman empire, 11, 12, 15, 29, 67, 113
Romans, 7, 11, 37
Rome, 13, 92, 98, 104, 114, 117, 119, 163, 183, 185, 186
see also Vatican
Ross, Alexander, 143
Royal Institute for Inter-Faith Studies, 184, 192
Runciman, Stephen, 85, 86, 87, 88, 89, 91
Runnymede Trust, 1
Russell, Bertrand, 189
Russia, 126
Ruth, 5
Rutter, Eldon, 146

Saadya Gaon, 55
Sabaeans, 26
Sacy, Silvestre de, 147
Safavid Empire, 125
Sagamu, 188
Sahara, 125
Sahas, Daniel, 38–41
Said, Edward, 142, 148–9
St George's House, 183
Ṣalāḥ al-dīn (Saladin), 88, 91, 104, 149
Salamanca, 96
Sale, George, 144
Salerno, 100
Salibi, Kamal, 72
Ṣāliḥ, 24
Ṣāliḥ, Sheikh, 135
Samarqand, 61
Sanūsī, 129, 142–3
Saragossa, 99, 113
Sarah, 35
Sa'sa'a ibn Khālid, 53
Sassanian Persian empire, 15, 16, 22, 34, 38, 47, 50, 72, 73, 113
Satan, 57, 94
Saudi Arabia, 126, 183, 191, 192
Schleiermacher, Friedrich, 149–50
School of Oriental and African Studies, 68
Schuon, Frithjof, 166
Seale, M. S., 41
Sebeos, 35
Second Vatican Council, 153–4, 155, 177, 183
Secretariat for non-Christians, 177, 181
see also Pontifical Council for Inter-Religious Dialogue
Seljuks Turks, 61, 74, 84, 91
Septuagint, 6
Serbia, 109–11

Sergius, 94
Severus of Asmounein, 37
Seville, 189
Sezincote House, 146
Shāfi'ī, al-, 50
Shahrastanī (al-), 143
Shaizar, 91
Shalimar Gardens, 194
Shamil, 129
Sharī'a (Islamic law), 50, 60, 63, 70, 165
Sharpe, E. J., 143, 151
Shī'ī Islam, 62, 66, 72, 87, 111, 118, 120
Shiraz, 123
Shirk (polytheism/idolatry), 27–8, 46, 192
Shu'ayb, 24
Sicily, 88, 98, 163
Siddiqui, Ataullah, 161
Sidon, 64
Siger of Brabant, 102
Sigismund, 110
Silvester II, 97
Sirjwas, 65
Sistine Chapel, 104
Skyreholme, 193
Slavs, 113
Sloan, Samuel, 146
Smith, Wilfred Cantwell, 3, 156–8, 159, 166, 190
Song of Roland, 81, 92, 99
Sophronius, 44
South Africa, 191–2
South Arabia *see* Yemen
Southern, R. W., 92–3, 96, 97
Spain, 13, 34, 36, 69, 79–84, 89, 93, 97, 98–102, 109, 112, 119, 127, 165, 189
Spanish Martyrs' Movement, 81–4, 92, 113
Sri Lanka, 182
Sudan, 2, 126, 142
Sufi Islam, 116, 124, 129, 147, 154
Sulaimān the Magnificent, 117
Sumatra, 129
Switzerland, 112, 182, 183
Syracuse University, 159
Syria, 14, 15, 16, 20, 34, 37, 38, 43, 44, 47, 53, 54, 56, 69, 72, 86, 88, 89, 112, 114, 117, 125, 145
Syrian Orthodox Christians, 23
Ṭabarī, al-, 42, 66–7, 143
Tabriz, 123
Taghlib, tribe of, 16–17
Ṭālbī, Muḥammad al-, 162–6, 183, 185, 188
Tambaram, 152
Tanzīmāt, 128
Tawḥīd (unity of God), 192–3
Teissier, Henri, 181
Templars, 88
Temple, William, 160
Temple University, 159
Termagent, 92
Tertullian, 9, 70
Theodore Abū Qurra, 40, 53, 54, 55, 58
Theophanes the Confessor, 56–7
Thomas, David, 63, 76n28
Thomason, James, 131, 133
Thomason, Thomas, 133
Three Wise Men, 23
Tibawi, A. L., 134
Timbuktu, 125
Timothy, Catholicos, 52
Tobacco Protest, 129
Tokat, 123
Toledo, 79, 93, 98, 99
  Toledan Collection, 98
Torah, 20, 27, 55
Toronto, 69
Tours, 80
Translation movement (Arabic to Latin), 98–102
Translation movement (Greek to Arabic), 52, 54, 67
Trappist monks, 187
Tribute *see Jizya*
Trinity, 57, 62, 66, 121, 192–3
Tripoli, 87, 183
Tritton, A. S., 45–6
Troeltsch, Ernst, 150
Troll, C. W., 130
Troubadours, 99, 100
Tuareg, 125
Tunis, 60, 89, 98, 114, 115, 116, 126, 163, 164, 185
  University of Tunis, 183
Turkey, 64, 73–4, 123, 126, 166, 184, 186, 187
Turṭūshī, al-, 163
Tyre, 88

Ulfilas, 113
'Umar ibn 'Abd al-'Azīz, 46, 58
'Umar ibn al-Khaṭṭāb, 42, 43, 44, 45, 46
see also Covenant of 'Umar
Uniate churches, 117
United Kingdom, 142, 186
see also England
United Nations, 68
United States, 127, 158, 159, 190
see also North America
Universities, 99–101, 116
'Uqba ibn Nāfi, 79
Urabi, Aḥmad, 129
Urban II, 84, 91
Usāma ibn Munqidh, 91
Uzbekistan, 61

Valencia, 99
Vandals, 71, 79
Varthema, Ludovico di, 145
Vatican, 180, 181, 183, 184
Vatikiotis, P. J., 128
Venice, 89, 112
Verdi, 128
Vermes, Geza, 7
Vézélay, 87
Vienna, 111, 126, 181
Vienne, Council of, 96
Vikings, 80
Volney, Comte de, 145

Waardenburg, Jacques, 24
Walīd, al-, 47
Wāqidī, al-, 42
Waraqa ibn Nawfal, 20, 23, 24
Washington DC, 146, 185
Watt, William Montgomery, 29, 99
Werff, Lyle Vander, 122, 124
White Fathers, 125, 127, 164, 185
William of Malmesbury, 93
William of Rubroek, 117
William of Tripoli, 116, 117
Windsor, 183
World Council of Churches, 156, 161, 177, 180, 181, 182, 183, 184
World Islamic Call Society, 183
World Muslim Congress, 182, 183
Wycliffe, John, 111

Xavier, Francis, 120
Xavier, Jerome, 120, 121

Yaḥyā ibn 'Adī, 55
Yathrib *see* Medina
Yazdagird III, 34
Yazīd I, 93
Yeats, W. B., 189
Yemen, 16, 22, 42
Yorkshire Dales, 193–4
Yoruba, 188
Yugoslavia, 2
Yūḥannā ibn Ḥaylān, 55

Zealots, 6
Zebiri, Kate, 191
Zengi, 87
Zionism, 161, 182, 190
see also Israel
Zoroaster, 104
Zoroastrianism, 73
Zwemer, Samuel, 124–5, 134, 185

CPSIA information can be obtained at www.ICGtesting.com
Printed in the USA
BVOW032002050812

297041BV00001B/161/P

9 781566 633406